THE LETTERS OF EVELYN UNDERHILL

EVELYN UNDERHILL

1933

The Letters of
EVELYN UNDERHILL

Edited with an Introduction
by
CHARLES WILLIAMS

With Two Illustrations

Christian Classics
P.O. Box 30
Westminster, MD 21157
1989

The present printing of *The Letters of Evelyn Underhill*
has been undertaken at the suggestion of Christopher L.
Bazemore, manager of Newman Book Store, 3329 Eighth St.,
Washington, DC 20017

First published 1943 by Longmans Green & Co., London
First printed in paperback 1989

ISBN: 0 87061 172 0
Library of Congress Catalog Card Number: 89 062318
Printed in the U.S.A.

CONTENTS

ILLUSTRATIONS

INTRODUCTION

I

Evelyn Underhill was born in the afternoon of 6 December, 1875, at Wolverhampton. Her father was Arthur—afterwards Sir Arthur—Underhill. He was a distinguished barrister and a bencher of Lincoln's Inn, son of Henry Underhill for some time Town Clerk of Wolverhampton; her mother was Alice Lucy Ironmonger. The family home was always in London—a pleasant well-to-do home of what used to be called the Tory kind. She was educated there, except for some three years (1888-1891) till she was sixteen at a private school at Folkestone; afterwards in London she went to King's College for Women, where she read history and botany.

Her young experience, however, included also the sea and Europe. Her father was an enthusiastic yachtsman; he was founder and for many years Commodore of the Royal Cruising Club. In 1888 she went for her first cruise in his yacht *Amoretta*. The log-book which she kept records her learning to sail and to sketch. She became a good small-boat sailor—she could race and win prizes; she had all her life a passion for efficiency.

The family were friends with their neighbours, the Stuart Moores, whose yacht often sailed in company with the *Amoretta*. The Stuart Moore boys were her chief—almost her only—young companions. A letter written to her mother when she was fourteen says: "I hope you enjoyed the Nevilles' dinner-party; have they got an eligible child as a companion for me? if so, mind you let me know her." In that sense she was a lonely child—which not all only children are, for she had (it is clear) all her life a great capacity for and enjoyment of friendship. But two things began during that childhood. One was her companionship in activity with Hubert Stuart Moore, who afterwards became her husband; the other was her own personal activity of writing. She had

7

begun this before she was sixteen, for she then won the first prize in a short-story competition organized by the magazine *Hearth and Home*, and she occasionally followed this story with others. It was after 1898, when she was twenty-three and living with her family in London, that in general her own friendships began. She moved, though not exclusively, in one of the "literary sets" of the day. She knew Maurice Hewlett, and at his house met Laurence Housman and Sarah Bernhardt. She also became acquainted with May Sinclair—now too little recollected; for the present writer and for others of the then young her novels had a quite unusual attraction; with Arthur Machen— whose interests were, in some respects, very like her own, though in the expression of them she turned rather to actuality and he to myth; with Mrs. Baillie Reynolds and Mrs. Belloc Lowndes, Mary Cholmondeley and Evelyn Sharp, Mrs. Ernest Dowson and Mrs. Wilfrid Ward; and with Arthur Symons. But her chief friendship was with Ethel Ross Barker, and this was one of the most intimate of her life; it ended only with her friend's death in 1920.

In 1890 she had first gone to France; she wrote of it: "France is charming." But from 1898 she began a habit of going to Europe with her mother in the spring of every year—a habit which lasted until 1913. In 1898 they went to Lucerne, Lugano, Como, and Milan; and she alone went on to Florence. In 1899 she was at Florence again; in 1900 she first saw Chartres; in 1901, Assisi. In 1910 she went first to Rome. She wrote from Florence during her first (1898) visit: "Once you have found it out (what Italian painters are really trying to paint) you must love them till the end of your days"; and again: "This place has taught me more than I can tell you; it's a sort of gradual unconscious growing into an understanding of things." She was then twenty-two.

Meanwhile, in 1902, her first book had been published. It was a book of humorous verse, called *A Bar-Lamb's Ballad-Book*. It was concerned with the law, and was no doubt written under the legal influence of her father and her future husband. Astonishingly, the book remains amusing forty years afterwards. Two quotations from it may be risked. The first is the explanation that legal heirs are

> Dimly perceived through a philoprogenitive mist.
> Moreover, they may not even be descendants:
> They are sometimes your Maiden Aunt,
> Or the Cousin that you particularly object to,
> They may also be your Step-brother's Son,
> Or, very occasionally, your Grandmama.

The second is from the poem on the case of Jones *v*. Lock, where "A father put a cheque into the hands of his son nine months old, saying, 'I give this to Baby for himself,' and then took the cheque back, put it away, and shortly afterwards died. Held that there was no valid gift of the cheque to the son."

> The elder children, grown adult in greed,
> Cast doubts upon their parent's dying deed;
> Safe in possession, little did they reck
> If he had said, "This shall be Baby's cheque."
>
> The outraged infant thought,
> "I'll go before the Court,
> And ask, by my next friend, for some redress."
> Alas! not more, but less
> Were his possessions when the suit was done,
> For the defendants won.
> The gift, without delivery, was not good;
> No valuable consideration shown:
> Such acts are ratified by this alone.
> The plaintiff, much astonied, went away,
> The action lost, and all the costs to pay:
> And homeward riding in his little pram
> Allowed his Nurse to call him "Martyred lamb!"
> Refused his bottle, wailed in infant grief,
> And called the Judge a wicked, naughty thief.
> In after life, 'tis said, he always swore
> "Possession is *Ten* points of *English* Law."

A*

In the year (1902) in which this book appeared, she had begun work on her first novel. It was published, under the title of *The Grey World*, in 1904; and another, *The Lost Word*, begun in 1904, appeared in 1907. The third and last novel, *The Column of Dust*, appeared in 1908. All three had a reasonably good reception, but they are not, it must be admitted, as good as one expects them to be. *The Column of Dust* has a superb theme; it has possibilities of wit, terror, and sublimity. The wit is there, but hardly the terror or sublimity. The description of the working of a magical rite at the opening is good; and so, in a different way, is the other Rite of the Helpers of the Holy Souls towards the close. But though the moral of the rest of the book is not less than noble, its literary effect is less than exciting. She had not, on the whole, an imaginative style; the reason may be that her imagination moved too near to serious faith to allow itself, in her writings, much leisure.

Her other activities about this time included a partial collaboration with J. A. Herbert, Deputy Keeper of MSS. at the British Museum, in a book on illuminated MSS. Eventually, however, this was abandoned, and the book was issued under his name alone. From 1907 onwards also she was beginning work on her book *Mysticism*, which appeared in 1911. Among the occupations of her leisure was bookbinding, which she had taken up much earlier and in which she became extremely proficient.

There remain two dates of her personal life, both of the first importance. In 1907 she was married to Hubert Stuart Moore. Their house was at 50 Campden Hill Square, a short walk from her parents' home. In 1911 began her friendship with Friedrich von Hügel.

II

It is necessary to pause here. In 1911 she was married; she had published her first serious book; she knew von Hügel. She had already begun to correspond with "inquirers"; her first known letter of the kind is given among those that follow, dated 29 November, 1904, and by 1911 there had been others. Of what sort, at the age of thirty-six, was her mind?

It was said above that she knew Europe and the sea. It would be possible and even easy to make play with the sea-likeness; she might, in a careless moment, have done so herself, for she had, in her careless moments, a slight tendency towards such fancies. It may well be supposed indeed that something of her ardour and her delight enjoyed the sea as they enjoyed that other sublimer sea which the author of the Apocalypse saw stretched before the eyed creatures and the Throne. Such images, however pleasant, are literary. But the experience of Europe was not only literary but historical, and not only historical but contemporary. In 1892 she had written in a paper headed: "My Thoughts and Opinions written on the eve of my seventeenth birthday, December 5, 1892": "I hope my mind will not grow tall to look down on things but wide to embrace all sorts of things during the coming year." Many girls at seventeen might have aspired so; some might have succeeded. What was remarkable about Evelyn Underhill was that, during the next few years, she not only "embraced" friends; she saw and "embraced" Europe. It has, in the fifty years that have since passed, become easy and indeed fashionable, to talk of "the West," of "our culture," and even of "Catholic culture." It was not so easy in the first decade of those fifty years, nor did she talk of it. But she knew, at first obscurely, what it was.

It may have been partly due to the fact that she had had, as she said, no "orthodox education." It was true both in a general and in a particular sense. "I wasn't," she wrote, "brought up to religion." At home it seems to have been of no importance; at school it was something more, for she was certainly confirmed (11 March, 1891, at Christ Church, Folkestone, and made her first Communion at St. Paul's, Sandgate, on Easter Sunday), and a few great names had passed across her mind. "Last

Sunday we went to a lecture in the church, it was on Milton's *Paradise Lost*, and was *horribly* uninteresting, all about dogmas and conclusions to be drawn from the poem and such stuff" (21 June, 1889). "The colporteur came to-day, and I have bought some lovely sensational moral stories for Sunday reading. . . . Mine are called 'Run down,' 'Martin Luther,' and 'Ruth Erskine's Crosses.' Oh! please can you tell me who Spinoza was, he was mentioned in the sermon last Sunday; he seems to have been a not very nice person from what Mr. Wakefield said." In spite of these rather unfortunate instances, she does not seem, though she may not have been told many of the right things about Europe and Christendom, to have been told, too forcibly, too many of the wrong. Even so, the wrong things—meaning the merely incorrect—were in the air. She escaped them, or she threw them off. She came from England and the sea to Europe, and she did not patronize it. It was the first mark of her honour.

In the same paper of "Thoughts and Opinions" she says that her ideal woman "should have a due sense of proportion." It was perhaps something of this quality that caused her, six years later, to write of the Italian painters that they had taught her a gradual growth "into an understanding of things." She was then enjoying them as art; at that age one may enjoy religion as art; it is permissible and proper. Also the Italian painters were meant to be enjoyed as art. But she was becoming aware that the inner diagram of that particular art—as indeed of much other—was not only art but religion. And in this art a particular, a defined, religion. She was already becoming aware of That which is called the Church.

It must be repeated that that was by no means common at the end of the nineteeenth century, especially for a nature not habitually pious or docile. Her mind was, for a woman, unusually inclined to the abstract. She says herself: " Philosophy brought me round to an intelligent and irresponsible sort of theism which I enjoyed thoroughly but which did not last long. Gradually the net closed in on me. . . ." She had joined (in 1904) an occult

companionship known as the Order of the G.D., and belonged
to it for some years. She was not yet impressed by the person
of our Lord; when she wrote of "the Christian net" she was
accurate. A diagram and an energy which she certainly had not
expected had appeared to her, and she already understood many
things about it. She understood, for example, many saints. Most
of us are, naturally, a little eclectic about the saints; the present
writer, for instance, has never been able to feel much excitement
about St. Francis of Assisi and St. Thomas More (though he
does not think that creditable to him). Dr. Inge has been a little
lordly about Angela of Foligno. But Evelyn Underhill quite
early understood not only that they were saints but that they
were different saints. She wrote intelligently not only about
Francis but about Angela. She submitted herself to detail; she
was, as has been said, in all things efficient.

She had seen the Catholic pattern. The Church had appeared
to her. She was not, at first, prepared to yield wholly to it. In
February 1907 her friend, Ethel Ross Barker, was staying at the
Franciscan convent of St. Mary of the Angels in Southampton,
and she went there to join her for a week-end. It was a convent
of Perpetual Adoration. She noted in a diary (4 February, 1907):
"The wonderful week began." She wrote (14 May, 1911):
"The day after I came away (the Feast of the Purification), a
good deal shaken but unconvinced, I was 'converted' quite
suddenly, once and for all, by an overpowering vision which had
really no specifically Christian elements, but yet convinced me
that the Catholic religion was true." By Catholic there she meant
the Roman. On her return to London she wrote to Robert
Hugh Benson, whom she knew and had heard preach, putting her
chief difficulties—difficulties of the reason—before him. He
replied immediately and sympathetically; the correspondence
continued, and by the beginning of April she had all but determined to make her submission.

But her way was not to be as simple as that. Something
occurred which was not so much itself the hindrance as the

occasion of the discovery of the real hindrance. Her engagement had been announced on 3 July, 1906, and she was to be married in 1907, and her future husband was, not unnaturally, unprepared to assent to what he regarded as an alteration in their relations. He insisted that she should delay at least six months. She was unwilling to do so, but she was convinced that it was her business to do so; that is, she was not convinced of the complete authority of the Roman Church. She made this clear to Benson. "I think," he wrote to her, "you are perfectly right to offer to wait—for your own sake as well as for his—until the thing becomes clear and established." She was married on 3 July, 1907; on the same day Benson "very gladly" said Mass for her intention; he wrote that he could see that "You are not yet certain of the Catholic position, and that the Church is not yet plain to you. That being so, let me congratulate you on your marriage, and wish you every conceivable happiness—above all, the happiness of one day receiving the full gift of Faith."

A further development in the same year greatly affected her. In September the encyclical, *Pascendi gregis*, of Pius X against Modernism was issued. She says: "The Modernist storm broke." It had effects in England. George Tyrrell became excommunicate; it was not clear what others would be similarly affected. Evelyn Underhill, though she had this vivid sense of the Catholic and Roman pattern, was not clear on her duty. Or rather, she was clear; the Papal Encyclical appeared to her to demand, on some points, a surrender of her intellectual honour. It is easier now to see that this need not have been so; and even to see that on the points where she was then obstinate, she eventually came to the orthodox belief. But as things were then, she was thrown, with others, into a most difficult position. She dissented, and was inflexibly called; she assented, and was inflexibly refused.

The matter on which she found difficulty was probably that discussed in von Hügel's letter to her of 26–9 December, 1921: the question of the historicity of certain alleged facts. Von

Hügel's discussion of this may be found in that letter (*Selected Letters*, edited by Bernard Holland). The immediate point, however, is not the intellectual controversy, but the effect on Evelyn Underhill of the position in which she found herself. She was between two impossibilities; say rather, she found herself face to face with an Impossibility—something that could not be, and yet was. She wrote in 1911: "I cannot accept Anglicanism instead; it seems an entirely different thing. So here I am, going to Mass and so on, but entirely deprived of the sacraments" (14 May, 1911). And again: "It is all wrong, but at present I do not know what else to do." Nor, in fact, does one. One is apparently left to live alone with an Impossibility. It is imperative, and in the end possible, to believe that the Impossibility does its own impossible work; to believe so, in whatever form the crisis takes, is of the substance of faith; especially if we add to it Kierkegaard's phrase that, in any resolution of the crisis, so far as the human spirit is concerned, "before God man is always in the wrong." That is not, by itself, the complete truth; we should have to add to it the opposite and complementary phrase that, also before God, man is always in the right; but the other is the more important for our own sense of any resolution. The only rightness there is in the Impossible itself —"to whom be glory in the Church for ever through Christ Jesus."

But before the resolution of the crisis, whatever that may be, it is necessary to live with that Impossibility. One may be united with it by faith—that is blessed. But one is also united with it by another, more painful, method. The Impossibility, however we write about it, is not impossible only in a high and abstract intellectual sense, but in a low and deadly. It is the details of the Impossibility that press home—the sordid, the comic, the agonizing. "I asked Him," wrote Léon Bloy (*Letters to his Fiancée*), "to let me suffer for my friends and for Him both in body and soul. But I had envisaged noble and pure suffering which, as I now see, would only have been another form of joy.

I had never dreamed of this infernal suffering that He has sent me." It is in the non-relation of human life to any decency that the human heart finds its—exile? not exile, for it has then no proper sense of its home. All it knows is that everything is "most contrary to its disposition." It weeps without hope; it grudges without charity; it brags against others with a beguiling plausibility; it hides itself from others in a pride of spiritual derision; the thing it cannot bear is naked love—nor till it can bear it can it find it, nor till it can find it can it bear it. This is the inward Impossibility, which remains no less impossible because the mind tries to sweeten it to something other than itself—perhaps even with every kind of literary delicacy, the equivalent in our day of the visions and locutions of the past. There is but one outer test of true faith—"the incessant production of good works"; there is but one inner—patience.

In this situation Evelyn Underhill turned to a study of that Way of the Spirit which is called Mysticism. She began work on a book on the subject. It was called *Mysticism*, but it was also called by a sub-title—*A Study in the Nature and Development of Man's Spiritual Consciousness*. The portentous phrase does her some injustice; she was not like that. She was truly concerned with real things; the word "reality," though she was inclined to use it, has by now a certain cheapness about it. She wrote in the Preface:

This book falls naturally into two parts; each of which is really complete in itself, though they are in a sense complementary to one another. Whilst the second and longest part contains a somewhat detailed study of the nature and development of man's spiritual or mystical consciousness, the first is intended rather to provide an introduction to the general subject of mysticism. Exhibiting it by turns from the point of view of metaphysics, psychology, and symbolism, it is an attempt to gather between the covers of one volume information at present scattered amongst many monographs and text-books written in divers tongues, and to give the student in a compact form at least the elementary facts in regard to each of those subjects which are most closely connected with the study of the mystics.

The present writer must have read it first within a year or two of its appearance. What then remained in his mind—and still remains—was not the analysis of the relation between mysticism and magic or symbolism, and not the psychological analysis, but the authentic sayings—or rather the general sense of the authentic sayings. It was a great book precisely not because of its originality, but because of its immediate sense of authenticity. Open it now three times at random—

(1) "The just man goes *towards* God by inward love in perpetual activity and *in* God in virtue of his fruitive affection in eternal rest."—RUYSBROECK.

(2) "There is none other God than He that none may know, which may not be known. No, soothly, no! Without fail, No, says she (the contemplative soul). He only is my God that none can one word of say, nor all they of Paradise one only point attain nor understand, for all the knowing that they have of Him."—*The Mirror of Simple Souls*.

(3) The soul "is so full of peace that though she press her flesh, her nerves, her bones, no other thing comes forth from them than peace."—ST. CATHERINE OF GENOA.

These three sentences were exhibited by three random openings, and so it is with the whole book. To the reader, Evelyn Underhill, as the author, was altogether occulted by the dark or shining fierceness of the sayings she had collected. In the Preface to the twelfth edition (1930) she wrote that the first term of the mystic life must be sought "in the Vision of the Principle, as St. Gregory the Great taught long ago." It was that Vision of the Principle which these sayings illuminated and to which they pointed. But it was also that Vision of the Principle which now, for her personal life, involved the Vision of an Impossibility. She was united with it by faith alone. The book is not only a noble book on its subject; it not only witnesses continually to the authenticity of the saints; it is also one of her own "good works" and an expression of her own patience. It appeared in 1911; in the same year she wrote (15 May, 1911): "But I cling to St. Paul. . . . Is it not amazing . . . when one can see the action of the Spirit of God; so gentle, ceaseless, inexorable, pressing you bit by bit whether you like it or not towards your home? I feel this more and more as the dominating thing—it seems so odd that everyone does not feel and notice it happening, don't you think?"

It might, however, be held that when she wrote that book, and still more obviously when she wrote *The Mystic Way* which followed it in 1913, her attention was still a little disproportioned. Given her condition at the time, it could hardly be otherwise. The existence of the Impossibility, her doubt of certain historicities, her inevitable reliance on the workings of the interior Spirit, all tended to give her work a tone, which she did not altogether mean even then, and of which she afterwards disapproved, of interior interpretation. The Christian dogmas and the Christian miracles held a hint of the symbolical—not as they must do because they mean more than we can know, but as they ought not to do because so they deny themselves. Thus in the preface to *The Mystic Way* she spoke of Christianity beginning "as a mystical movement of the purest kind." "The sequence of psychological states" which is the Mystic Way is a fact "attested by countless mystics of every period and creed"; "yet its primary importance for the understanding of our earliest Christian documents has been generally overlooked." The book, she says, ends "with a study of the liturgy of the Mass: the characteristic artform in which the mystical consciousness of Christendom has expressed itself." No doubt these phrases, and others like them, could be understood in an orthodox sense, but no doubt also they would not be normally understood in any such sense. *The Mystic Way* is a valuable book for those who know the Faith, but she herself came to distrust and dislike it as "false doctrine" and the reason is clear. She even modified, or at least indicated a modification of, *Mysticism*. In the preface to the twelfth edition (1930) she wrote:

Were I, now, planning this book for the first time, its arguments would be differently stated. More emphasis would be given (*a*) to the concrete, richly living yet unchanging character of the Reality over against the mystic, as the first term, cause and incentive of his experience; (*b*) to that paradox of utter contrast yet profound relation between the Creator and the creature, God and the soul, which makes possible his development; (*c*) to the predominant part played in that development by the free and prevenient action of the Supernatural—in theological language, by "grace"—as against all merely evolutionary or emergent theories of spiritual transcendence. I feel more and more that no psychological or evolutionary treatment of man's spiritual history can be adequate which ignores the element of "given-ness" in all genuine mystical knowledge.

This change in her intellectual tendencies came, no doubt, partly from the influence of von Hügel. In a letter of thanks for *The Mystic Way* (13 May, 1913), he wrote that he had not read it properly, but: "I see how fine the structure of the book is and how carefully you seem to have borne in mind the all-important place and function in religion of liturgical acts, of the Sacraments, of the Visible, of History. You will remember that I was not quite [*sic*] about this side of the question in your *Mysticism*, and the able reviewer of this new book of yours in *The Times* . . . seemed to me clearly insufficient on this profoundly important point. I am so very pleased too that the structure of your book proclaims the three stages of the New Testament, the Synoptics, St. Paul, the 4th Gospel."

III

By 1913 then she had known the first great crisis of the Impossible, and had set herself to be reconciled to it by faith and by obedience. She knew the dear intimacies of mortal existence. She knew, also, a master. Of what kind was his influence?

The letters between them do not exist. She was his friend from 1911 to 1921; in 1921 she put herself formally under his direction. He died in 1925. The only definite account of their relations is what may be deduced from a paper called *Finite and Infinite: a Study of the Philosophy of Baron Friedrich von Hügel*, with a further note on *Von Hügel as a Spiritual Teacher*. These were included in a volume called *Mixed Pasture*, published in 1933. They may, roughly, be analysed as follows.

She puts, first, the doctrine of "the Reality of Finites and the Reality of God"—the title of the Baron's unfinished Gifford Lectures. This involved the double set of duties—to this world and to that other. So put, it sounds easy and accepted, but in fact both the Baron and Evelyn Underhill carried this definition further and made of this "limited dualism" a kind of unity. She writes: "'A polarity, a tension, a friction, a one thing at work in distinctly another thing'—this was for him a fundamental and inevitable character of our spiritual life." It was this sense of organism profoundly living and working in organism which caused him to doubt abstractions and even "pure mysticism." " 'The mystic sense flies straight to God and *thinks* it finds all its delight in him alone.' But a careful examination always discovers many sensible, institutional, and historical contributions to this supposed ineffable experience."

She says of him: "I cannot but think that this intense consciousness of the close-knit texture of the realities within which we live and move—will come to be recognized as von Hügel's ruling intuition, and one of the chief contributions made by him to religious thought." The present writer is not in a position to judge whether this is a faithful interpretation of von Hügel. But he is fairly certain that it was a centre of Evelyn Underhill's own thought and experience. She continues to quote: "We all need one another . . . souls, all souls, are deeply interconnected. The Church at its best and deepest is just that—that interdependence of all the broken and meek, all the self-oblivion, all the reaching out to God and souls . . . nothing is more real than this interconnection. We can suffer for one another—no soul is saved alone and by its own efforts." Elsewhere she writes that "Baron von Hügel was fond of saying that the Church came first and the mystics afterwards." The Church is something more than the totality of the mystics. " 'L'esprit pour vous,' said Huvelin to his great pupil, 'c'est un esprit de bénédiction de toute créature,' and this was the spirit the Baron strove to culti-vate in all his pupils in the interior life." The principle of this is God; nay, as the theologians teach, God is Himself each One working in the Others, the "co-inherence" of the Trinity; and it might be added that it was in this sense also that He made man in the image of Himself.

On one of the few occasions on which the present writer met Evelyn Underhill, she permitted herself to speak of one of his own novels which had something of this sort of theme. In it he had written of two characters: "He endured her sensitiveness, but not her sin; the substitution there, if indeed there is a substi-tution, is hidden in the central mystery of Christendom." It was a well-meant sentence, but she charmingly corrected it. She said something to this effect: "Oh, but the saints do—they say they do. St. Catherine said: 'I will bear your sins.' " She spoke from a very great knowledge of the records of sanctity, but I should be rather more than willing to believe that she spoke from a lofty practice of sanctity and from a great understanding of the laws that govern, and the labours that are given to, sanctity.

The three elements which she finally stressed in von Hügel's work were the transcendental, the incarnational, and the institu-tional; all these he encouraged in his pupils and in her. She was at heart so naturally orthodox that, in a way, it even seems unnecessary. But it is possible, as was said before, that she might have over-tended to a wholly subjective understanding of the Way. In the period of her difficulty she might have come to interpret the Church and the Mysteries of the Church as purely symbolical, and the historicity of the tale as false. It might have happened; it did not. Von Hügel "had himself faced every scientific and critical difficulty, yet remained a devoted son of the Roman Catholic Church." His pupil took the lesson to heart. By 1919 (7 January) she was writing to a correspondent of "guides who seem to me rather doubtful—e.g. Molinos, as to whose aberrations I agree with Baron von Hügel, and (especially) Mrs. L——, a lady whose spiritual practices were doubtless better than her declarations on the subject." But she retained, as all high disciples of high masters do, a vivid judgement of her own. She wrote (28 August, 1924): "The Baron dosed me with Fénelon at one time, till I told him that a Perfect Gentleman giving judicious spiritual advice to Perfect Ladies was no good to me—since when his name has not been mentioned between us!" Not that she underrated either Fénelon or his advice; "Surtout, chère Madame, évitez les fatigues" was a maxim, at certain times, of Fénelon, of von Hügel, and of her own.

She had always had a high sense of the relation of the soul to others. In *The Column of Dust* she had written of the Vespers of the Dead said by the Helpers of the Holy Souls. It is worth quoting a few paragraphs:

But presently she woke from her dream, called forth by the high and urgent voice which led these poignant ceremonies. She heard it cry with a strange accent of authority—a certainty that its invocation could not be in vain—"*All ye orders of Blessed Spirits!*" and the congregation took it up, finished the phrase, "*Pray for the faithful departed.*" They had gone, it seemed, beyond the limit of their first petitions. The supplication of divine omnipotence was over. Now they extended their appeal, humanized it, claimed the help of the triumphant dead in caring for their poorer kin.

"Saint Gregory—Saint Augustine—Saint Ignatius!" cried the appellant voice: and the eager chorus followed with its supreme demand, "Pray for the faithful departed." None were excused from this duty. One after another, the torch-bearers of the faith were claimed, petitioned: and with so assured an accent that Constance almost expected a quiet presence to answer from beyond the radiant mist.

It went on, that roll-call of the happy dead; and with each name the reiterated, imperative, united cry for help. They called them down into this little chapel, claimed their kinship; insistent on the necessity of their suffrages, expectant of their brotherly aid. They were reminded of their humanity, these elect and shining spirits, snatched from the study, the brothel, the battle-field, the court. "You," these intent and amazing women seemed to say, "you, even more than we, should work, should plead for them. You have achieved: you have entered the Light: you are *there*. We do our best, but we are so far away. We lack your transcendent opportunity. Therefore we remind you of your fraternal obligations—*all ye holy doctors, popes, and confessors, pray for the faithful departed.*"

This awareness had developed, and under von Hügel's influence had recovered that visible, that institutional, order which it might have lost. It included, to her degree, both the dead and the living; it meant for her now chiefly two things—the poor and the Church. "God, Christ, and the Poor," she quoted from her master, and she attended to all. She came, at one period, to make a habit of visiting in North Kensington and spending two afternoons a week in the slums there. And she encouraged the same thing, whenever possible, among those who came to her for direction. The strange sense in which the poor, merely by being poor, are thought of as being the Body of Christ; almost as if the mere not-having made a man closer to the Incarnate than ever, in itself, could the having, seems to have been familiar to her, as indeed were all the aspects of mystical thought. "We are sewing the miserable little patches we call charity and social service into the rotten garment of our corporate life. . . . Thousands of us are eating what we suppose to be the Bread of Eternal Life at our brothers' expense." When that happens, it is certainly true that "we eat and drink our own damnation." She says, in a paper read at the Copec Conference at Birmingham, 1924, that the mystics had a hard name for this kind of thing. "They called it 'adoring Christ's Head and neglecting His feet.' 'Surely,' says one, 'He will more thank thee and reward thee for the meek washing of His feet when they be very foul, and yield an ill savour to thee, than for all the curious painting and fair dressing thou canst make about His head by thy devout remembrances.' " She quoted in another paper, read in 1922 at the Inter-Denominational Summer School of Social Services, a great passage from Walter Hilton concerning the City of God—"it seemeth . . . six cubits and a palm of length. By six cubits are understood the perfection of a man's work; and by the palm, a little touch of contemplation." This, she said, was the true formula—"skill and vision." "St. Teresa said that to give our Lord a perfect service Martha and Mary must combine."

Because her own business was chiefly to train young Marys, she did not forget their and our debt to the Marthas, and she was humbly and acutely aware of those unknown and harassed Marthas at the expense of whose pain we all live. Even in religion, though she wrote "unless one can stretch into one's own devotional life to make it avail for them . . . it remains more or less a spiritual luxury," she also wrote: "One comes away . . . nearer God. They give one far more than one can ever give them." Her sense of the spirit never left her blind to the bibliographical details of a book, nor did she forget this world in her attention to the other. But the other had still its own problem here, and in 1921 she solved it as best she could; she became a practising member of the Church of England.

It would be unfair to represent this as a compromise—conscious or unconscious; in fact, of course, it cannot be a compromise. It is impossible to compromise on the Church of England; her sacraments are sacraments or they are not. It is possible to believe either; it is possible to refuse decision. But it is not possible honestly to say that they will do instead of something which ought to be substituted for them. We cannot accuse Evelyn Underhill of any such dishonesty. So far therefore she must have modified her earlier position. She no longer said: "I cannot accept Anglicanism"; she did accept it. It is to be admitted that she accepted it at first without enthusiasm. She had been baptized and confirmed into that Church. But she had not been brought up in it; she had not learned from it the great dogmas nor seen by its light the illumination of her experiences. It had not been to her, as it has been to so many, "the Vision of the Principle," so that, whatever great doctors and august traditions others may acknowledge beyond it, it is still to them control and direction, origin, nourishment, and glor . Her realization of the Vision had been related to the Holy Roman Church, and there for her the metropolitan centre of Christendom lay. The letter to Dom John Chapman (9 June, 1931) presents the facts as far as she could see them, and no-one else is likely to see them better. "I . . . solidly believe in the Catholic status of the Anglican Church, as to orders and sacraments, little as I appreciate many of the things done among us. . . . The whole point to me is that our Lord has put me *here*, keeps on giving me more and more jobs to do for souls here, and has never given me orders to move. . . . I know what the push of God is like, and should obey it if it came—at least I trust and believe so." Von Hügel had gone into the matter in 1921, had said that she was only to move if God called her, and "was satisfied that up to date I had not received this call." She had, in her earlier days, experienced the impact of the Impossible. The only proper result of that, in any life, is to accept the working of the Impossible along such possibilities as it condescends to create. She never forgot the one, but she never refused the other. To call such obedience—whether it takes place in religion, in politics, in any love-affair, or whatever—a compromise is to underrate, in her as in others, both the fidelity and the labour. It is necessary to maintain both, as and how the Impossible decrees. This she did; it was the meaning of her submission. Her period of attention and patience had lasted for some fourteen years. The proof of her calling—or, at least, the value of it—was in her motherhood of souls.

Of the poor and the Church she had—at least, since her conversion in 1907—always been conscious. There was, however, something else which von Hügel did for her; it is described in a letter not reprinted in the body of this volume. The sentences are so important that they ought to be quoted: the date seems to be about 1927: "Until about five years ago I had never had *any* personal experience of our Lord. I didn't know what it meant. I was a convinced theocentric, thought most Christocentric language and practice sentimental and superstitious and was very handy to shallow psychological explanations of it. I had, from time to time, what seemed to be vivid experiences of God, from the time of my conversion from agnosticism (about twenty years ago now). This position I thought to be that of a broadminded and intelligent Christian, but when . . . I went to the Baron [this refers to the 1921 directorate] he said I wasn't much better than a Unitarian! Somehow by his prayers or something he *compelled* me to experience Christ. He never said anything more about it— but I know humanly speaking he did it. It took about four months—it was like watching the sun rise very slowly—and then suddenly one knew what it was.

"Now for some time after this I remained predominantly theocentric. But for the next two or three years, and specially lately, more and more my whole religious life and experience seem to centre with increasing vividness on our Lord—that sort of quasi-involuntary prayer which springs up of itself at odd moments is always now directed to Him. I seem to have to try as it were to live more and more towards Him only—and it's all this which makes it so utterly heartbreaking when one is horrid.

The New Testament which once I couldn't make much of, or meditate on, now seems full of things never noticed—all gets more and *more* alive and compelling and beautiful. . . . Holy Communion which at first I did simply under obedience, gets more and more wonderful too. It's in that world and atmosphere one lives."

She adds two notes on this. The first is, as might be expected, a reminder to herself that such "consolations" have a danger about them. Their best characteristic indeed is that they have, when real, not only a beauty and goodness in themselves, but also, as it were by a proper accident, an encouragement of lucidity and accuracy. Our Lord, it may be said, increases not only faith but scepticism, each in its proper relation to the other. She continues (secondly): "This makes it so much more difficult than before to meet on their own ground the people who have arrived at a sort of all-overish theism and feel 'Hindus are often nearer God than Christians,' and that there are 'other ways to Him' and so forth. . . . When they bring out all the stuff about Christ being a World Teacher, or the parallels of the Mystery religions, the high quality of Buddhist ethics, etc., I just feel what shallow, boring, unreal twaddle it is! But feeling that doesn't win souls for God."

The operation between von Hügel and Evelyn Underhill was, of course, invited. Neither he nor she was apt to "interfere" otherwise. It would be a highly improper course for anyone to attempt to "compel" anyone into a state which they themselves refused. But, that allowed, it seems to be an example of the working of organism within organism about which she wrote in speaking of him. It is an example of what is known by the Church as the Communion of Saints—meaning those living in the Mystical Body. The result was to establish her heart and mind more and more clearly and deeply in the "sound doctrine" and high devotion which is the response of the Communion of Saints to our Lord.

Her experience developed during 1923–4. In February, 1923,

she wrote: "Yesterday I *saw* and *felt* how it actually is that we are in Christ and He in us—the interpenetration of Spirit—and all of us merged together in Him actually, and so fully described as His Body. The way to full intercessory power must, I think, be along this path. Quite half of what I saw slipped away from me, but the certitude remains: 'the fragrance of those desirable meats,' as St. Augustine says. Curious how keen all Saints are about food." And at Easter in the next year she noted: "One comes to realize the institution of the Blessed Sacrament as the first moment and sum of the whole Passion—'He gave Himself in either kind.' That is really the whole story; and the same demand is more and more completely made on us." The Union, after Its own manner, was authentically begun in her, and her authenticity testified to it, both by her own words and by those she copied. Thus in the same year she noted privately, from the *Mirror of Simple Souls*: "The soul feels no joy, for she herself is joy." Both parts of the phrase are intense.

IV

From 1911 onwards her life consisted of religious work, either private or public, interspersed with holidays abroad as long as possible. The private work meant, in general, cases of direction; the public, her addresses, retreats, and books. Most of the letters which follow exhibit the first; a few notes on the second may be given here.

These thirty years, from 1911 until her death in 1941, are divided almost equally into two parts by the death of von Hügel in 1925. She had begun taking retreats in 1924, after the experience described in the last section. But she had taken part in public religious activities before then. Thus in 1912 she had joined the Committee of the Religious Thought Society, and took a good part in its work. She had always, as long as her health permitted, to yield to the demands of her own very practical and efficient nature; if she took part in anything, it had to be an active part. Thus, during the 1914–18 period of the war, she worked in the Naval Intelligence (Africa) department in translation and the preparation of guide-books—an activity with which, as earlier with the sea, a delicate fancy might play as consistent with her other and lordlier vocation. "I am gradually finding out that most devout persons," she had written in 1913, "are docetists without knowing it, and that nothing short of complete unreality will satisfy them." In fact, the accusation is largely true, though not quite in the sense that she then meant. But spiritually, she would have asked nothing better than to be considered an efficient translator and preparer of guide-books in a time of war. She came to disapprove of *The Mystic Way* because she thought it, on the whole, an inaccurate guide-book; just as she also rather disliked the two little books (*The Spiral Way* and *The Path of the Eternal Wisdom*) which she published under the pseudonym of John Cordelier because she thought the style faulty and flowery. This is a great tribute to her authenticity; she was, to the very end, prepared to purge and elucidate her literary expression. She accepted criticism with a free and disengaged heart. Not that— though it seems curious to say so—she was ever primarily a writer; she was something rather less but much better than that, as other writers will realize.

But as she was no Docetist, so she was no Manichean. She had, by nature, a vivid sense of the "reality of finites." It will be seen, from certain phrases in the following letters, what a love and interest she had for her cats. Von Hügel had written to her (26–9 December, 1921), in one of his letters of direction: "I much like your love for your cats. I deeply love my little dog; and Abbé Huvelin was devoted to his cat. We all three can and will become all the dearer to God for this our love of our little relations, the smaller creatures of God. Again it was God incarnate, it was Jesus of Nazareth, of Gethsemane, of Calvary, and not pure Theism, that first taught this." The present writer has indeed wondered if some movement of the mind along there lines was not part of the preparation for the apprehension of our Lord previously described. Certainly her apprehension of this world must have been; when she talked of "Reality" it was not an exclusive but an inclusive Reality which she meant.

In the same way she was devoted to flowers and birds, as to all living creatures, and had a keen interest in archæology. She and her husband often arranged their holidays with these concerns in view. Thus they went in one year to Monte Generoso for the sake of the Alpine flowers, and in other years to Drummond Castle and Malham Tarn for the sake of the English. She had a passion for mountains, though she saw a certain irrationality in her ardour—"they are only heaps of earth." But if the Omnipotence deigned so to create, why not adore the Omnipotence and (in another kind) the creation? So, and not otherwise, the single operation proceeded in her.

In 1921 she gave the Upton Lectures on Religion at Manchester College, Oxford; they were afterwards published as *The Life of the Spirit and the Life of To-day.* She was also a member of Copec and made a contribution to one of its published reports. She was now generally recognized not only as a "great Christian writer" but as a person capable of communicating spiritual initiative and power. It was inevitable therefore that she should be continually asked to give retreats, addresses, and quiet days, though it is said that on the whole she rather disapproved of quiet days, "as being too short to produce much effect and often too little detached from ordinary life." In this, as in everything, she did not much care for the exceptional or the incidental; it was normal life, and the food of normal life, with which only she was concerned. It was for that reason that she particularly loved the Retreat House at Pleshey, because it became for her part of a great and awful normality, and certainly no Retreat House can better deserve the praise. A number of her addresses were from time to time published in book form.

Her books, on the whole, fall into two classes; one might carry on the divisions maintained above (but only so as "not to

break the back of the poor phrase") and call them either translations or guide-books. The first consists of the actual translations
and critical editions which she brought out. Among these are
her editions of Ruysbroeck (1916), of *The Cloud of Unknowing*
(1912), and of *The Scale of Perfection* (1923); the books on
Ruysbroeck (1915) and on Jacopone da Todi (1919); *Eucharistic
Prayers from the Ancient Liturgies* (1939); and such other books,
or parts of books, as *The Mystics of the Church* (1925). She is
said not to have cared much for this last, and to have regarded it,
more or less, as a piece of hack-work. Every writer who has had
to do hack-work will sympathize. But it has, in fact, a quite
particular value. One may again use the word *authenticity*; it
exhibits, with high intelligence, the many and various authen-
ticities of the saints. She had—what so many religious writers
have not—a real religious impartiality, a holiness of judgement,
consistent with her own predilections but overruling them.
Her natural efficiency may have played its part in this; it
was as distasteful to her to be wrong intellectually as to be
wrong morally. Taste, by itself, will not save souls, but taste
may be a subsidiary instrument, and a taste for recognizing
differences in souls is very useful both in recording sanctity and in
encouraging sanctity. She was, in every way, revolted by jargon,
and this remains true even if occasionally she herself seems to
yield to it. She wrote (20 September, 1911) of an edition of the
Lady Julian: "I consider his idea of editing truly beastly. 'Reaction and Nightmare' is hardly a felicitous title for her chapter
about the vision of the fiend, to my thinking! Nor is 'littleness of
the Kosmos' a likely phrase on the lips of a fourteenth-century
mystic." Nor, perhaps, on any except a Greek's or a fool's.

In this group also her journalistic work should be included;
it provided, and (if it is ever possible to collect any of it) would
continue to provide, valuable footnotes to the "translations."
She was a well-known contributor to many periodicals, and for
some time Theological Editor of the *Spectator*. When that paper
changed hands and she had to resign this post, she began work

for *Time and Tide*. Her relations with this paper were particularly delightful to her, for she found there (as others have done) friendship and freedom; the last thing she ever wrote was a review for it. She is reported to have been among the better kind of reviewers—exact to space and time.

The other class of books, "the guide-books," are those which serve as direct exhortations to the Way. Such are *Practical Mysticism* (1915) and *The Essentials of Mysticism* (1920). These titles may seem a little cheap, but the books are not so. They are, on the whole, a psychological examination of the Way. She was always very well aware of the psycho-physical dangers, both in herself and in others; it was one of the reasons why she eased her students as much as she urged them. But to know the dangers, and to remark that sometimes they should be evaded ("Surtout, chère Madame, évitez les fatigues"), does not mean to renounce heroism. She records, if without extreme enthusiasm yet with real apprehension, certain moments in the lives of the saints most difficult for some of her readers to understand, but she expects her readers to understand them. She says in the *Essentials of Mysticism* of Sœur Thérèse de l'Enfant-Jésus: "Her superiors seem at once to have perceived in her that peculiar quality of soul which is capable of sanctity, and since it is the ambition of every community to produce a saint, they addressed themselves with vigour to the stern task of educating Thérèse for her destiny. . . . When her health began to fail under a rule of life far beyond her strength, and the first signs of tuberculosis—that scourge of the cloister—appeared in her, the Prioress, in her ferocious zeal for souls, even refused to dispense the ailing girl from attendance at the night-office. 'Une âme de cette trempe, disait-elle, ne doit pas être traité comme une enfant, les dispenses ne sont pas faites pour elle. Laissez-la. Dieu la soutient.' This drastic training did its work."

In the same way she had noted in an essay included in *The Essentials of Mysticism* the paragraph in which Angela of Foligno has scandalized generations:

THE LETTERS OF EVELYN UNDERHILL

I elected to walk on the thorny path which is the path of tribulation. So I began to put aside the fine clothing and adornments which I had, and the most delicate food, and also the covering of my head. But as yet, to do all these things was hard and shamed me, because I did not feel much love for God, and was living with my husband. So that it was a bitter thing to me when anything offensive was said or done to me; but I bore it as patiently as I could. In that time, and by God's will, there died my mother, who was a great hindrance to me in following the way of God; my husband died likewise; and in a short time there also died all my children. And because I had begun to follow the aforesaid way, and had prayed God to rid me of them, I had a great consolation of their deaths, although I also felt some grief; wherefore, because God had shown me this grace, I imagined that my heart was in the heart of God and His will and His heart in my heart.

She did not altogether defend it. But neither did she obscure it. There it was, and we shall not understand the Way without understanding that.

It is worth noting these one or two extreme examples, because of the letters. These were written to many different correspondents, and (carelessly read) they might leave an impression of too great ease, of an almost over-emphasis on relaxation. Such an impression would be unfair to Evelyn Underhill. She did not, certainly, wish to take too great risks with her inquirers; she was, like von Hügel, reluctant to interfere. But also she was very clear that we ought all, and especially those upon the Way, above all upon this particular Way, to wait upon the Lord. We ought to be quick but not flurried. She is continually, delicately, insisting on this. "I know you do feel tremendously stimulated all round; but remember the 'young presumptuous disciples' in the *Cloud*! Hot milk and a thoroughly foolish novel are better things for you to go to bed on just now than St. Teresa" (7 February, 1923). "It is not God but your too eagerly enjoying psyche which keeps you awake and tears you to bits with an over-exciting joy" (1 March, 1923). "You have been relying

33

too much on experience, and not enough on the facts of faith"
(24 November, 1923). "You need not have worried about
penances and mortifications need you? When the hour strikes
they are there all right; and so on with everything else, only never
the expected thing" (20 June, 1924). "Don't be in a hurry with
your convert! It is not everyone who is equal to 'giving themselves freely' at the beginning. . . . She will probably do best
on a sugar diet for a little while and in due course find out for
herself that it is not adequate" (31 July, 1925).

All these are from the last section of Letters, but they could
be paralleled elsewhere. She was concerned to free her friends
from that faintly deceptive psychic chat within themselves which
so often produces spiritual cant, however unintentionally. And
she had perhaps an especial grasp of the fact that a soul may so
ask for a thing that it receives, in the end, that gift and no other—
and then cannot bear it. It exclaims then, and the whole universe
—we must not say the Creator—answers only: "Vous l'avez
voulu, Georges Dandin!" Fortunate he who can see it so;
blessed he who can use it so.

Of her own temptations little can be said. The letters in
which, if at all, she exposed them do not seem now to exist. In
an early MS. book of notes she had made at the age of fifteen a
list of "My Faults." It runs to nineteen entries, namely: "Selfishness; pride; conceit; disorder; moral cowardice; self-deceit;
scepticism; thoughtlessness; revengefulness; exaggeration; want
of truth; changeable; double-dealing; teasing; unkindness; dis-
obeidience [sic]; dishonourableness; profanity; idleness."

It is a pleasant thing—and yet not without its significance.
Long afterwards, von Hügel said that she was inclined too
"vivaciously" to attend to the state of her own soul. Her
vehemence was apt to commit the same error as another person's
sloth; it confused attention and destroyed reason. Her sins
indeed in general seem to have chiefly derived, as one would
expect, from what again von Hügel called "the vehemence and
exactingness of your nature." It was she, rather than others, who

34

suffered from this. What better? But here and there, for a moment, one can see it might have been otherwise. The single final egotism—the psychic (the word is hers) awareness of the self—was a trouble to her as to all sincere and generous souls. It exists, of course, in all human beings; the only difference is between those who allow it to infect, and perhaps to corrupt, the spiritual and those who do not. This infection leads to those sins which are exposed in the great oration on love delivered by Virgil to Dante half-way up the purgatorial mountain. She, who loved Dante, would have permitted the reference.

These temptations took, on the whole, two forms. There was sometimes a moment's spiritual envy, a transient jealousy; of these once she wrote: "Severe steps must be taken"—as, for example, when one or more of her people suddenly veered towards another teacher. She knew, as well as any of us, that our business is so to give that "by taking oneself one makes the recipient independent." The phrase is Kierkegaard's, speaking of the omnipotence of God, but all Christians who happen to be made teachers should give in this way, and Evelyn Underhill laboured to do so; that she had sometimes to labour does not derogate from the result and does increase her honour. She demanded from herself a Dantean courtesy of largesse in all relations. She once observed of herself that she was apt to exhibit "a condescending attitude to family claims," which was "insincere and to my own disadvantage." Her comment is an example of her intelligence. Many might have thought such an attitude of condescension wrong, but they might have supposed it to be only too sincere. She knew it was not so; she was pretending even while she soared. She was not to be easily deceived.

Yet, in another sense, the fear of deception lay close to her. She was apt at times, though these seem to have grown fewer as the years went on, to be attacked by a violent emotional scepticism. Her old tendency to explain everything subjectively recurred now as a temptation to suppose everything—objective

35

or subjective, dogma or experience—to be spiritual hallucination. She retained for long a desire for spiritual certitude, and she suffered acutely from the lack of it. The equal (or all but equal) swaying level of devotion and scepticism which is, for some souls, as much the Way as continuous simple faith is to others, was a distress to her. It is doubtful if she ever easily managed to drive those two horses together in her own life, however she was wise to instruct others. There is nothing improper in this; it is indeed but part of that great principle which was intentionally exhibited on, and unintentionally defined under, the Cross of our Lord: "Others he saved; himself he could not save." We are here talking, of course, not only of intellectual belief and intellectual doubt, but rather of that felt in the blood and in the soul—"utter and intimate unbelief." She wanted to be *sure*. Benson had written to her long before: "I really do not think you have enough reverence for the stupid." She was taught, in a spiritual sense, so to reverence herself.

Both these temptations, it may well be thought, are only indications of her conflict with the final psychic egotism; say, that this itself was perhaps something more, some conjoining of sacrifice with sacrifice. She wrote (in 1932): "The number of hours I've spent apparently in prayer but really raging in hell these last 18 months don't bear thinking of. Hard continuous work or people one has to talk to, are the only things that keep it off; and here, I'm a great deal alone and entirely at the mercy of furious and miserable thoughts, a large part of which I know are imaginary but for all that can't escape from. . . . I simply dare not let my mind be passive. What I mind most is that it makes one feel absolutely wicked and vile, and I don't *want* to be wicked. And all the books, and everything else one has always loved, are implicated, and merely make one feel sick, and so everything is spoiled and there is absolutely nothing left." Whether, before she died, she was freed "by high permission of all-ruling heaven" from such suffering, it is impossible to say. It seems likely that she was, for the preoccupation of the war brought other, and perhaps less obviously personal, pain. But here, rather than at any other point—here in relation to that great principle of grace by which we do not know what we are, what we achieve, or what we appear—may be quoted what one of her friends said of her later:

"It was in October 1937 that I met her first—invited to tea with her in her Campden Hill Square house. She had just had one of her bad illnesses. The door of the room into which I was shown was directly behind the big arm-chair in which she was sitting facing a glowing fire. As I entered she got up and turned round, looking so fragile as though 'a puff of wind might blow her away' might be literally true in her case, *but* light simply streamed from her face illuminated with a radiant smile. . . . One could not but feel consciously there and then (not on subsequent recognition or reflection) that one was in the presence of the extension of the Mystery of our Lord's Transfiguration in one of the members of His Mystical Body. I myself never saw it repeated on any later meeting though others have probably seen the same thing at other times. It told one not only of *herself*, but more of God and of the Mystical Body than all her work put together."

Such an outpouring of light has been observed elsewhere—in certain great men (such as, I think, Leonardo) and by lovers in lovers. It is as if the physical flesh itself had become, or at least had seemed to become, its unfallen self; as if that Original which was seen in the Transfiguration chose at certain moments to exhibit something of its glory in its created derivations. That such a phenomenon was observed in her is credible enough; it was her reward, and (after the proper heavenly manner) it was given to others.

V

It is not possible, in an Introduction of this kind, to speak properly of her friends. Yet not to allude to them at all would be to omit something of which she was very conscious, to which she vividly "submitted," and from which (as from her husband) she continually, under God, "derived herself." The requests for their prayers for this or the other effort which she sent in her letters, the criticism of her work which (by general testimony) she invited, show this. That great sense of exchanged derivation —that is, at bottom, of the Communion of Saints—which is the very manner of life of the Kingdom of Heaven, was always present to her. It is the root of humility. The phrase "to pray for . . ." has become (except indeed to the best practitioners) a little tainted by our spiritual poverty; it is not verbal but vital; it is our mode of being, or perhaps it would be better to say it is the carrying of our natural mode of being on into the arch-natural. She gave and took in marriage and all its high exchange of dependency; thus, except for her public duties, she kept her evenings for her husband when he returned from his legal work; and so also, in proper degrees, she gave and took in friendship; and carried those friendships very far. They were to her part of the apprehension of the Union, and her concern for the Union lived in them, though of course not solely. They were in Catholicity, but also Catholicity showed in them.

Two relationships may be mentioned as examples—one Italian, one English. The Italian was her intimacy with Maria, the *Sorella minora* (or Sister Superior) of a community of followers of St. Francis. She first heard of them through other friends and presently herself visited them. She afterwards wrote of them in the *Spectator* (11 February, 1928): "The head of the household and foundress, who is known as the Least Sister, came down the lane to welcome me. . . . Those who recognize her type will discover without surprise that her delicate courtesy, her serene and wide-spreading love conceal a Teresian inflexibility of purpose: a profound sense of the pain and need of the world, and a passionate desire to help it. As we sat in the woods, I asked her to tell me something of her conception of the spiritual life. She replied, in words startlingly at variance with her peaceful surroundings, '*In tormento e travaglia servire i fratelli.*' "

Such a phrase struck to Evelyn Underhill's heart. She quoted, in the same article, another which must have been almost as precious to her: "We receive good," Maria had written, "from the experience which each soul brings to us; from an example, from a fraternal warning, from that gaze with which we follow every creature in reverence of heart, learning to love, venerate, help, and pray."

There grew up between the two women—and lasted for a good while—an exchange of this duty and desire, and therefore of power. They were both "members" (to use a too defining word) of an unorganized Confraternity which "worked in the hiddenness," and had "no propaganda, no public reunions, no rule but that of a common loyalty and intention and a mutual reverence and love." That intention was the achievement of the Union, in all proper degrees, after all proper methods, but especially on earth as it—now and already—is in heaven; that is, by the Union on earth, as much as may be, of the Church with her Lord; that is, by the Church visibly at unity with herself; that is, as a means, by the drawing of all professing Christians into concord and peace. Such Confraternities, from time to time, exist—so unorganized, so hidden; they may not last; they spring and cease; but invisibly one succeeds to another; they are gates in the heart for the elect, who indeed become elect partly by their own election of such opportunities. The prayer of this company was that of St. Catherine of Siena: "Come, Holy Spirit, into my heart; draw it to Thee by Thine ineffable love, and bestow on me charity with fear. Keep me, O Christ, from every evil thought. Warm me and illuminate me by Thy most sweet love, that every pain may seem light to me. My Holy Father, my sweet Lord, I pray Thee help me in my every service."

The other friendship which may be mentioned, only as an example, was English. On one of her afternoons of visiting in the slums and all-but-slums of North Kensington, Evelyn Underhill was directed to the home of an invalid, a certain Laura Rose. In the course of their first conversation, she asked what books Mrs. Rose liked best, and was answered: "St. John of the Cross." This immediately set up a knowledgeable kinship between the two women. Evelyn carried books to the invalid, and derived instruction from her; when she had to return to London from the country (she preferred the country to London —but even the great have their weaknesses!) she sometimes said: "London has one advantage; it holds Laura Rose." Mrs. Rose was a contemplative by nature; she had small education, in the ordinary sense, but she knew her leaders. Evelyn Underhill recognized the power. In 1936, after long ill-health, Laura died. She is here recollected, not only for herself, but because her first answer is typical, as it were, of so many of Evelyn's friendships: "What do you like to read?" "St. John of the Cross."

VI

The last period of her life was marked by two withdrawals. The first was physical and involuntary; the second, spiritual and voluntary. She suffered very much from ill-health, especially from asthma; and she was gradually compelled to give up all her public speaking and taking retreats. She was peculiarly anxious not to be too tender to herself; in spite of all her good advice to others, she was herself liable to err by doing too much rather than by doing too little. Yet she thought it an error, and desired not to err. She wished to be wholly at the disposal of the Lord who determined proportion as well as direction, and she had generally, so devoted, a very clear spiritual judgement on what she could and could not do.

Her other withdrawal was of a more limited kind. Evelyn Underhill was never anything of an eccentric; she had in her a metropolitan spirit of the City. It will be remembered that, in 1914–18, she had taken as active a part in the war effort as was possible to her; she had spoken at meetings and worked in the Admiralty. By 1939 her views had changed; it would perhaps be more accurate to say that her power had changed. It is impossible now to contemplate the steady movement of her spirit along its clarifying purpose towards its end and not to see this as a part of that same movement. To say she had become a pacifist is a crude way of putting it, though, of course, correct. It would be truer to say that that grace which had disposed itself within her prevented her from being anything else. It does not, of course, follow that this is everybody's Way or everybody's vocation. But it is at least quite likely that it might, at any moment, be anybody's or at least any Christian's. The practical question which always has to be solved is which of the claims to such a vocation are genuine (not attributing any guiltiness of self-deception to any claimant). We do not perhaps succeed very well with our tribunals; more care might be taken with their personnel, and a certain number of practised confessors included, at least on the ground of their being among the better kind of psychoanalysts. But it is difficult to see what other course can be taken; the State has a right to share in the final decision, as the Church has a duty to share in the decision on any claim to the Religious Life. Evelyn Underhill's long life of authenticity was, in her case, the best guarantee of that authenticity. Pacifism in her was the last development of the Way which she had followed; it was, in her and for her, our Lord's chosen method. He who had seemed to her first, under veils, an Impossibility, and then, in another sense, a Possibility, now deigned, in this matter, to be something of both. For she had no doubt about her duty and no doubt about "the excellent absurdity" of her duty. She joined the Anglican Pacifist Fellowship, and she wrote for it a pamphlet, *The Church and War*. It is a quite uncompromising pamphlet: "On the question of war between man and man she [the Church] cannot compromise."

It might be held that, in uttering this judgement, Evelyn Underhill was again allowing some licence to her earlier faint tendency to tell the Church what it ought to believe. The Church has never been pacifist, and it has certainly never thought it was compromising by not being pacifist. It has steadily discriminated between love and submission, and enjoined the one without, in all cases, recommending the other. Such a small gibe at her would not, it may be hoped, have wholly displeased her; she was very generous. But obviously such a small gibe refers only to a hasty phrase or two in her writing. It has nothing to do with her own spiritual choice.

In the same way that argument, which ever since 1907 had at times obtruded itself, about the claims of the Church of Rome or (to put it another way) about the Catholicity of the Church of England, had faded. It seems likely that, under the influence of von Hügel, she had understood better than before the nature of the choice which might have been presented to her. "You will," he had written, "remain spiritually weak and inconsistent, if you do not, however slowly and indirectly, resolve this bit of amiable naturalism in the ocean of the supernatural love of, and waiting upon, God." She had certainly assented to this. If she had understood it to be sin to remain in the Church of England, she would (humanly speaking) certainly have surrendered. But she not only did not so understand it; she definitely thought it her proper place. She may sometimes have said with a smile or a sigh the equivalent of: "They order these things better in Rome." But her submission was to the Catholicity of the English Church, and beyond that to the Union of Christendom. She joined the Fellowship of St. Alban and St. Sergius, largely owing to the interest in the Orthodox Churches and their Liturgy which her studies for her last large book, *Worship*, aroused in her. She set before the text of the book a quotation from Elizabeth Waterhouse's *Thoughts of a Tertiary*: "All worship was to him sacred, since he believed that in its most degraded forms, among the most ignorant and foolish of worshippers, there has yet been some true seeking after the Divine, and that between these and the most glorious ritual or the highest philosophic certainty, there lies so small a space that we may believe the Saints in Paradise regard it with a smile." Her beliefs (*mutatis mutandis*) were expressed perhaps still better in a phrase which she took over with joy from her Roman Catholic Italian friend Maria: "The Venerable Roman Church does but preside at the Universal Agape." It was the Universal Agape to which and for which she gave her life.

Worship was published in 1937. It was a good book; it was a topical book; and (universal though its subject was) it was also a highly personal book. It was "about" that to which she had all her life given herself, "about" adoration, and it was her own devotion and her own experience which found such phrases as "Worship is summed up in sacrifice"; "The devotional and liturgical path is at once Evangelical and Eucharistic"; "This is the ordained consummation of Christian personal worship: the mystery of creation, fulfilled in the secret ground of every soul." There are fewer quotations from the saints here, though there are more from the Rites, but all have the same authenticity about them. She knew very well the point at which, as she says, "the Rite assumes a life and authority of its own." She had known something similar during those other years, long ago, in Florence. The "understanding of things" which had begun in the Florentine pictures had entered on its greatest and, in this life, final movement. The second war opened; she was profoundly shocked and hurt, but she was not in any sense overcome, and she made herself a means of its crucial union with our Lord When she had written about the Cross, she had always meant the Cross. She had so worked that the great Ignatian phrase might have been applied to her—"her eros was crucified." Add to that one of her own quotations from Ruysbroeck: "I must rejoice without ceasing, though the world shudder at my joy." The lower eros was fastened to the cross, as far as her will could; the Divine Eros had fastened himself. She knew something of that cross on which (could it be said with belief!) they interchanged felicities. The shudder at that joy terrifies the world, but then the world has only one choice—between terror at that and terror at itself. Evelyn Underhill had all her life been aware of that necessary and supernatural terror; all her war against psychic deceptions, in herself and in others, was meant to purify all towards the terror and the joy. It is credible that she knew at least the momentary presence of the joy. If the present writer has seemed, here and there, to say a little less than he might about her writing, it is because that, on the whole, was the least (though no doubt a valuable) part of her intense vocation. Her vocation was rather to be—a guide? no; say rather, in the end, a light. The light might, and certainly did, illuminate and guide, but first it merely shone. This light she was; this (she so being) communicated to her, through her obedience, her vehemence, her faith something of the secrets of its own clarity.

The war had begun. But Evelyn Underhill's own secret wars were, it seems, ended. She might suffer, but now it was not from her own conflicts. She continued, as far as she could, to assist and instruct. A group of young women who wished to read theology had come together in London in 1939; she had been of use to them, and when on the outbreak of the war they were scattered she continued to write to them all a quarterly letter. These letters were afterwards collected in *The Fruits of the Spirit* (1942). In the autumn of 1939 she gave instructions on prayer to the children of the village of Washington, on the Sussex Downs, where she was then living, and conducted meetings for prayer in the church. In 1940 and during at least a part of the great air attacks at the end of that year, she was in London again. But apart from these merely outward movements, she grows secret. It would be useless and indecent here to multiply words. She continued to write a little; she continued, in her last and best activity, to pray and adore. She ingeminated "Love!" On Sunday, 15 June, 1941, she died; she is buried in the churchyard of St. John's Parish Church, Hampstead. The present writer, as it happened, was at her beloved Pleshey when the news of her death came to it. There is erected to her, in the chapel there, under the bell which rings always threefold in adoration of the Blessed and Glorious Trinity, a memorial plaque. She had begun by a passion for abstraction and pattern; she had learned to know the Incarnation, to adore in the Eucharist, to reverence the stupid, to love every creature. But the lettering on the plaque does not chiefly commemorate that. As if returning, by divine permission, all her gathered knowledge and growing illumination to that profound belief on which she had first set her heart, filling the diagram with richness, and exhibiting sweetness in the Strong, it takes all back into the Alone. But the Alone Itself is full of otherness. The lettering recognizes not only Its uncreated alienness from us but also our created likeness to It, when it says, quoting that lofty genius, John Donne, who smiled and moaned and was at peace to no other end: "Blessed be God that He is God, only and divinely like Himself."

Note on the Letters

Many of Evelyn Underhill's letters are not now available. The whole correspondence between her and von Hügel is missing, and indeed most other correspondence between 1912 and 1924. This is particularly unfortunate because the most critical period of her own development is thus left without record.

The following selection has been made from letters very kindly put at my disposal by Mr. Stuart Moore and by her friends and correspondents. I am under a serious obligation to all, and especially to those who have eased the task of selection. I may be permitted here to name Mr. Stuart Moore himself, Miss Lucy Menzies (the Literary Executor), Miss Clara Smith, and Mrs. R. V. Vernon. It is much to be hoped that I have not disappointed them in fulfilling the task.

The Letters have in general been arranged chronologically, one set alone excepted. The various series are distinguished by different sets of letters, in some cases (but not in all) the initials of the recipient. The last section consists of a selection from a particular correspondence made by the Bishop of St. Andrews. The Bishop was of the opinion that this group of letters should stand by itself, and indeed it is clearly desirable that in a book of this kind there should be one example of Evelyn Underhill's continuous work. My responsibility here is therefore limited to a necessary abridgement of the Bishop's choice.

I

1899–1919

O all ye works of the Lord, bless ye the Lord; praise Him and magnify Him for ever.—*Song of the Three Children.*

Lo, these are but the outskirts of His ways; and how small a whisper do we hear of Him.—*Job.*

Hotels Schweizerhof and Luzernerhof,
Lucerne.

March 28th [1899].

To Hubert Stuart Moore.

I got your letter this morning; *dearest* I *do* hope you are not very lonely and are going to have a nice happy healthy time. Oh, *do* be careful of yourself. We have just heard of Mr. Pyke's death, and it has made me *so* nervous. I'm quite *sure* the bar is getting to be a very dangerous profession. It seems awful the way quite youngish people die off. Do *do*, my sweetest boy, have all the fresh air and exercise you can, and avoid chills and being run down. I suppose Mr. Pyke's death is good for you in a way but how awful for his poor wife. I'm sure that nasty Admiralty Court isn't healthy, I'm thankful to think you won't sit in it all day now. *Do* have some nice walks in your holidays, and after you get home, go for some long bicycle rides. *Please* do.

I only wish you were here, I wish it all the day long. To-day has been exquisite. Very hot, sunshine like you never see in England, and yet brisk and refreshing. We have been nearly all day on the lake, going to Brunnen and back. It was so bright and clear we could see right across to the Bernese Oberland, even the Jungfrau which I had never seen before. The snow mountains and bright green lake and the quaint little square-sailed boats looked heavenly. I wanted you *so* much. You would just have enjoyed it. After tea we went up to the Glacier garden, where a real glacier once was, and you can see the deep holes in the rock and the boulders that fitted in and ground them out.

There is also a real Alpine Club hut, like you sleep in when you are climbing a mountain, from which it appears that mountaineering is a bit *too* uncomfortable for my taste, only a little hay to sleep on, and no head room worth mentioning.

I'm so anxious to get to Lugano and get my darling's next letter. I wonder if you got my photograph before you went away. If so, tell me *exactly* what they are like, and if they are better than the proofs. I am sure those proofs were printed on Matt P O P so you could tone and fix them if you wished. Our talk last Saturday has made me feel intensely that nothing matters very much to us except each other. It seems as if our two lives had rushed together and fused into one, and overshadow everything else. I feel as if all I say and do here was only a pleasant dream, and my real life was left behind in England for the boy to take care of till I come home to it and him. Do you understand? And do you ever feel like that about your girl? Tell me.

Chartres.
Tuesday night.
[April 17, 1901.]

To the Same.

This is an absolutely heavenly place, far exceeding my expectations, and we have dropped into such a comfy old-fashioned inn with a sweet old landlady in a bag cap. Only fault, they overfeed us horribly. The town is full of old houses with high gables and carved fronts, there are lots of quaint corners but no smells, and it is delightfully clean and airy. The day has been sun and shower with a high wind—something like my temper is occasionally. The Cathedral is a dream of beauty with nine magnificent doorways set in deep porches and crammed with sculpture. Nearly all the stained glass was put in before 1300. Nothing one can see in England can give you an idea of it. It is more like translucent enamel set with diamonds than anything else I can think of. I wish you were here, and I think you would like it, though the place swarms with priests who would set your Protestant teeth on edge.

Lengua da Ca,
Alassio.
Saturday, March 26th [1904].

To the Same.

I meant to answer your letter this morning but it was such a lovely day that immediately after breakfast we went off for an expedition into the hills; first drove to the first village above here through the olive woods; then climbed up through delicious little waggly stony streets, so narrow that when we met a donkey with panniers it had to lean up against the wall to let us pass; then up through more olive woods and out on to the healthy part of the hills: then we popped through a narrow little gap in the cliffs, and came out suddenly on the north face of the hills, and were looking right across an immense valley, all blue and purple with little white towns, to the Maritime Alps which stretched right along east and west as far as you could see, and were simply shining with freshly fallen snow. Yesterday was very cold here with rain, so it must have been snow on the mountains. We devoted the wettest part of the day to bookbinding and in the afternoon went to two tea parties. Tea parties simply swarm in Alassio and our average has been two a day since I came out.

The people are intensely funny and a rather smart lady who told me that it was "the continental Cranford" about summed the whole thing up. There's a funny little artist who talks a lot about the "reverent imitation of nature" but hasn't quite managed it yet, and a parson who said the other day that "even some of the most *distinguished* Early Christians did at times fall into sin," a remark which I am cherishing very fondly for future use.

Yacht *Wulfruna*,
Helford, St. Martin.
23 September [1904].

To J. A. Herbert.

Thank you so much for your kind letter. I am very glad indeed that you like the book.[1] I am sorry the phrase "Imagina-

[1] *The Grey World*. The quotation is the famous paragraph on "Imagination, the real and eternal world, of which this Vegetable Universe is but a faint shadow" from *Jerusalem*.

tive Life" seems wrong. It was used in rather a technical sense by Willie, the same sense in fact, as that intended by Blake in the quotation I have prefixed to the book, which is supposed to give the key note of such philosophy as it possesses. I can't think at the moment of any locution which says just the same thing; and this one seemed to have the advantage of a respectable ancestry.

[Undated.]

To J. A. HERBERT.

> Most worthy pard, my jaded wits refuse
> To reach the heights of your triumphant Muse.
> I merely send these little rhymes to say
> I'm glad we've got the plate of Sainte Abbaye.
> (And, by the way, I rather wonder when
> Our Magnum Opus goes to Methuen?)
> As to Abênteuẽr Gesämmt—well!
> Why can't the wretch in French his legends tell,
> Or decent Latin? I don't like to worry you
> To translate this. So many works to flurry you
> There are, with Titus Vesp. and all the rest.
> Perhaps to wait a while would be the best.
> Thanks many for the loan of Odo's tale.
> I hope my understanding will not fail
> To grasp the crabbed tongue in which it's writ
> And make it for the British Public fit.
> I also want to find a redaction
> Of Virgin's Hand on lock, with detailed action.
> (See Ward) a pretty tale, but rather terse:
> A virtue that does not infect *my* verse.
> Farewell! I'll write again to mention when
> I come to the Museum at stroke of ten.
> Meanwhile, good wishes to you all I send,
> And am your feeble and exhausted friend.

> > E.U.
> > Explicit.
> > Ora pro me.

3 Campden Hill Place, W.
Nov. 29, 1904.

To M.R.

I must thank you very much for writing to me as kindly as you have done. I think it is so good of those who have read, and have cared for what they have read, to write and tell the author, who knows little of what her work is doing, once it has gone out into the world. As you say, the finding of reality is the one thing that matters, and that always mattered, though it has been called by many different names.

Of course, on this side the veil, the perfect accomplishment of the quest is impossible; we can only come to the edge of the sea that separates us from the City of Sarras. Few get so far: but for those who do, it seems that there is a certain hope. It is of course quite difficult for me, from one letter, to judge of your position; so I hope you will forgive me if I say anything you do not like.

But you say in one place, that the more urgent the want of reality grows, the less you see how to effect it. Now, this state of "spiritual unrest" can never bring you to a state of vision, of which the essential is peace. And struggling to see does not help one to see. The light comes, when it does come, rather suddenly and strangely I think. It is just like falling in love; a thing that never happens to those who are always trying to do it.

You say also, as regards beauty, that you find its sensuous side dangerous and distracting. This is true at first: but when once it has happened to you to perceive that beauty is the "outward and visible sign" of the greatest of sacraments, I don't think you can ever again get hopelessly entangled by its merely visible side. The real difficulty seems to me to come from the squalor and ugliness with which man tries to overlay the world in which he lives.

I have been so much interested by your letter and hope you will forgive this imperfect reply.

Perhaps you will write to me again when you are in the mood. Those who are on the same road can sometimes help one another.

Grand Hotel,
Venice.
April 20th [1905].

To HUBERT STUART MOORE.

We arrived last night all right though rather late. It was very funny to see all the stations full of soldiers and guards along the line, but otherwise I don't think one could have told that anything was wrong. The arrival here is perfectly beautiful. About ten miles away, the land begins to break up into marshy patches, tussocks of grass and pools of water; then more water and fewer patches of land, and then suddenly the last bit of land is all gone and the train runs over a great smooth grey sea, for 3 miles, on a bridge just raised above the surface of the water. For a bit you are "out of sight of land" and then at last you see the towers of the city ahead of you. It's just perfect arriving in the evening like that with everything very grey and dim. I *did* wish you were here. And then it was so exciting to step out of the station pop on to the canal and see all the usual station bustle being done by swarms of gondolas, all black and fringed, such long thin graceful creatures all shooting and twisting about. And there was a full moon and after dinner we went out on the Grand Canal, and saw Venice by moonlight. We have to-day secured our own gondola; such a nice man, named Vittorio, with whom I have to hold long conversations for the Commodore.[1] We spent the morning in the gondola, going in and out among the canals, seeing the palaces etc. . . . There are a lot of English yachts here, and also heaps of lovely sort of Istrian boats rather like Dutch schoots but painted the most splendid colours which come with cargoes of firewood. And people go off to them in gondolas and buy a bit when they want it. It's so nice everything being done by boat, and stepping out of the front door bang into the water. I spent the afternoon in St. Marco, and managed to get a slight first idea of it. But you can't describe it.

It's like nothing you ever saw; but when the Westminster Cathedral is done, that will be a sort of parody of the interior. It is all mosaics with gold backgrounds. Five domes, with

[1] Her father.

wonderful processions of figures circling round them: and all the arches, spandrils and lunettes mosaic-ed too, and the lower walls marbled. And all the detail is so marvellous. Every minute you come on pierced marble screens, and lovely bas-relief panels set here and there in the walls, both inside and out, to vary the marble panelling: and all sorts of strange green and rose and purple marbles that one never sees anywhere else. The pavement is made with them too, and with jade and lapis, all in Byzantine patterns. But it isn't a bit garish *I* think, just a masterpiece of colouring. The Commodore however thought it horrid, and fled to the shops, where he bought paper knives made to imitate the prow of a gondola.

There's one lovely mosaic of the body of St. Mark being brought by ship to Venice. The ship is all aback, the sailors are asleep, and St. Mark appears and wakes them up, very anxious, and evidently saying "*Do, do* take more care of my body."

Grand Hotel,
Venice.
Saturday night [April, 1905].

To the Same.

I do hope the cold weather has gone in England and you are having a nice sunny healthy holiday. It isn't very hot here, a fresh sea breeze all the time but it has been nice and sunny to-day. At twelve o'clock the Easter feast began, and all the flags were hoisted on the flag staffs in front of St. Mark's. Huge great banners about 50 feet I should think: three Italian ensigns, and two crimson and gold flags with the Lion of St. Mark. It makes the piazza look simply gorgeous, with these great things floating out, and all the mosaics and white domes of the cathedral behind, and the crowds of pigeons wheeling about, as thick almost as our birds at the Helford, only rather a different colour. Inside St. Mark's, the gold altar front is unveiled for Easter: 11th century Greek work all set with jewels. I'm going to try and get a seat in the choir for High Mass to-morrow so as to gaze on it undisturbed.

We spent the morning at the picture gallery. A tremendous

lot of big rambling Veronese and Tintoretto things to wade through, but also, to console one, a lot of lovely Cima and Bellini and Carpaccio: things rather in the style of our pet St. Jerome in his study at the National Gallery. There is the whole set of the story of St. Ursula by Carpaccio done to decorate the guild-room of the St. Ursula guild. The first one, where she is in bed asleep and the angel comes and warns her of what she is to do, is too sweet. Such a neat room, with her clothes neatly folded at the foot of the bed and her crown (she was a Princess) laid on the top! The Commodore liked Titian's big fluffy Assumption (I'm sure he secretly agreed with the celebrated American who said she was "a remarkably fine young woman") but he got a bit restless over the other things—kept asking patiently "Is this by a *celebrated* artist?"

In the afternoon we went a long gondola ride to a church on the far edge of the city looking out to the lagoon where we found several lovely pictures and a perfectly darling old sacristan who used to go about with Ruskin when he was here writing *The Stones of Venice* "two hours every morning, signora, for years and years and years." He knew all about the pictures, knew Berensen, but said "he had always his own idea about who painted the pictures, that Signor Berensen: nevertheless, he loves art." He had been attached to that church for 50 years: such a sweet old thing.

Grand Hotel,
Venice.
May 1st [1905].

To the Same.

We've been pottering about seeing our pet things a second time, and digging out a few isolated pictures in different churches, as to-morrow will be our last day in Venice. This afternoon was roastingly hot so we took a steamer to the Lido and lay out on the sands looking at the Adriatic—*so* blue, just the colour of turquoise: but it seemed very shadeless and dusty there after Venice, which has no dust, and heaps of shade in the narrow alleys and canals. We walked along to St. Niccolo di Lido, where my patron saint, St. Nicholas, is buried, quite forgotten now, poor dear, though he did such lots of nice miracles in the Middle Ages! His Church was locked so I couldn't go and pay my respects to his tomb.

By way of a complete change from Tintoretto and St. Marco, last night a very smart professional palmist arrived here and proceeded to give a most absurd lecture with limelight illustrations of characteristic paws, in the hotel drawing-room. I learnt from it several curious things, chiefly that my affections are more sensual than platonic, that I have no self-confidence, am inconstant, but literary, and that people who sleep with their thumbs tucked inside their clenched hands are by nature maniacs. I hope you don't do that. The lecturer pleasantly added, "All young infants clasp their thumbs in this manner." So nice for fond mothers.

Grand Hotel de la Poste,
Albi.
Tuesday night [24 April, 1906].

To the Same

We only stopped one night in Toulouse, as it was such a big dull noisy town and we didn't like it a bit. There were two interesting churches but nought else. One was a splendid *huge* Romanesque church, St. Sernin, with a most lovely Gothic crypt full of the most extraordinary collection of relics I ever saw—supposed to be the best there is. They are all in splendid silver gilt and jewelled reliquaries, some like Gothic shrines and some life-sized heads and some ark-shaped coffers with carrying poles. There were bits of 6 Apostles, the True Cross, the Crown of Thorns, most of the saints one has heard of and many one hasn't. A perfectly darling old priest exhibited them to us, and also St. Dominic's chasuble and a lovely bit of Xth century Byzantine brocade in which St. Louis wrapped up the Crown of Thorns when he brought it from Constantinople to France. But it was rather a grisly show. "Here, Madame, we have *almost half* of the body of St. Barnabas. His head is unfortunately at Rome and his left arm at Montpellier." "Here you see the head of St. Thomas Aquinas. No, Madame, he is not buried in Toulouse. He is buried in Italy: but a pious Dominican cut off his head

55

and brought it here," etc., etc. The collection includes a bit of Susannah (of the Apocrypha) and *most* of the body of St. George (whose actual existence is very doubtful) and a bit of the wedding veil of the Blessed Virgin. But it's a very marvellous show and most of the mediæval relics are no doubt genuine. They also have an immense Byzantine crucifix with the figure carved in wood and covered with thin sheets of gilded copper, which was brought to Toulouse in the Crusades.

Gubbio.
April 16, '07.

To the Same.

Of *course* I don't want you to copy out Father Benson's letter for me. I shall be interested to read it all the same when I get back. I hope he has really answered your questions and not just vapoured: but it's awfully good of him I think to take so much trouble about us. What he really means—I think—about conscience and judgement is, that the spiritual instinct one has must never be surrendered or tampered with because one's intellectual judgement or reason does not seem to justify it. Of *course* I *know* you are not "keeping anything back"—any more than I am myself.

I'm glad there is such a nice lot of dinner and tea things—but, did you find any little dishes for entrées, etc. I s'pose we shall still want an every-day dinner set shan't we? I think it's a splendid idea to put those cupboards in the front room. *Don't* go and destroy family papers that may be of interest: surely it's a pity: they don't take up such a fearful lot of room, you know. *I* don't mean to "start" naked like that—I shouldn't like it. But of course I agree with getting rid of real rubbish: I must start on mine when I get back. Will it be a *very* tight pack to fit in, do you think? We must leave room for Jacob, you know.

I am very well and happy and *do* hope you are too.

Goodnight dearest. All my love.

Siena.

April 22, 1907.

To M R.

I was so very glad to hear from you again: I remember your letter well, and have thought of you more than once, and wondered how you "got on." At the same time, I do feel a horrible sense of responsibility in answering your letter. You see (most naturally since we do not know one another) you have written with considerable reserve: therefore I don't feel a bit sure that what I shall say will be the right thing for *you*. So, if my remarks seem to you to go against your own intuitions (and these are the only valid finger-posts in the last resort) I do beg of you to trust your own judgement, take no notice of what I have said, and above all do not try to twist yourself to accept my statements. *If* they are true, you will come round to them at the right time.

The first point is: you say "Now I ask myself, shall I remain awake," etc. It is absolute waste of time to ask oneself such questions as this. You *are* awake: it is your job to remain so. Do not ask yourself, or worry yourself, or doubt. If you choose to exert your *will*, you can hold on to your vision—it rests with you to do this. I allow it is hard work—particularly, perhaps, under modern conditions. But surely it is possible to you to be alone, quiet for a little time each day? Then you can shut out all the trivialities of existence and "reset your compass." Further, this terror of losing the Light and getting entangled in the material world is a sign, less of insight, than of "spiritual adolescence." It is horrid whilst it lasts, but one tends, I think, to outgrow it. When you are *really sure* that every bush is "aflame with God" you will no longer feel contempt for the triviality of the bush. You will see that the material world, although of course an illusion in the form in which it appears to us, is an illusion which has strict relations with reality. It is the dim shadow of the thought of God. Under these conditions it falls into its right place in the scheme of things. This aspect of the material universe, as the veil through which, under the present dispensation, we must see the Divine, received its final sanction in the Incarnation of Christ.

I do not know of course how far the dogmatic side of Christianity appeals to you. I *do* think that if you study it, you will find there the solution of many problems and doubts. This statement does not of course apply to much "popular religion": I make it more in reference to mystical Catholicism. I do believe as you say, that one may call one's Supreme Reality by many names: but the old names have a way of proving themselves the best in the long run, and the old-fashioned recipes of prayer and meditation still remain, under various disguises, the "only way." Sooner or later you will "see," if only for a minute: but no one can anticipate that moment, it comes when one least expects it. It does not last, but the certainty which it conveys does last. All you can do, really, is to have faith and go on quietly without worrying. "Live the life, and so shalt thou learn the doctrine."

I think I must say this to you—avoid like poison the modern creeds and sects, mostly of American manufacture, which serve up a sort of travesty of Christianity, and distort the words of Christ to the purposes of their own philosophies. I mean the "New Thought" "Higher Thought" and so forth. These lead nowhere. Follow where you feel that you are being led, wherever that may be: but do not have fears about losing what you have found, that only puts you back. "In that thou dost seek Me, thou hast already found Me."

If you think it worth while to answer this letter, *please* don't hesitate to do so. Probably I have not told you anything that is of the slightest use; but if you will say where I am wrong, or a little more definitely what your own position is, perhaps I could be more help. Anyhow I could tell you the names of books that have helped me in the past, if you would like that: some of them might be of use to you—but one never knows.

> Grand Hotel la Vittoria,
> Bibbiena.
> Friday [1907].

To HUBERT STUART MOORE.

My own darling boy, I was so glad to get your letter at Arezzo this morning: I only hope you are telling me the truth

58

and are *really* feeling purry *and* closer to one another in spite of the "depression." After all, as I have thought as I now think for many months, if it was to separate us you ought to have felt it coming on long ago and as the chief result has been to force us to talk openly to each other about all the real things which we sedulously kept from each other before, the final effect in spite of difference of opinion ought to be to make us much more real companions than in the past, when we each had a watertight bulk-head carefully fixed to prevent undue explorations. Also I do think it must be a great gain to *you*, all round, if I can make you see the real beauties of Catholicism, as well as the merely superficial corruptions on which you had been led to concentrate yourself. It is better, after all, to walk along a rather muddy path to Heavenly Syon, than not to get there at all!

Orvieto.
Wednesday evening [25 April, 1907].

To the Same.

Yesterday afternoon we had a beautiful drive to some Etruscan tombs outside the city. The drive was much nicer than the tombs I thought (this letter will be *very* disconnected as I am surrounded by 5 chattering Americans comparing coloured post cards. One has just observed, "My! ain't this general resurrection with the skeletons popping out of their graves just *sweet*!"). The tombs are like caves in the side of a hill. The path down to them amongst the flowers was beautiful, there were things like blue marigolds and also some lovely shaded violets which I have never seen before. Inside the tombs there were fragments of frescoes rather like the things on Greek vases but very decayed and hard to make out by candle light. Also there were huge spiders and oh! my darling boy, centipedes nearly 5 inches long! They ran up the walls and then fell down with a most horrid flop close by you. Also drips fell from the roof and you were not sure whether they were water or insects. Altogether my mind was *much* too distracted to pay proper attention to the remains of prehistoric art. But the drive back winding down the hill and getting views all the time of Orvieto standing right up on its rock against the sky was simply enchanting. We've spent lots of time in the Cathedral. There are some gorgeous frescoes by Signorelli and Fra Angelico, and some faint delicate lovely 14th century ones in the choir. The Signorellis are all about the last judgement, and all the souls—saved or damned or "un-decided"—are naked—marvellous studies of the nude, but somehow a nude heaven seems as unspiritual as Carlyle's naked House of Lords seems unpolitical. They are extraordinarily interesting and original though—the intense surprise and half awakened state of the newly risen, and the bewildered inability to enjoy themselves of those who find themselves in Paradise. Goodnight. The chatter is *so* colossal I *cannot* write. All my love, darling.

Siena.
Sunday night.
[1 May, 1907].

To the Same.

We've not done much to-day owing to the weather: first Mass at the Cathedral, and then went into the Cathedral-Museum till lunch time. There I had rather a find. I think I told you about the choir stalls illustrating the Nicene Creed which I have been studying here and which no one has described so far. I've taken elaborate notes of them and intend to write an article on them. To-day in the Museum I found 9 small Creed pictures, the remains of a set from the Cathedral sacristy, which show interesting differences from the inlaid ones, which are much more curious. These are the only two sets of Creed pictures I've ever seen, and will be most useful to compare with each other. I *think* the pictures are a bit the older: they look like late 14th century, but are supposed to be by a man who died in 1422.

The big Duccio Madonna looks lovelier than ever. I could sit with her all day! She was rather discounted this morning by a terrible parson with his rabbity daughters who arrived and began to read aloud, in a sort of preaching voice, "This celebrated picture, one of the finest works of the Sienese school," etc. I don't know how the pictures bear it: I'm always expecting them to come out of their frames and kick.

I have written to Charlotte and told her that we should probably want a pair of purple curtains for the dining-room. Purple is such a dreadful colour for fading that I'm sure it won't be worth while to have anything but her fast dyed pure stuff. Materials fade most horribly, and last time I was at Alice's I noticed the things she bought when she moved into that house, and they have already gone quite faint and dingy. I think very few draperies but very good ones is the right line to go on, don't you? And first class linen in preference to cheap silk. I wondered whether you would see about having the mattresses re-made by Shoolbred's whilst the furniture was away, or whether it would be better to wait till we had bought the single beds for front room? How are you going to do the different things you meant to do yourself to furniture, and the circlets for the wedding, with the house in an uproar?

A lady in Liverpool, who wrote to me three years ago, after reading *Grey World*, to say I had "made her see what Reality really is" (!) has just written me another, rather pathetic, letter, asking me to help her out of her spiritual tangles. I think this sort of thing is a most horrible responsibility, and rather ridiculous when the person applied to is still in just as much of a tangle as anyone else. A. also has been shying her "honest" but rather shallow doubts at my head. I wish I could make them see that I am *not* an authority. Suppose I tell them all wrong, how awful to feel afterwards that they were trusted to you and you didn't do as well for them as you might have done. Don't *you* ever go and "rely" on what I say, will you? I mean in that particular connection, of course. Good-night, darling.

Tuesday morning—between Siena and Pisa.
[3 May, 1907].

To the Same.

I'm very sorry to leave my darling Siena: in spite of the pouring rain on Sunday, she has been very seductive this year. Yesterday we practically gave up the whole day to St. Catherine! First we went down to her house which on this day of the year is completely thrown open to the public, all the little chapels and oratories into which the rooms have been turned, trimmed up, and with candles burning. Swarms of people going from room to room and venerating the relics, which were all exposed. Everyone in the highest spirits. A very nice little priest blessed my medals before her crucifix. Then we went up to St. Domenico for High Mass, then I rushed off to the Hospital where there are some subterranean chapels in her honour, and the tiny little cell where she used to go and rest when she was nursing the sick. This also is only open this one day. The little cell was full of flowers, laid on the recess in which she used to sleep, and they give you some to take away with you. Half the boys and youths of Siena were in the various shrines, in their confraternity dresses, tremendously content and happy, fussing about and giving away blessed bread, etc., etc. In the afternoon (or at least from 5.30 to 8!) was the big function at St. Domenico. Every imaginable candle in the church was lit—the shrine itself just a blaze of lights, it really looked *lovely*. They had vespers and a rather terrible sermon, during which everyone kept passing through the chapel in which St. Catherine's head was exposed. Thanks to J.W., who has really been very attentive, *we* went into the sacristy, and to the back of the shrine, where you can climb up and actually stand and look into the reliquary. We also saw St. Catherine's altar-stone and a lot of other "special" relics. Then, just as it was getting dusk, the procession—two pages in mediæval dress, with the banners of St. Catherine's own ward (the Goose) and St. Domenico's ward (the Dragon), then the confraternities, carrying a huge silver bust of the saint, and a bishop and various priests in magnificent copes, and all the little girls who had made their first communions that morning, dressed like small brides and carrying immense candles, and then everyone else who could get hold of a lighted candle following on behind. It went three times round the church, everyone singing the local Italian hymn of St. Catherine, which is as "catching" as a music hall ditty! There must have been well over a thousand people in the church. After that, the Te Deum and Benediction —and then we went home, very late, to dinner.

I had rather a find in the afternoon. We plunged into an old curiosity shop near the Cathedral, and found it was of the rabbit warren nature—innumerable dirty little rooms leading out of each other. One was full of old books, largely sermons, law books, etc., but I found amongst them a very agreeable 4to in old vellum—the Italian edition of the Flos Sanctorum, 1690, with lots of woodcut vignettes and in a very good state. I looked longingly at it, but was sure it would be too dear: asked the old man how much it was. He said, "This is a very old book, with many pictures, it is worth much." I remained silent. He said, "By good fortune I got it for 2½ francs." I said, "What do you want for it then?" He said, "As I got it for that, you may have it for three francs!" It's rather big to get into our box, but I *had* to get it.

3 Campden Hill Place, W.
May 12, 1907.

To M.R.

I am so glad you have written to me again: I hope you will continue the correspondence how and when you feel inclined (not at 3-year intervals!) if it seems good to you.

I have read your last letter very carefully. You say, I am to consider that you are an Anglican. But—there are Anglicans and Anglicans! The question, for instance, whether you really believe in the Sacraments, as actual vehicles of Spirit and not merely beautiful and helpful ideas, is a vital one. The keys of the Catholic position (and Anglicanism is of course a slightly diluted Catholicism) are,

A. The Incarnation and
B. A mystical continuation of the Incarnation in the Sacraments.

You see, if you accept these things as *realities* for you, you have at once something to "go upon." I wonder also which are the dogmas which struck you as repellent? Many are of course most difficult on their concrete and historical side, and some hardly affect the inner life of most people. But a formal creed is not a *faith*: it is, as the Roman Catholics rightly call it, the "symbol" of the faith.

I am afraid, if you did deliberately turn your back on the light.

you *must* have rather a horrid time getting back. The restlessness and sense of being "unable to grasp" is dreadful I know: the only comfort is, that it is better than apathy—and it is the experience of all the mystics that the "way of purgation" has to come before the "way of illumination." You may also take it for granted, of course, that so long as you want the peace and illumination for your own sake, you will not get them. Self-surrender, an entire willingness to live in the dark, in pain, anything—this is the real secret. I think no one really finds the Great Companion till their love is of that kind that they long only to *give* and not to get.

I am sending you a short and very mixed list of books. If you care to tell me which (if any!) you like, I could then perhaps tell you some more—or if I can be of any other sort of use, I shall be so glad.

CLASSICS

The Confessions of St. Augustine.

This is to me the most wonderful record in the world of the awakening and return of a soul to God. I think everyone must see in it clues to their own experience. It is like a living voice from the 4th century, telling of the same longings, the same difficulties, the same quest.

L'Ornement des noces spirituelles de Ruysbroeck l'Admirable.

Translated by Maeterlinck. Have you read this? It is "difficult" but most wonderful.

The Theologia Germanica.

The Revelations of Divine Love, by the Lady Julian of Norwich.

I think, of course, that the Roman Missal is, next to the New Testament (almost the whole of which is incorporated in it), an unmatched treasury. Have you ever read with attention the whole Canon of the Mass? If you can "do with" books of devotion, there is one called *Ancient Devotions for Holy Communion* which is free from sentiment, has many beautiful things, and the whole Mass in English and Latin. It is published by Kegan Paul and costs 3s. 6d.

MODERN BOOKS

The Soul of a Christian, by F. Granger.
    (I *strongly* recommend this.)
The Soul's Orbit, by M. D. Petre.
Oil and Wine, by George Tyrrell.
Lex Credendi „   „   „
A Modern Mystic's Way.
The Rod, the Root and the Flower, by Coventry Patmore.

Do you know Francis Thompson's poem *The Hound of Heaven*? It is in a little anthology called *Lyra Sacra*. I am sure you would like it and probably also much in Coventry Patmore's *Unknown Eros*.

3 Campden Hill Place.
May 15, 1907.

TO THE SAME.

I am so glad you are going to read the Missal. But do not be "put off" if at first it strikes you as a rather commonplace liturgy and you are left wondering what I see in it. Everything, really, is there: but like other valuable things it has to be hunted for. As to *understanding* the Mass, no reading or other intellectual process makes one do that, I think. You see the Mass is either (*a*) a gross superstition or (*b*) an enormous spiritual fact. Intermediate theories, that it is a "helpful symbol," "true for those who believe in it," etc., are not really tenable. Now it is quite easy to think it is (*a*); but quite difficult of one's own accord to realize that it is (*b*). This means that one's perceptions must be exalted to the spiritual plane, if only for a moment—and such an exaltation is of course the true object of ceremonies, liturgies and much meditation. But *don't* worry and excite yourself or pull yourself up by the roots to see how you are getting on! That way lies spiritual insomnia, the most deadly disease in the world. Let yourself go more, and trust more: you will get in the end what you are meant to have.

3 Campden Hill Place, W.
Corpus Christi, May 30, 1907.

To the Same.

Please don't apologize for writing . . . if I can help you the least bit, I shall be paying back some of the debt I owe those who have helped me; it is rather a luxury to administer counsels of perfection to others instead of to oneself!

I feel like writing you a rather bracing, disagreeable, east-windy sort of letter. When I read yours my first impulse was to send you a line begging you only to *let yourself alone.* Don't keep on pulling yourself to pieces: and please burn that dreadful book with the list of your past sins! If the past really oppresses you, you had far better go to confession, and finish that chapter once and for all! It is emphatically your business now to look forwards and not backwards: and also to look forwards in an eager and optimistic spirit. Any other course is mere ingratitude, you know. There is a dispirited tone about your letter as if you were taking your own variations of mood and inevitable failures far too seriously—feeling your pulse too much. You say reading the *Modern Mystic* "increased your responsibility more than you can bear." This also is morbid (I am really horribly rude this evening!). Your responsibility ends when you have made sure that you are honest in will and intention, and are doing your best. There are no unbearable responsibilities in this world but those of our own seeking. Once life is realized as a succession of acts of loving service, undertaken in a spirit of joy, all that moonshine vanishes. I nearly quoted a text at you: but instead of that, here is a "bit" which contains much food for profitable meditation I think. I wonder if you know it already?

"There was a saint who said, 'I must rejoice without ceasing, although the world shudder at my joy.' *He did not think he could save his soul without it.*"

People seem often to forget that Hope is a cardinal virtue necessary to salvation like Faith and Love: an active principle which ought to dominate life. I do think it would be so much better if you would go on quite simply and *trustfully* for a bit. After all, we value far more in our human relationships the sort of love that gives itself joyously and eagerly without introspection than the sort which is perpetually occupied with its own unworthiness or shortcomings. I wonder whether you are living too lonely a life for your temperament. You sound a little bit like it.

Of course you are *quite* right when you say that feeling must precede doing: but unless it finally results in doing, it is mere emotional satisfaction, of no value. The direction and constancy of the *will* is what really matters, and intellect and feeling are only important in so far as they contribute to that. Don't be bullied by Tyrrell: he is often splendid, and also often quite wrong, being cursed with a cleverness that runs away with him.

Have you read R. H. Benson's *Papers of a Pariah*? I'm not "recommending" this as a "serious" work—but it is rather a pleasant book which has several things in it which I thought extremely well put, and I think you might like it. I wonder what you thought of the Missal! I observe that you preserve a discreet silence on the subject! I hope the one you got had the liturgy in Latin as well as in English. It is untranslatable somehow. Don't you think the office for to-day is beautiful? Have you read the *Pange Lingua* in the original? I forget whether it comes at Corpus Christi or Holy Thursday in the Missal for the laity, being sung on both days.

Yacht *Wulfruna*.
Aug. 2, 1907.

To the Same.

I think the *central* fact of the Mass is the Presence on the Altar. From this are deducible the other aspects of communion, sacrifice, and adoration. To limit the meaning of the Eucharist to any *one* of these things is implicitly to deny the Presence in its full signification. One of the best introductions to the history of the Early Liturgies is Neale's *Essays in Liturgical History*, if you can get hold of it. They have it at the London Library I know. Bright's translations of early collects are also good: and there is a wonderful collection of scraps from all these sources in *Ancient Devotions for Holy Communion* about which I think I told you. It's a Roman book, though! Also the Mozarabic Rite has lately been edited I think. Perhaps you would like Dr. Abbott's

Silenus the Christian. Duchesne is of course good: but more about ceremonies than liturgies. Remind me when I go home to send you some little booklets on the Holy-Week ceremonies, which are rather interesting in a slight way.

It is odd how quickly the Christian Liturgy arrived at its full splendour; and how every alteration made since has resulted in blemishes rather than improvements—unless the editor happened, as in the case of St. Thomas Aquinas, to be both a poet and a saint. But of course the Platonizing of Jewish conceptions which went on at and about Alexandria during the first 4 centuries A.D. was an intellectual process almost unparalleled in history, and the Fathers of the Church which it produced were very superior, mentally, to most of their sons!

I wonder if you have read any of St. Augustine's sermons as well as the *Confessions?* He, of course, inspired many of the mediæval mystics—as for instance Julian of Norwich, one of the wisest and most beautiful.

50 Campden Hill Square, W.
Oct. 9, 1907.

To THE SAME.

It is perfectly disgraceful of me to have left your last letter unanswered so long. But we have only been home a fortnight, and there has been so much to do—my house not being really in order yet—that correspondence has been considerably neglected. . . . I am glad you were pleased with Ruysbroeck. He is one of the truly illuminated, I think, and belongs with St. Teresa and the matchless Lady Julian of Norwich (I forget whether you have read her: if not, I could lend her to you if you like).

I send you with this the Holy Week pamphlets, and also a book of scraps (all the best really) from Plotinus, the best of the Neo-Platonists. I wonder if you know Boehme. There is an excellent introduction to him, by Martensen—not a particularly new book. As to St. Augustine's *Sermons*, the only edition I know is old (about 1840), big, and probably out of print. But you would get it surely at a library? I wonder if you know of Dr. Williams' Library in Gordon Square? There is no subscription; they send you two books at a time, and their collection of theological and mystical books is magnificent. I am sure you would find it most useful.

It seems to me from what you say in your letter, that things are going on so well with you that it would be superfluous, not to say highly impertinent on my part, to lecture or argue. If I am right about the Eucharist—and I can only tell you what I see or believe I see—you will see it too, sooner or later. The question after all, is not what the Church of England says is there, or what any one else says, but what *is* there.

There are plenty of learned persons saying all the time that what you have already found is not there at all. But their arguments will never be valid to you again, any more than the arguments of Anglican divines against adoration of the Blessed Sacrament are valid to me. Direct spiritual experience is the only possible basis; and if you will trust yours absolutely you are safe. When one thinks of the distance you have gone in the last few months, it is incredible that you should ever be depressed or distrustful again!

50 C.H.S.
Nov. 20, 1907.

To the Same.

I see I have got two letters of yours to answer! This is quite dreadful of me: but it is consoling to reflect that you must have found out long ago that I am a very bad correspondent.

I *am* so glad you are happy: I always thought you would be, if only you would let yourself. People who care about these sort of things at all have a fund of happiness at their disposal which outside circumstances, "hard lives," etc., can't touch. Only so often they are perverse, and won't take advantage of their privileges—like an over-scrupulous nun, haggling over whether she is quite good enough for her Maker.

I am so sorry you thought you had got to return Plotinus if you had not finished with him. There is never any hurry really: and I will always tell you if I happen to want books back. Dr. Williams has got a very fine complete edition of the Life and Works of St. Teresa in French—together with other Spanish

mystics—three large and heavy volumes! It is most unsuitable
for Dissenting ministers but I'm sure you would like it. There is
a nice little edition of Tauler in the Library of Devotion for
1s. 6d.—without the remarks of the odious Miss Winckworth.

I cannot think why you are "put off" by a thing like the Mass
of St. Gregory. Are you going to disallow all the visions of all
the Saints? And, if the substance of what he saw was God, surely
it was just as reasonable for him to perceive its accidents under
one form as under another?

50 C.H.S.
Dec. 30, 1907.

To the Same.

Thank you so much for your last letter—and for the very
pretty card, quite the nicest I had! Of *course* I will be glad for
you to tell me more about yourself if you feel that it will help
you. It is so much easier to tell a person one has not seen, and
you need *never* see me unless you like!

You say reading St. Teresa has made you feel anxious to get
on quicker (but *no one* can get on quickly with this particular
job) and you do not know what to do next. I do not one bit
want to go on harrying you with advice: but I just submit it
for your consideration that there are certain attitudes of mind to
be cultivated, and certain methods of devotion to be learned,
which are quite essential and quite definite. They are really, I
believe, the thing to do next. Of course I can only gather vaguely
and approximately the point you have reached and the use you
are making of the light you have got—so all I can do is to tell
you the things I have found out for myself, on the chance of one
or two of them fitting in.

Now it seems to me that one's life only attains reality in so
far as it is *consciously* lived in the Presence of God. This
consciousness can be attained and clung to by a definite act of
the will—or rather by a series of graduated acts. Once you can
breathe that atmosphere, *it* will determine most questions of
conduct for you—become a sort of norm or standard, by which
all other proportions are judged. Secondly, as a means of getting
at this, there is the regular and systematic practice of meditation:

by which of course I do *not* mean thinking about a pious subject but the "deep" meditation which tends to pass over into unitive prayer. You probably know that experience already: but so many people, instead of regarding it as a part of their regular spiritual food only do it when they "feel in the mood" or "when they can." But once the will is in proper control you can always enter into the silence, though often enough without finding anything (consciously) there. That, I think, does not matter much. What *does* matter is, never to give up, once you have started on the way, in spite of the horrid discouragements and ups and downs. I expect it is "more than my place is worth" to mention the extreme usefulness of the rosary in this connection? So many people seem to think it a sort of calculating-machine for the saying of Hail Marys: whereas it is really a wonderful psychological device for assisting the meditative state—a sort of "First Steps for Little Contemplatives." At least I find it so but perhaps you would not!

50 C.H.S.
Jan. 16, 1908.

To the Same.

I feel a horrid diffidence in advising you on your last letter: it seems very presumptuous to do so—because, in a way, you have enough of your own to go on, and I, in advising you, can only go on my own experience, which may not be a bit of use to you. So, I shall probably make mistakes, and you *must* exercise your own judgement in accepting what I say. We are both in a very confusing forest, and the fact that I say I think I have found a path in one direction is no valid reason for you to alter your course.

Now, first, you have, you know, the "root of the matter"—and as long as you cling to that, you *can't* go far wrong. As your favourite St. Augustine said, "Love and do what you like!" If you like wrong things, you will soon find the quality of your love affected. This same condition of love governs everything else (e.g. it rules out, once for all, the idea of cash payments. Whether they are in force or whether they are not, the true lover, whether on the earthly or heavenly plane, has no thoughts to waste on them). It seems to me that your immediate job must be to make this love active and operative right through your life—to live in the light of it all the while, and act by it all the while—to make it light up your relations with other people, with nature, with life, with your work, just as much as it lights up immediate communion with Our Lord. Try to see people by His light. *Then* they become "real." Nothing helps one so much as that. Prayerful and direct intercourse is only half one's job; the other half is to love everything for and in God. This is of course only a long-winded way of saying that one has got to let faith issue in charity. When you have learnt to live within the love of God in this human and healthy sense, the question of sin will cease to be such a bogy as it is at present. Your attitude towards sin is really almost Calvinistic! ! *Don't* dwell on it! Turn your back on it. Every minute you are thinking of evil, you might have been thinking of good instead. Refuse to pander to a morbid interest in your own misdeeds. Pick yourself up, be sorry, shake yourself, and go on again. Of course, it is deplorable that we should all hesitate to make temporal sacrifices for eternal gains— Thomas à Kempis is very bitter on the subject if you remember— but look back on the time when this aspect of the subject would not even have occurred to you, and ask yourself if your present unrest does not indicate progress? So with sins—as we advance, our conscience gets more delicate, and acts of self-help which once seemed almost laudable, now look hideous. Of course, because you had a "good time" before Christmas, and enjoyed devotion, you are now having a reaction and a flat time. But sticking to it in the flat times is of far more value both as service and as discipline—than luxuriating in religious emotion. It is what strengthens your spiritual muscles. Even the best people— even the saints—have always had to bear it: sometimes for years. It is a natural condition in the spiritual life. I know it is perfectly horrid when it happens—and I do *not* mean to be unsympathetic! But you must get enough grip to go on trusting in the dark. All the prayer in the world will not get you into a state in which you will always have nice times. You must not get slack: you must make a rule of life and go on with it steadily.

Now about meditation. Perhaps it may not be your "line." It is entirely a matter of temperament I believe. Some people cannot do it at all. Personally I can do it to a certain "stage": but I know others who, with less practice, can pass easily and naturally into far deeper stages. In spite of all the mystics have told us, we are in it working with almost an unknown tool. Try to get rid of the visual image. Do you remember St. Teresa said of one of her nuns, "Sister X . . . has so *little* imagination that she always sees an image of the thing on which she meditates."

Try this way.

1. Put yourself into some position so easy and natural to you that you don't *notice* your body: and shut your eyes.

2. Represent to your mind, some phrase, truth, dogma, event —e.g. a phrase of the Paternoster or *Anima Christi*, the Passion, the Nativity are the sort of things I use. Something that occurs naturally. Now, don't think about it, but keep it before you, turning it over as it were, as you might finger some precious possession.

3. Deliberately, and by an act of will, shut yourself off from your senses. Don't attend to touch or hearing: till the external world seems unreal and far away. Still holding on to your idea, turn your attention *inwards* (this is what Ruysbroeck means by introversion) and allow yourself to sink, as it were, downwards and downwards, into the profound silence and peace which is the essence of the meditative state. More you cannot do for yourself: if you get further, you will do so automatically as a consequence of the above practice. It is the "shutting off of the senses" and what Boehme calls the "stopping the wheel of the imagination and ceasing from self-thinking" that is hard at first. Anyhow, do not try these things when you are tired—it is useless: and do not give up the form of prayer that comes naturally to you: and do not be disheartened if it seems at first a barren and profitless performance. It is quite possible to obtain spiritual nourishment without being consciously aware of it!

Read *Holy Wisdom* by the Ven. Augustine Baker.

P.S. The dear cat sends his love; he was much flattered, as he perceives you to be a lady who understands cat-nature! His name is Jacob, because he supplants all other cats in the affections of those who know him—or so he thinks!

Hotel St. Jean-Baptiste,
Carcassonne.
Thursday night [25 April, 1908].

To HUBERT STUART MOORE.

I got your Sunday letter and Monday p.c. when we arrived here this afternoon. I'm *so* sorry you had such a disgustingly dreary holiday with no real sailing or anything; I can't bear to think of it—but if only the fresh air and idleness has done you good, it will be something.

You were a *darling* to send flowers to the Convent for Easter —nothing you could have done would have pleased me more, as you know. Sister Eucharistie wrote a delightful letter, saying how beautiful they were and that she put them on the High Altar near the Blessed Sacrament. I *do* love you for having done that. It's lovely to think that there was something of ours there then— "offering the homage of their beauty," as she says in her letter.

Via Michele 6,
Firenze.
Saturday [27 April, 1908].

To THE SAME.

I am now quite raving mad about Italian pictures and you will find me a horrid nuisance on the subject. I thought I knew how to appreciate them before I left England, but now I know that I knew less than nothing. The Botticellis here are *entrancing*; after a bit they cast a sort of spell over you, and you can't get away from them. Those really great old painters don't throw themselves into your arms, like modern pot boilers, and say "Look what pretty things I paint"; you have to find that out for yourself, but once you have found it out, you must love them till the end of your days. Please bear with this nonsense, the place makes me incoherent and I've no one here to talk to, at least on these subjects.

74

50 C.H.S.
2nd Sunday after Easter, 1908.
To M.R.

Here are your other Carcassonne pictures: I hope you will like them. It *was* nice of you to write me a "welcome back" letter! I liked it very much: as much as Jacob's very furry and demonstrative greeting. We had a nice smooth and sunny crossing, and I feel very glad to find myself at home again!

I wonder if you have yet discovered Auch? It takes a little looking for: and I have not yet met anyone else who has been there. It's on a side-line, west from Toulouse: a rather miserable, empty, unsuccessful-looking town, full of empty houses and closed shops, with a Cathedral which also looks desolate outside but is "all glorious within." Your window is, as you saw, 16th century and very good of its kind. It is in the Chapel of the Blessed Sacrament, and is one of a series which go completely round the choir-chapels; really magnificent Renaissance glass with all the splendour of the period and none of the paganism.

As for *O felix culpa!*—I feel a certain evil joy in telling you that it comes from that despised manual of Christianity, the Roman Missal! ! you will find it in the *Exultet*, sung at the blessing of the Paschal Candle on Holy Saturday. It, and the music to which it is always chanted, are supposed to be the most ancient things in the Liturgy. I think I shall never forget the first time I heard it: it is so strange, wild and poignant. And they are expressive words, aren't they? They lift one straight away from the morbid and emotional hash with which the average curate profanes the Passion.

Benediction *is* nice, isn't it? If you want the whole text of the service you can get a little book called *The Garden of the Soul* for 6d. which contains that, and Mass, and Sunday Vespers, the Way of the Cross and some devotional odds and ends. The first Hymn is always St. Thomas Aquinas' *O Salutaris Hostia* and the Collect is always the one for Corpus Christi *Deus qui nobis*. Next time you are in London you must go to Benediction at the Chapel of the Assumption in Kensington Square. They have it every day at 5, and the nuns sing quite charmingly. . . . It is a tiny place so you would be able to see quite well.

I wonder how you will like Boehme. Often enough he is over my head altogether. He seems like a person dazed by his vision and stuttering with the violence of his effort to express it.

I found some more Ruysbroeck while I was away. *Œuvres Choisies* by E. Hello. Snippets are always horrid: but in this there is a long piece of the *Treatise on Contemplation*, and two Canticles, and various other precious things. Would you like me to lend it to you presently?

50 C.H.S.
May 9, 1908.

To the Same.

I am sending you a Holy Week Book to see the *Exultet* in Latin just to take the taste of the English version away. The bit you quote is terrible; I have never come on quite such a bad example as that. There is no hurry about returning this book as I am not likely to want it yet awhile.

Isn't the Lady Julian lovely? But Methuen's 3s. 6d. edition is much better than the Kegan Paul one and has quite a nice Introduction instead of that stuffy little essay of Tyrrell's. Tell me when you want Ruysbroeck. There is a little life of him at the beginning, which is rather nice to have.

I was amused to find you had seen the picture in the *Bookman*! It is more like a nigger boy than anything else, having been taken in the back of the chemist's shop at Scilly, at the end of a day's fishing! Heinemann annoyed me by demanding a portrait for publication, which should be "mystical and strike a personal note"! Whereupon in a spirit of pure devilry, I sent him that! He was annoyed—but used it!

June 16, 1908.

To the Same.

Your letter got to me late as we were spending Whitsuntide in the depths of the New Forest—in a tiny cottage with forest ponies browsing at the door—*so* nice! I wonder was this the region where you felt you could not follow me? It is inaccessible: far away from the Blessings and Fonts and all other circumstances of ecclesiastical splendour. A perfect example of what a pious friend called "the godless desolation of rural England." All the same I *do* rather miss churches when I have not got them to run to—don't you?

I was amused by your description of your violent and successful hunt for those *Corpus Christi* verses. I imagined you and the bookstall boy vainly searching *M.A.P.*, *Home Chat*, and *London Society*—and finally running them to earth in the least expected spot! I am *so* pleased you liked them—it never occurred to me you would want to see them at all. I thought the middle stanza had some horrid stuffy lines in it but I could not get it any better. I want to do a little book some day of those sort of verses for all the year: but so far only the Christmas, Mid-Lent and Holy Week ones are done and nowadays I seldom write rhymes.

I wonder if you idolize Corpus Christi day as much as I do? It is my "secret love" among all the feasts of the year I think. In the afternoon I generally go to the Convent of the Sacred Heart at Roehampton where they have a procession of the Blessed Sacrament and Benediction in the lovely old garden. I wonder if you would like it?

I nearly forgot the most important part of this letter: namely, that Jacob sends his best love and says that—most fortunately—he is, as you wished, Tabby: but emphatically NOT COMMON. He has been told he is Pure Persian, and is inclined to believe it. He celebrated my return yesterday by catching a mouse and eating it, with every circumstance of cruelty, in the garden whilst I was having my tea. There *are* moments when it is difficult to adjust even the nicest cat to an optimistic scheme of Creation!

This is a horribly frivolous letter. I don't know why a bit. Perhaps the after result of last night's women writers' Dinner—which this year was madder and more amusing than ever. My opposite neighbour was a lady who has made herself a religion of Conic Sections, and told me that Curves were the key to the Universe and an infallible corrective of pantheism: and that Sex and Psychology were in it all—a dark saying indeed which I have not yet unravelled! Next to her sat Mrs. Tay Pay O'Connor who interrupted the discourse on Curves to ask her if she knew Mrs. Cecil Raleigh, who had done so much in Drury Lane Melodrama. Add to this a large Chorus of successful Suffragists, full of Saturday's demonstration: and the usual hare-and-hounds business of anxious admirers chasing successful authors in order to have the pleasure of saying, "I *do* so like your book!"—and it is not surprising if every scribbler in London is feeling weak and light-headed to-day!

Good-bye. I will send Ruysbroeck in a day or two. His remarks on Hell, coming from such a quarter, are painful reading: but much of the rest compensates.

St. Martha's Day, 29:7:08.

To the Same.

I am writing this to Liverpool on chance of its catching you before you go. Not that my remarks on the subject are likely to be of the slightest use as I am quite as much (or more) feeling my way in the dark, as you are! So, you must please only read it as a tentative expression of opinion, founded merely on my own experience as far as I have gone yet.

The first point is—do you wish to develop in yourself (1) "balanced faculties" or (2) to be a "specialist"? If (1), then utter repression of the senses is obviously wrong, and indeed impossible to those who live the active life at *all*. If (2), then such repressions *may* be right for entirely exceptional souls. But please note that the great contemplative saints are not found amongst such souls. Remember St. Francis with his love of birds and music, sun and air: St. Teresa's eau-de-Cologne: Ruysbroeck's and St. Bernard's passion for the forest. As to what you say about the cloistered life, I don't know whether you have ever known any nuns or monks personally? I know a good many and as a matter of fact, they live the life of the senses just as much as anyone else, only in a peculiarly simple and detached way. If you want to find the person who combines spiritual passion with appreciation of a cup of coffee—go to a convent. It is just there that you find this type in perfection. I believe the whole secret to lie in "detachment": and it is difficult to conceive how anyone who has once seen the "vision splendid" even for a moment can fail to have this detachment in

78

THE LETTERS OF EVELYN UNDERHILL

some measure, or fail to see bits of it, hints and shadows, in most of the evidences of sense. I think that the R.L.S. point of view, *lit by this experience*, may be spiritual; *not* lit by it—it is only a sort of cosmic cheerfulness and rather shallow at that!

The Church has always, of course, held up as the Christian ideal a mixture of the active and contemplative life—the one lit up by the other. Our Lord's human life was just that, wasn't it? Social intercourse regulated by nights spent in the mountain in prayer. We *ought* to be strong enough to use our senses without letting them swamp our souls: to enjoy them, without ever forgetting the greater joy of the "deep yet dazzling darkness."

The condemnation of "*lust* of the eyes" seems to me to just point the distinction between lust and reasonable love. Just as, in the same way, it is right to love other people *in* the Love of God—but not to have violent and exclusive passions for them. This shuts off the spiritual light just as completely as an attack of hatred and malice! I am sure that nothing which can co-exist with the consciousness of the spiritual world hurts us—and it seems to me that all pure beauty can so co-exist if we choose. Of course in moments of meditation (and indeed, I think, of prayer) all sensual images are in the way. But even in the cloister, unitive prayer *cannot* be continuous. A rightly detached soul can "switch off" the world of sense at those times without despising it. The two things are so *very* near together. So that it *is* the "garment that ye see Him by"—if you know Him first. And, as pain is plaited right through nature and supernature as we know it, I don't see that this longing to hurt oneself (it *can* become hysterical if not looked after, as I know to my cost, so beware!) militates against the other part.

Consider again St. Francis: the "heavenly melody" and the Stigmata lived side by side in his experience. I do not believe anyone ever lived a more perfectly Christian life than he did. It is shamefully ungracious not to glory in the works of the Lord because one is preoccupied over the fact that one is a miserable sinner. The fact that we say the Confession and the *Agnus* at Mass does not make us modestly omit the *Gloria*. I am certain we should stretch our spiritual muscles till they permit selfless joy as well as selfless pain. If it were otherwise, Gethsemane would have made Cana in Galilee impossible. Surely you have perceived for yourself the difference between created things as seen in the indescribable atmosphere which theologians call "the love of God," and seen in the ordinary worldly light?

I remember you told me once the first thing you "found out" was a sense of intense refinement. The first thing I found out was exalted and indescribable beauty in the most squalid places. I still remember walking down the Notting Hill main road and observing the (extremely sordid) landscape with joy and astonishment. Even the movement of the traffic had something universal and sublime in it. Of course that does not last: but the after-flavour of it does, and now and then one catches it again. When one *does* catch it, it is so real that to look upon it as wrong would be an unthinkable absurdity. At the same time, one sees the world at those moments so completely as "energized by the invisible" that there is no temptation to rest in mere enjoyment of the visible.

This is all very scrappy and unsatisfactory I know; but if there is anything I have left out that I *could* answer, do tell me.

P.S. Did you notice this in St. Bernard? "Experto crede: aliquid amplius invenies in Silvis quam in Libris. Ligna et lapides decelunt te quod a Magistris audire non possis."[1] And this: "Quidquid in Scriptures valet, quidquid in eis spiritualiter sentit, maxime in silvis et in agris meditando et orando se confitetur accepisse, et in hoc nullos aliquando se magistros habuisse nisi quercos et fagos joco illo suo gratioso inter amicos dicere solet."[2] Isn't that rather nice? I hope you will find the oaks and beeches equally improving to the mind!

[1] 'Believe me who have tried. Thou wilt find something more in woods than in books. Trees and rocks will teach thee what thou canst not hear from a master.'—*Letter to Henry Murdach*.

[2] Whatever strengthens him in the Scriptures, whatever he feels of spiritual worth in them, he confesses that he had found chiefly when meditating and praying in the woods and fields, and in this respect he is wont to say among his friends with that gracious playfulness of his that he had had no other teachers but the oaks and beeches.

Vézelay.
August 29, 1908.

To the Same.

I have been "thinking you over" a lot since we were here. Oddly enough your letter partly anticipates what I wanted to say to you: but does not quite answer it. What struck me about you was, not that there was any danger of your relapsing into "comfiness," but that your tendency was to make your religion a *tête-à-tête* affair. The communion of Saints and all that is implied by that does not occupy a sufficiently prominent place in your creed, I *think*. (All this must be read with the usual reservations because so often my judgement is wrong.) This is a trap specially set for those who are attracted by the personal and mystical aspect of religion and find their greatest satisfaction in unitive prayer. Now, you say you have taken up two new bits of work: but you carefully refrain from mentioning what they are. I don't in the least want you to tell me: for probably having to answer questions about yourself fills you with the same misery and loathing that it does me! But I do hope it is work which brings you into immediate personal contact with those you are helping—which appeals to your human qualities. Half an hour spent with Christ's poor is worth far more than half a million spent on them. It is *necessary* to a sane Christianity. *Experto crede.*

I remember some years ago being told that I was all wrong because I had not learned to recognize Christ in my fellow-creatures. I disliked the remark intensely at the time—but it was true.

I do not mean by this that I want you to undertake a prolonged course of slumming: but since you *are* doing work, do let an hour a week be given to *something* of that kind. Never mind about extra devotions at present. You are doing enough in that way I think: but remember that you are to be a companion-in-arms, a fellow-worker, as well as a lover and secret friend: that you are to further the coming of the Kingdom by your outer as well as your inner life. Do this not only as a "response," a "sacrifice," but as a natural act of friendship to your brothers and sisters. The kingdom of heaven is not a solitude *à deux.*

It is the vice of a false mysticism that it often produces this impression.

On the other hand, saying fervent things, if one truly feels them, is never humbug even though one is too weak to live up to one's aspirations. So don't worry about *that*. Just as it is not humbug to say prayers one longs to feel, even though the emotional power fails at the moment. *Never forget that the key of the situation lies in the will and not in the imagination.*

I know it is difficult to take the same interest in other things: sometimes one simply can't. I cannot give you any prescription against that and after all, although it is regrettable in some ways, I am not sure it is wholly a vice. One cannot have more than one centre to one's life (at least, not without suffering pretty badly for it—and I hope you will not try that!) and once you are adjusted to Eternity, Time is bound to look a bit thin. Metaphysics produced this effect in me far more badly than religious mysticism, because they proved that the world was illusion without providing any reason for its existence.

Now, after this drastic lecture, you cannot say I have not taken your parable to heart, can you? I should like even to say a little more on the merits of those vocal and formal prayers for which you manifested such a truly Protestant contempt, but that will keep for another time if you feel you want it!

We are enjoying ourselves here immensely and I already feel much better. The quiet is heavenly: and we are staying on till September 7, as Hubert thinks it is "better for me" than rushing about. . . . The company has been very amusing: two French lady artists and the Director of the *Bibliothèque des Arts Décoratifs* at Paris, a delightful person, both cheerful and brilliant who became very friendly and is going to take us round the Musée in person when we return to Paris. We walked over together to Pierre Perthuis yesterday afternoon. What a perfectly lovely place! It was very clear after a rainy morning and the view from the high bridge was marvellous. The old gentleman whose garden contains the ruins of the cloister, dortor and refectory and the monks' garden and vineyard here, asked us in yesterday and showed us round: gave Hubert a local fossil from the "grotte" and me a bunch of roses!

50 C.H.S.
Sep. 26, 1908.

To the Same.

I am afraid you will think this letter has been a terrible long time coming, but we only got home yesterday morning: and whilst we were away I never once had enough leisure to really settle down to it. We had a splendid time, particularly at Autun, which is a most gorgeous place both for scenery and "monuments" and at Château-Chinon which is as good as Switzerland without its disadvantages. We wound up with 5 days of shopping and sight-seeing in Paris: a little of everything, with the Sainte Chapelle at one end of the scale, and new autumn hats at the other. We liked none of the places better than dear Vézelay though; and shall certainly go back there another year. It was quite affecting saying good-bye to all our friends—particularly Madame Bobelin, who for some unknown reason loved me dearly and kissed me fervently (to my great amazement) in the middle of the narthex.

I return your bath with our unlimited thanks. We have severally blessed your name every morning for it. It *was* kind of you to lend it. Now for business.

A. About your work. I think you are doing very well indeed: and I should have thought, with your regular work, you have undertaken as much as you can properly manage. You say you will do more if I think this is the right line for you. I think, as I told you, that it is an essential ingredient in your life, but this does not mean that it is to overpower all the other ingredients. You must leave yourself time and energy for prayer, reading, meditation, and *also* please, for social intercourse with beings of your own class. The "right line" for you, in my opinion, is to check your own tendency to excess of individualism. But do not, in your zeal, overdo it in the other direction. I do so want your life to be properly balanced. To live alone, and be shy, and have a turn for mysticism, makes an individualistic concept of the relation between yourself and God almost inevitable. Such a concept is not untrue: it is half a truth, and when held together with the other half—the concept of yourself as one of the household of faith, related to every other soul in that household, living and dead—it becomes actually true. If this were *quite* true to you, intercessory prayer would become as natural and necessary as passing the salt to your neighbour at table instead of remaining in profound contemplation of your own plate.

B. This, too, is where formal prayer comes in, for in (the best) formal prayers—the Psalms, and prayers of the Saints—we are making our own the best aspirations of the best minds. To say that you cannot pray for the things they prayed for—that your wants are not theirs—is merely to say that you are not really in the stream of Christian tradition. To use these prayers confirms one in this tradition. They are educative to the soul which wants to learn to pray, just as good literature is educative to the mind that wants to learn to write. Also is it not rather arrogant to refuse to avail oneself of the help of experts? They got to the place you want to get to, and their prayers presumably helped them to do it. By using these prayers you enter into their atmosphere. You ought to pray *to* the saints too—ask them to help you. "The best way of knowing God is to frequent the company of His friends," said St. Teresa, and it is just as important to keep in touch with your brothers and sisters out of the body as in the body.

Don't be depressed about your girls' Bible Class. Of *course* they have not an elementary sense of religion: not one per cent of the population has at their age: and only a smallish proportion I think, at any age! The main thing is in that sort of work that you should make them like *you*, and that you should make it perfectly clear to them that *you* believe absolutely in your religion and care intensely for it. Let all your religious appeals, if you make them, be as emotional as possible. You will not make them grasp religion now, because they do not feel the need of it: but some time in their lives a crisis will come in which they will either accept or reject religion. *Then* the remembrance of your teaching, or rather the personality of the teacher who represented Christianity to them, will become of paramount importance; and the fact that it is connected in their minds with some one who was friendly *and* helped them, will count enormously. So you really have no cause to feel sad: that sort of work has mostly to be done in faith: and at the very lowest you are acting as a civilizing agent, which is one way of furthering the coming of the King-dom. To have got on friendly terms with the girls is a great thing. It means that you have an influence over them though they would probably rather die than let you know it!

Do not attempt "intellectual teaching"—go for their feelings quite simply and do not be afraid of letting them see yours! Religion *cannot* be communicated without enthusiasm. They must see it in you before they will get any idea of it for themselves —and this can be done independently of talking about it. I agree that the secret-love-affair style is very pleasant for the individual worshipper. But it is fatal in a missionary.

I *wholly* agree with the lady who asked you not to be a snail. The extra time which you proposed to put into more good works might be devoted to *that* department for the present, don't you think?

I got such a nice little old book in Paris of the *Meditations and Soliloquies of St. Augustine*, which I had not read before. It is Latin but very easy. Would you like to see it later on? And was there not some other book I was to lend you? . . .

Which Viollet-le-Duc has the account of Vézelay in it? Is it the Dictionary of Architecture? I want to read it up before my memory gets faint at all. We found Nevers a nice place and extremely cheap. There is one of the finest Romanesque churches I have seen—excepting St. Hilaire at Poitiers—and this is much less restored than St. Hilaire. It is all of a piece, not Gothic, and with all its dear little clusters of apses undisturbed.

Oct. 22, 1908.

To the Same.

This is not a "director's" letter at all, so you may at once banish the usual sensations of trembling—and probably those of pleasure also!

It is really to ask you whether you feel like being *extremely* angelic and helping me at your leisure with the job I have on hand just now? I am writing—or trying to write—a "serious" book on Mysticism and of course want to make use of the German mystics and some of them have never been translated whilst others have been done from such a controversial point of view that one dares not trust the translators. I am particularly hung up over Meister Eckhardt and Mechthild of Magdeburg, but there may be others. Now if I sent you the books, *would* you read them leisurely through, check any passages I sent you and extract and translate for me any bits you thought specially good bearing on points of which I would send you a list?

This is a perfectly barbarous proposal and please do not hesitate to refuse point blank if you do not like it. I know you know German well—and I don't know it at *all*!—and so I thought perhaps I might venture to *ask*, anyhow. This letter is very scrawly for the usual reason—Jacob! Having settled myself in most unascetic ease for an afternoon's letter-writing on the sofa, he said that he wished to be nursed; which has complicated matters. He sends his love, and is larger than ever! I have not any MS. to send: it is all in little bits, being added to and corrected, and won't settle down. I suppose you do not happen to remember whereabouts in the Lady Julian a passage comes saying that salvation or perfection or something "cometh of the pure love of the heart and of the light of the reason and of the steadfast mind"? I have used the quotation and lost the reference! ! !

I think you sound as if you were doing very well—and quite enough in the parochial department! Please hold the scales level, and don't let tract-distribution take the place of meditation! Tell me how your girls go on—I feel most interested in them. It is such splendid kind of work—I wish I did it, but the young never like me unfortunately. Good-bye. Be sure you say NO if you feel like it.

Nov. 21, 1908.

To the Same.

It is very evil to have left your last letter unanswered so long: but then, I *am* evil—and truly sincere persons always express their character in action. You, by the way, are very evil too: your behaviour about "business arrangements" approaches the frontier of *crime*. Did you seriously think that I ever intended you to slave for me like this as a sort of graceful act of friendship?

You have just waited till you were indispensable; and then taken a Mean Advantage! ! However—I will be even with you in the long run and what I says I'll do, that I does do. Meanwhile I am deeply grateful for what you are doing, even on these preposterous terms.

The book gets on *very* slowly, as the further I go the more material I find. I enclose a plan of the chapters, which I shall keep to more or less. You will see from this the sort of extracts likely to be useful. It is a study of mystical method and doctrine, *not* of specific mystics: so that bits bearing on my points are more useful than bits showing *their* peculiar characteristics.

. . . Vaughan says Eckhardt's "Spark of the soul" is equivalent to Plotinus's "divine intuition." Do you think this is so? I should like a bit or two about the said "spark of the soul" but this will do much later on.

Yes, I shall have to include Suso, also Tauler; but fancy I can get enough for my purpose in English. Mechthild has not come yet, and I *fear* must be out of print which is dreadful as she is really peculiarly lovely: even in the horrid shoddy rhymes of her only translator (who of course gives *no* references!).

This morning I found at the L.L. David von Augsburg catalogued as a 14th century mystic. He is Vol. I of Pfeiffer's series, of which Vol. II is your Old German Eckhardt. I know nothing of him, nor, apparently, does Vaughan.

Nov. 24, 1908.

To the Same.

I cannot *think* of an unctuous book for you! Most of those I have read lately are of a strenuous cast, excepting Richard Rolle, who is at present the beloved of my heart. But he is only obtainable in the E.E.T.S. Northern English text: horrid stuff to spell out. I think I must edit him for modern readers some day.

Isn't this lovely:

"In the beginning of my conversion and singular purpose, I thought I would be like the little bird, that for love of its Lover longs . . . it is said the nightingale to song and melody all night is given, that she may please him to whom she is joined. How muckle more with greatest sweetness to Christ my Jesu should I sing . . . by all this present 'life that is night in regard to clearness to come. . . . Worldly lovers soothly words or ditties of our song may know, for the words they read, but not the tone and sweetness of that song they may not learn. Oh good Jesu, my heart thou hast bound in thought of thy Name and now I cannot but sing it!" There's oil of joy for you!

Have you read Molinos? I could lend you a little thing of his if you like. He is nice—but *not* sticky.

I do not know what to say to you about Confession. My own feeling about it is, that if practised it should be done regularly, as a normal part of your life, without fuss or excitement, and not as a sort of spiritual spring-cleaning. This (the spring-cleaning style) is quite as upsetting as its material equivalent. It means, in my experience, agonies of contrition often extending over weeks, and paralysing in their effect: and I doubt its usefulness except for slack persons who will not face the facts of their own character without a stimulus of this kind. Regular confession *made to a priest, who looks upon it as normal and not in the least interesting,* I believe to be an excellent way of keeping your house in order. But, if it means anything at all, it is something so big that the personality of your confessor and whether he sees through you and you mind being seen through, etc. etc. simply does not come in. It is a sacramental act: you are not confessing to a sympathetic curate, but to Christ as embodied in the Church. You are a member of a family and are confessing to that family that you have not lived up to the standard set. This is why in the Roman form you confess not only to God and the priest, but also to the saints, each one of whom, as members of a potentially perfect Church, is injured by *your* imperfection.

Jan. 22, 1909.

To the Same.

I should be rather glad if you would send me your extracts from Mechthild and my notes (but not the book). I should like to look through them as on the strength of Mrs. Bevan I had arranged to use several passages which may not, from what you say, be admissible. You shall have it back again later if you like to revise: and if I re-arrange the language at all you will have to tell me whether I am Bevanizing or not! I have used heaps of your Eckhardt, he seems to fit me nicely somehow: but Tauler, though excellent, does not so far seem any good for this job.

Tell me sometime from the history the date of David von Augsburg, and who he was and what he did. It sounds a charming sort of book. Send it and Martensen back when you have quite done with them, not before.

Have you got Tauler's *Sermons for the Sundays after Trinity* in German? If so and if I use any pieces from the Wicked Winckworth (neither your French vol. nor the *Inner Way* contains those sermons) perhaps you would not mind comparing them with the original to make sure she has not falsified in the interests of "evangelical truth"?

I have had St. Bernard *On Consideration*. Most of it is tiresome stuff about the duties of a Pope (it's a letter addressed to Eugenius), but Book V, on the Consideration of heavenly things, has some lovely passages, and a splendid definition—"What is God? The best object of thought." The last phrases I should like to use as a colophon—

"But perhaps after all He is more easily found by prayer than by dialectics. Here then let us end our book—but not our search for Him." Isn't that beautiful?

I am so sorry you are "left to yourself." It is a cheerless experience but can be a fine piece of discipline if you choose to make it so. The causes I think are partly material—the inevitable fatigue of a spiritual sense which cannot live always on the stretch and is now resting. I think it helps one to go on if one remembers that one's true relation to God is not altered by the fact that one has ceased to be aware of it. Other things being equal, you are just where you were before, but are temporarily unable to see the Light. And the use of the disability, just like the use of any other sort of suffering, is to prevent you from identifying fullness of life with fullness of comfort. Your ideal of spiritual life must be right up above all the pleasure-and-pain oscillations of your finite, restless self: and you will not have any real peace till you have surrendered that self altogether, and tried to grasp nothing, not even love. When you absolutely and eagerly surrender yourself to the Will, you will cease to writhe under that sense of deprivation. You will take it all in the day's work and go on steadily. These are the sort of times when verbal prayer, if one has assimilated it and made it one's own in more genial seasons, becomes a help: and enables one to go doggedly on, praying *more* not less, because the light is withdrawn. To do otherwise would be a confession that you have been living by sight and not really by faith at all.

As to "having too good an opinion of one's own capacities," I don't think we *have* any spiritual capacities except those obtained and developed by prayer, and one can hardly feel cocky about those, can one? The true attitude is to rest with entire trustfulness on the Love of God, and not care two straws what happens to one's self. If you are *there*, how little the question of whether you see you are there can matter. It is rather an honour to be allowed to serve Him in the darkness instead of being given a night-light like a nervous child.

This does not *mean* to be a scolding letter and I hope it does not sound like one. It consists chiefly of rebukes I have administered to myself on similar occasions.

I am so glad you like *Holy Wisdom*. I think it very solid and trustworthy.

Sexagesima, 1909.

To the Same.

Please I really am sorry not to have answered your letter before—and it *was* nice of you to write to me for the Purification. I did not know you knew—so it was rather a surprise altogether! All the week a bad cold has induced limp sensations and a decided disinclination to do more writing once the daily tale of bricks was accomplished—so that is the real reason.

Are you still being a Martha I wonder? Don't go and have a distracted Lent over it: it is such waste, one does not pick it up all the year. Better a dusty lodging than a dusty soul after all—though I am not sure you will agree with me. . . .

I have got such a nice edition of Suso—quite complete—and am translating pieces from it. I expect I shall have to ask you to compare them with the original, as unless the French was almost literal (which I doubt) the final result may be much like Bevan. There is something disastrous about French for the purposes of religious writing. I have just had the Abbot of Farnborough's lectures on the Liturgy—and he translates *Sursum corda,* "Haut les cœurs!" Very exact no doubt—but there seems something lacking, doesn't there?

I have also had Madame Guyon's Autobiography (the original edition) and I will not conceal from you that it is highly diverting in parts, though of course I shall have to try and treat it respectfully. "Divers Croix chez M. son Père" is the title of the chapter dealing with various events when she was twelve years old and her Mama and Papa did not quite fall in with her plans for her own salvation.

Feb. 17, 1909.

To the Same.

What a woeful letter! You are so very meek that I haven't the heart to scold you much, though you really have been naughty this time. Just when you were most "beset" and might anyhow have found it a bit difficult to hold on, you calmly gave up your one chance of beginning the day fair and square! Where *had* your sense of proportion got to, when you thought you had not time for your morning prayers?

Now you will not get out of your present depressing situation by expending emotion upon it. The only thing that can help you is exercising your will. To begin with, the question of whether your waking thoughts are going to be devoted to reality or Miss E . . . is one which is entirely within your own control, or can be, if you give a few days to it. Your waking-up thoughts are largely governed by those with which you go to sleep. *Refuse* to take the worries of the world to bed with you. Shut them down the minute they begin to emerge. Absolutely nothing is to be gained by thinking over domestic complications when they are not present: it is imitating Martha's most reprehensible habit just at the moment when you have leisure to sit with Mary, and to gain from doing so a strength and peace and rightness of judgement which you can't get in any other way. You have got yourself into a state of spiritual fatigue and muddle, and you imagine, as you say, that your life is "dislocated." It isn't a bit: unless by dislocated you mean that it is not going quite so easily as usual and you are being given an opportunity to try your strength. Do be more trustful, more simple, more *childlike*. It is you yourself who are complicating things by not taking them bit by bit as they arise. Do this, and turn constantly to God by an act of the will, whether it gives you happy feelings or not. Adoration remains a grim duty when it ceases to be a joy: and is twice as much worth while under these conditions.

Now about Lent.

(1) Yes, of course I do think it would be a good plan to go to a week-day celebration: couldn't you go to Communion every week—during Lent only? Don't answer that it would be too exciting. It need not be if you handle yourself properly.

(2) Please say the Way of the Cross at least once a week during Lent; preferably in a church where the stations are set up, but if this is out of the question, say it by yourself. You can easily make your own meditations if you dislike those in the books. Stick to it even if it seems at first an arid and unsuitable sort of devotion. To me, the way in which it weaves together and consecrates every misery, injustice, humiliation, difficulty, weariness and squalor incident to human life, raises them to the *n*th degree of intensity and exhibits them in the full blaze of the Divine, is a sort of inexhaustible marvel.

(3) Put aside temporarily all ideas of unitive prayer, and devote yourself rather to plodding along, to intercession—using the whole strength of your will in it, not casually recommending people—and to curing faults. Pick one out and go for it steadily, noticing each day how many times you have committed it. *Don't* go to Church or to Communion primarily to "get help," but to offer service.

As to what to aim at. What you want is that steadfastness of spirit which is only obtained by *realizing* the greatness of God and the littleness of everything else except as a means to Him—meditate on these indubitable facts, and hold on to them with your will. *Amans Deum anima, sub Deo despicit universa*—and the odd thing is, that only when we "despise" them in this sense do we really cope with them efficiently. You will deal with the (domestic) problem much better when you regard it as a kinder-garten implement, useful to your education, but otherwise not of deadly importance.

I send you a bit of typing as you say you are ready for it: I hope you are not saying so to oblige me and inconvenience yourself. Don't do it until you really are comfortably at leisure. You will probably be annoyed (though I hope you won't feel it a "cross"!) to hear that one of Hubert's clerks, who had not much to do, has typed the first three chapters. I send the paper, as I thought it would be nice to have it all to match. Please make a carbon copy and give a 3-inch margin. My refs. at the foots of pages may not be always in the right order but mostly are I think. I have the opportunity of showing this chapter to a rather good theologian to check inadvertent heresies in it, which is really why I send it to you now. The other three chapters have been revised, lengthened and partly re-written and a rather long chapter on Conversion is nearly done, so I am not getting on so badly.

Many thanks for David. He seems nothing out of the ordinary, and I don't think I need inflict his Early German works upon you! Have you read Waite's *Holy Graal* yet? So queer and decidedly interesting. It contains at least one perfect epigram "God is the proper quest of the romantic spirit." I like that, don't you?

50 Campden Hill Square, W.
8 March, 1909.

To J. A. HERBERT.

Thank you very much for saying you will show Mrs. Limond some MSS. We are coming about 2.30 to 3 on the 15th. I think what remnants of my ancient lore still stick in my mind will enable me to lead her round the show-cases: but what I really wanted your kind offices for was to give her a sight of the Durham Book and Sforza ditto.

I wonder if you can give me a bit of information I rather badly want? Is there in the Museum—or elsewhere in London—a copy, printed or MS., of Richard Rolle's *Incendium Amoris*: the Latin not the English? It is not in Horstman's collection, which I possess. I am using him a lot for the book on mystics which I am writing just now, and Misyn's 15th century translation, called the *Fire of Love* (E.E.T.S.), looks suspiciously like being corrupt in places, so I must compare it with the original. I can't find the *I.A.* in the Catalogue and your esteemed colleague, Mr. Cyril Davenport, whom I roused from the agreeable occupation of making lantern slides this morning, could only tell me that if it was not in the Catalogue it was not in the Museum, unless possibly in a MS. which I should not be able to read! With which helpful and expert information I had to be content. . . . Rolle was such a popular writer in the XIV and XV that there must be lots of copies of the thing. If there are any other mystical treatises in the MSS. that you know of, and in a hand I could read, I should be thankful to hear. Horstman says that nearly all the English mediæval mystics are still in MS. and practically unknown. But he carefully refrains from mentioning names.

It is very exciting news about the MS. book. I suppose Methuen intends to publish this autumn? I know he is getting his list for that ready now, as he has just sent my new book (*The Column of Dust*) to press.

50 Campden Hill Square, W.
9 March, 1909.

To the Same.

Thank you very much indeed for all the splendid information about my Richard. I never meant you to take all that trouble— but am very grateful that you did! I will come and look at the most legible of the MSS. one day: probably I can find and check off the passages I am using without much trouble. I did find that much quoted ch. in La Bigne, but forgot to mention it. Why they always pick that one I can't conceive: it's good, but there are others better—particularly the nightingale passage and the bits about music. I want very much to edit Misyn, corrected by the original and arranged for modern readers, later on, when I have got my present job off my hands. Together with some of the things in Horstman it would make a very nice little book. And I think the "father of English mysticism" well deserves this trifling civility. When I am there I will also claim your kind promise to show me where and how hidden mystics may be catalogued. I am told to look out specially for Richard of Scotland, a pupil of the Victorines: but likely enough there is nothing in it. There is a striking resemblance between the casual advice of the learned and the crackling of thorns under a pot!

50 C.H.S.
St. Patrick's Day, 1909.

To M.R.

My very dear friend, I do hope I will get through this letter without saying something that will hurt you horribly by mistake. Believe me it's not meant to be hurting: so please try to read it as it is written.

Now to take your remarks in order.

(1) "It is so fatally easy to dispense with the regulations which I make myself." In giving way to such a feeling as this, and elevating your director into a sort of she-who-must be-obeyed, you are putting the whole thing on a wrong basis, and enfeebling your own will. If you regard any rule of life which you deliberately undertake as a promise made to God, an offering to Him—how *can* it be "fatally easy" to break it? Where is your sense of reality gone to?

At the present moment you seem to have got the perspective of your life all wrong: and you know it implicitly, and that is why you are so uncomfortable. You have got introspective again and are taking heaps too much interest in your own soul.

(2) "Your rule of weekly Communion is giving me a good deal of trouble." Why? And don't you think that this, again, is a self-centred and impossible sort of attitude to take up? "Behold the Bridegroom cometh" and you say, "But it's such a dreadful lot of trouble to get ready and I am never sure that

95

my hands are quite clean enough." I suspect you of going about your preparation in a thoroughly wrong-headed way: and pulling yourself up by the roots every time and meditating upon their discouraging condition; with the result that you think more of your own imperfection than of the Perfection which you approach. I had far rather you made no preparation at all than this. Our Lord did not say, "Come unto me all ye faultless": neither did He say, "Be sure you tear yourselves to pieces first." There are only *three* necessities of a good communion—Faith, Hope and Charity. To rely utterly on God and be in charity with the world—this is the essential. What you happen to be *feeling* at the moment, does not matter in the least. Do—*do* try and be more objective in your religion. Try to see yourself less as a complex individual, and more as a quite ordinary scrap of the universe.

(3) To the alarming list of innate vices which you have managed to get together I should like to add another: Pride. All this preoccupation with your own imperfection is not humility, but an insidious form of spiritual pride. What do you *expect* to be? A saint? There are desperately few of them: and even they found that faults, which are the raw material of sanctity remember, take a desperate lot of working up. You know best when and how you fall into these various pitfalls. Try and control yourself when you see the temptation coming (*sometimes* you will succeed, which is so much to the good). Pull yourself up and make an act of contrition when you catch yourself doing any of the things. *Never* allow yourself to be pessimistic about your own state. Look outwards instead of inwards: and when you are inclined to be depressed and think you are getting on badly, make an act of thanksgiving instead, because others are getting on well. The object of your salvation is God's Glory, not your happiness. Remember it is all one to the angels whether you or another give Him the holiness He demands.

So, be content to help on His kingdom, remaining yourself in the lowest place. Merge yourself in the great life of the Christian family. Make intercessions, work for it, keep it in your mind. You have tied yourself up so tight in that accursed individualism of yours—the source of *all* your difficulties—that it is a marvel you can breathe at all.

I hope you are going to get hold of a little personal work amongst the poor when you can? As for the inclination to cut connection with other people, *that* must be fought tooth and nail, please. Go out as much as you can, and enter into the interests of others, however twaddley. They are all part of life, remember: and life, for you, is *divine*.

As to the last crime on your list, however, "dislike of pain," you need not take a very desponding view. My dear child, *everyone* dislikes pain, really—except a few victims of religious and other forms of hysteria. Even the martyrs, it has been said, had "less joy of their triumph because of the pain they endured." They did not *want* the lions: but they knew how to "endure the Cross" when it came. Do not worry your head about such things as this: but trust God and live your life bit by bit as it comes.

There. God bless you.

50 C.H.S.
Wednesday in Holy Week, 1909.

To the Same.

I ought to have written ages ago: but these last days (*a*) the abrupt arrival of a new "case" for direction, of a very strenuous kind and (*b*) the fact that one of my dearest friends went through a very anxious operation last Monday, seem to have used up all one's vitality. I am so sorry. And now in Holy Week you will not be wanting a director's letter a bit: for the drama of these days provides far more than one can absorb as it sweeps over one. However, you can keep this till a more convenient season and I must send you a greeting for Easter Day. *Do* be happy on that day of days. Try being perfectly simple and trusting our Lord, and don't tie yourself into knots.

I do not think reading the mystics would hurt you myself: you say you must avoid books which deal with "feelings"—but the mystics don't deal with *feelings* but with *love* which is a very different thing. You have too many "feelings," but not nearly enough love. You don't love God in your fellow-creatures a bit. You ought to be able to love Him in Miss J . . . , but you do not, because Miss J . . . disagrees with your feelings.

Oh, *do* turn to, and do and be things for and to your fellow creatures for a bit. Devote yourself to that. Don't be afraid of "surface interests." Christ will be with you in those sorts of surface interests if they are whole-heartedly undertaken for His sake, and *not for your own soul's sake*.

These are the sort of things of a disciplinary kind which I think you ought to do. You have lost the knack of drawing strength from God: and vain strivings after communion of the *solitude à deux* sort will do nothing for you at this point. Seek contact with Him now in the goodness and splendour which is in other people, in *all* people, for those who have the art to find it.

But censoriousness and exclusiveness are absolute bars to making discoveries of that kind and you will not be happy till they are eliminated from your character. . . .

If this letter is very odious please forgive it. I am horridly tired and may not have put things properly. I always feel it is fearful presumption to scold you "being myself a full great wretch," as Rolle says!

Dinant.
Sunday afternoon [1909].

To HUBERT STUART MOORE.

This place is rather nice, and we hear the country walks all round are simply magnificent if the weather was fit for 'em. There's very good 5 fr. a day accommodation in the next village. I think the whole district would be very agreeable for our summer holiday one year if we were careful to avoid the more touristy places. The river is big and lovely, with great cliffs each side of it, and there are forests quite close all round. The railway travelling is v. cheap indeed, and so are most things in the shops. In the summer a steamer goes up and down between here and Namur. The towns seem rather full of neat villas and summer residences but the villages must be heavenly I think. Namur I didn't care for: but I got some nice old books. A little 17th century copy of St. Thomas Aquinas for 1 franc and a complete 4-volume breviary in leather, which I'd long hankered for, for 7½ francs! The old man said, "I think I ought to warn you, Mademoiselle, that this book is written in the Latin language." I was extremely pleased with the Curé in church this morning (I inadvertently came in for the sermon). He was a very robust person, who spoke like a commanding officer in the presence of very tiresome recruits. Having announced that certain services would take place this week, he suddenly added in a loud voice, "And I hope there will be more people at them than there were last week!" Everyone jumped, and he shook his head solemnly and said, "Far too few! far too few!" adding, "If you won't put yourselves out for the Blessed Virgin, you know, *she* won't put herself out for *you*."

50 C.H.S.
June 25, 1909.

To M.R.

Thank you so much for the MS. which arrived safely this morning: and also for putting in my missing references so kindly! You encourage me to leave 'em all out! I shall have another chapter (on Visions and Voices—it has been a horror to do) ready for you in a few days I think, though the deluge of summer parties rather interrupts work.

I think the *De Arrha Anima* experience is an intensive form of something which happens—or rather *may* happen—to almost anyone. I had one or two rather sharp pokings up of that kind during my blackest years—and do so still. If Grace were not more interested in us than we are in Grace, most of us would live and die in hell. It is so much stronger than we are that it *will* break in, in spite of our automatic resistance: and we are so immeasurably below it that we cannot attain to it or keep it by any voluntary activity merely because we want to.

I certainly would like very much to speak to Miss X. on the 29th: if I am not stricken with hopeless shyness when the moment arrives! But I cannot try to "evangelize" her unless she shows some slight desire for it, can I? You will just have to pray for her hard (excellent opportunity for practising the difficult art of intercession) and if she *should* cease to be "bored and incredulous" I promise faithfully to respond!

So glad you are feeling happy and practical and "expansive." Would you like to read Eleanor Gregory's *Horae Mysticae* when you have finished the *Book of Heavenly Wisdom*? It has lots of nice things in it, though many of her "mystics" are not mystics at all—as I often tell her to her great disgust!

Feast of the Visitation, 1909.

To the Same.

I have been meaning all the week to write and tell you all about the Bedford College party—but this week I have been to five parties and given two myself—and so there has not been a large margin of leisure.

You have probably heard by now that the B.C. one was on the most moist afternoon of the week—and everyone was jammed into the house, which was soon turned into a tin of nicely dressed sardines. When I arrived I could not find a soul I knew, so enlisted a large bevy of students to hunt (*a*) for Miss X . . . and (*b*) for my own hostess! Miss X . . . was discovered after a search which lasted close on an hour and just when I was thinking I must go on to my next party. She was very kind to me indeed; but there was a look in the tail of her eye as much as to say "keep off the grass." Has she any suspicion do you think that you effected the introduction for missionary reasons? She said she knew you and I became acquainted by correspondence, and that it seemed a good idea. Please, what do you want me to do next? I do not quite see that I can do anything unless she makes the first advance. We only talked for quite a short time and then my hostess found me and carried me off. The conversation rambled harmlessly round you, Vézelay and Bedford College. Would she come to tea with me if you told her to, do you think? I should be very pleased indeed if she would. I leave to you the task of inventing plausible excuses wholly unconnected with her soul.

I am glad the Vision chapter strikes you as "imposing." Really it is rather a fraud, being easier to get up than the more elusive parts of the subject. The only difficulties were in arranging it neatly and speaking what one believed to be the truth without hurting the feelings of the pious.

I am getting rather nervous about the accuracy of my French edition of Suso: I see Rufus Jones quotes a passage (I suppose direct from the German) which does not tally a bit with my rendering! Later on if I sent you the German and my MS. with the Suso passages marked, I *wonder* whether you would be a saint and an angel and compare them for me? I know quite well that asking in this calm way is impudence of the worst kind, but you know you encourage me!

You shall have Hilton soon: he is in use for the moment but will then be at liberty for a spell. I rather expect you will like him very much—though he is not such a poet as Julian. Do you know that some people believe him to be the author of the *Imitation of Christ?*

Thank you very much indeed for the information about the Cambridge Press. I have not written yet, as the friend who helps me with mediæval things knows a delegate or something and is going to consult him on my behalf first. It is not for *this* book, but for another thing. I've got a horrible lot of irons in the fire just now and do not know which to turn to first.

. . . Good night. I am nearly asleep so must leave off writing. I don't think I very much approve of your setting yourself penances for long past sins! Live hard, with both hands, and love as much as you can, and don't faddle with your experience!

Yacht *Wulfruna,*
Fowey.
August 28, 1909.

To the Same.

We have been as far west as Helford and now are on our way back to Plymouth: as Hubert and I leave for Luxembourg on Tuesday. We shall be at Diekirch from the 3rd to 6th September I think and then probably go to Vianden if we can get in there, then Houffalize, St. Hubert, Houget and back by Namur and Antwerp. But our plans are quite vague and really depend on how we like the district when we get there. . . . Send me a p.c. to Diekirch if you can, to say how you are getting on.

Cornwall has been behaving quite at its most beautiful, with lots of sunshine and only 2 or 3 soft drizzling days. The harvest fields all along the tops of the cliffs have been miracles of beauty. Don't you love harvest fields? They make me feel sort of wild whenever I see them.

We are lazing along now, with all our sails set, in a very very light breeze, past a beautiful bit of coast, all strange scraggy cliffs and white beaches. There is an old church on the top of the down we are just passing. This part of the country is full of XVth century churches, round-arched with carved timber roofs and often with fine old carved bench-ends. The cream of them, Lanteglos, is close to Fowey and by some miracle has fallen into the hands of a vicar with a taste for accuracy who has given it the correct small flat altars and other furniture according to Sarum use. It looks charming though a bit artificial. It has one of the nicest epitaphs I have seen for some time, on a 17th century Cornish merchant:

> Loe here a merchant
> Who both lost and gott
> By sea and land
> Such was his various lott
> But never lost hee less
> Nor gott hee more
> Than when hee left earth and sea
> For heaven's shore.

Don't you think that is rather sweet?

I enclose a bit of MS. for you to deal with at your leisure. Please make one carbon copy and begin each "station" on a separate page. There is *no hurry*. I will send you more as or when I do it and you can send me the whole thing together when finished. I have not done nearly so much as I intended of it whilst I have been here and shall probably do less in the Ardennes!

As it is a specially private document would you please take particular precautions to avoid any human eye falling on it whilst it is in your charge? And forget its existence afterwards, as quickly as you can? I do not know yet whether I shall print it or just keep it to administer privately; but if it *is* published, it will not be in my own name—so consider yourself sworn to secrecy by many deadly oaths. But I shall be very grateful for criticisms however violent. I am afraid it is scrappy and sentimental and full of vain repetitions: altogether quite different from what I intended it to be.

Good-bye.

Thursday night [1909].

To THE SAME.

Do not worry because you and Miss G . . . take different views of spiritual exercises. These things all become shams the minute they are allowed to be expressions of other people's opinions instead of your own personality. For this reason I am not going to tell you how often I think you ought to receive Holy Communion. But—if you feel a month is a long stretch, why wait a month? There is certainly no virtue in so doing. And there *is* a virtue in the frequency with which acts of pure love are renewed. The point in frequent communion is exactly the same as in frequent prayer or frequent attendance at Mass—and if you began to space those out at rare intervals, you would soon find yourself going backward. But have the thing out with *yourself* and find out what your own needs and dispositions are and do not let yourself be swayed by spiritual gossip—one of the most corrupting vices open to religious people!

Your other troubles you share with everybody who has any inner life at all—bar the Saints—at least, with all I have ever known, e.g. the constant and steady self-seeking although we know we are fools to do it, and the strange conviction that we are "losing the spirit of prayer" and slithering backwards in spite of our desire to run hard uphill! If by losing the spirit of prayer you mean losing the heavenly sensations of deep devotion I am afraid that does not matter a scrap. The more you are kept on the strain and the harder it is, the better. But these are the "harsh and repulsive doctrines" which you do not like! I think it is a very good plan to keep a diary of faults as a practical check, so long as you do not brood over the result. I believe almost the only way in practice to check self-seeking is to deliberately force yourself to do actual and concrete things in the opposite direction, however little emotional fervour you can put into them. On the religious side, intercession is excellent in this respect: one is always tempted to put in all the time in personal communications of deep interest and importance to oneself! And to make whole-heartedly a spiritual communion in the interests of another person is a really unselfish as well as a difficult act!

I think you are really getting on all right: but you must be prepared for a steady dying down of glamour and a throwing of you more and more on the normal resources of life. If your prayers really do the day's work for you—what more do you want? Not just deriving pleasure surely? Read the 2nd book of the *Imitatio*. It will do you a world of good!

I cannot write any more. Jacob has just jumped on my knee and is rubbing violently!

Wednesday [1909].

To the Same.

Here is a little scrappit of a chapter: the next is still under revision. I think although this is so short, it goes best by itself as an Introduction to the Second Part. *I hope you are keeping an account* against me: you must, are to, and shall. Then, when it has come to a reasonable sum I can pay it by cheque.

I am afraid I do not think the sense of "having no objective" is a bit bad for you. Remember, lots of people go through their whole lives without having, at *all*, the consolations which you have been calmly regarding as normal. And *no* one—not even the Saints—go through their lives without having the experience you are having now.

"There be many Christians most like unto young sailors, who think the shore and the whole land doth move, when the ship and they themselves are moved; just so not a few do imagine that God moveth and saileth and changeth places, because their giddy souls are under sail and subject to alteration, ebb and flow."

How do you like that? Here is another from the same.

"Hiding of His Face is wise love; His love is not fond, doting and reasonless . . . nay, His bairns must often have the frosty cold side of the hill, and set down both their bare feet amongst the thorns: His love hath eyes, and in the meantime is looking on. Our pride must have winter weather."

Good-bye.

Oct. 1, 1909.

To the Same.

Thank you ever so much for troubling to get *The Gospel of Play* for me to see. . . . It is perfectly splendid I think: and so is *The Gospel and Human Needs* which I have just got and am reading. I love his insistence on the romantic note, don't you? And think of it coming from a person who was described to me by one of his intimate friends as being, before his conversion, "a typical College Don, with no soul above savouries."

I send another bit of MS., though with diffidence, as you seem to find it so depressing! Yes! I do think all kinds of pain and struggle and all un-easy things done with effort, are or can be what I mean by the Way of the Cross. All people who live honestly, intensely and sincerely are treading it in spite of themselves: but it is better to know what one is about. I suppose taken alone it *does* seem rather an austere view of the universe: but I am sick of the feather-bed and dry champagne type of religion, aren't you? *That* is not "having life more abundantly" anyhow. And surely when it is patent that we are all being kept on the drive (unless we deliberately stagnate) and the whole world and all in it is kept on the drive, and that we are forced to spend our lives and use our energies in humiliating ugly sorts of ways, it is a source of exaltation not of melancholy to know that in this too we are accompanying the Spirit of Christ.

You write as if you were a bit low-spirited somehow. I hope you are not really. And *don't* look on reading the *Column of Dust* as a solemn and saddening ceremonial! It has not been written in that spirit, I assure you—nor am I the pious and pain-enduring invalid you seem to suppose. *Do* get these ideas out of your head! NO, everybody does *not* "find my works painful!" Some find them dull and some eccentric—and others read their own prepossessions into them! ! They don't tear them-selves into ribbons over them anyhow—and neither do I. I just write what comes into my head and leave the result to luck.

Luxembourg went on being nice to the very end. We went to Echternach and saw St. Willibrod's very gilded and objectionable shrine, and to Vianden, and for lots of splendid walks in the hills. Then we had 5 days at Houffalize and 5 more at St. Hubert (and I saw a stag in the forest, quite a sudden miraculous-looking one) and then stayed at Louvain on our way back. The Early Flemish pictures in the Cathedral are splendid and there is a most beauti-ful Gothic tabernacle for the Blessed Sacrament which stands on the north of the sanctuary, a little building all of itself, with a tall fretted spire. The woodcarving in some of the churches is wonderful even for Belgium, and altogether it is a distinctly fascinating old town.

The nicest scenery—at least the wildest—was at St. Hubert—miles of forest and moorland of unimaginable variety of shape.

Quite a large pilgrimage arrived whilst we were there, and came up the hill to the Abbey in procession, reciting the Rosary. I went in to the pilgrim Mass, but the atmosphere they created was too much for my enthusiasm and I ignominiously crept out at the Gospel! They say sometimes immense pilgrimages come there from Germany, on foot all the way.

The parish priest showed me St. Hubert's stole, which is supposed to have been brought to him from heaven by an angel. He rather spoilt the effect by saying, "It is a fine example of 6th century Byzantine weaving"—and it *was*.

I am extremely well and strong now. So there!

Dec. 1, 1909.

To the Same.

. . . I am glad *Ecstasy* is not entirely illegible. I have done it very badly I think: it was altogether too much for me—just piecing things together and guessing in the dark. But I have been working very poorly lately and now can hardly work at all, which is dreadful waste of time when one is shut up in the house. The book gets more and more difficult. I am past all the stages at which scraps of experience could guide one, and can only rely on sympathetic imagination, which is not always safe. Now I am doing the Dark Night of the Soul for which the chief authorities seem to be that gushing Madame Guyon who spent seven years in it, and Suso whose taste for consolations and annoyance when they were withdrawn will be rather congenial to you! ! ! Isn't that horrid of me? But prisoners do get malicious.

I did not mean, though, to be malicious in my suggestions about spiritual gossip. I am sure Miss G . . .'s influence must be good—so far as she is a saint: but the more of a saint she is, the more individual her life will be, and the less you will have to gain by comparing her practices with your own. And the more one talks over one's inward experience and compares it with that of others, the more one cheapens it. It is the most sacred and delicate of possessions and will not bear treatment of that kind. This is what I meant: and not a bit that it was a bad thing to talk of religion in a general way. But it *is* a bad thing to listen to descriptions of what another person feels, and a worse thing to begin judging your feelings by their standard. Each spiritual life is unique and its personal quality should be above all things respected. Of course if one is interested in religion there is nothing so interesting as talking of it with a sympathetic person : but it is a taste which should not be allowed to get out of hand.

I had tea and Benediction with your "other rival" as you call him, the other day. I do not direct him now: but we are firm friends and discuss things in a detached manner! Christianity is steadily transforming him and teaching him the meaning of life. It seems a really satisfactory conversion so far: particularly when one remembers how different he was before his rebirth.

Have you read *Christianity at the Cross Roads* yet? And what do you think of it? Wasn't *Punch's* review of the *Column (of Dust)* beastly? Quite the nastiest I have had. There have been about 40 now, representing all possible shades of opinion.

St. Thomas, 1909.
To the Same.

Scola Cordis[1] is the most absolutely charming thing I have seen for months: I have been playing with it half the morning and am longing to get to it again. Thank you so much: it seems to me a marvellous act of sacrifice to tear yourself away from it. I do not know what part I like best, the Emblems or the Odes. It is utterly fascinating. I had no idea Quarles was so uniformly fine. Eleanor Gregory put me on to the "vast triangled heart" and I supposed that was far above his general level but it does not seem to be. Didn't you like the one about the Crown of Thorns? I thought that beautiful. It will go away with me to Eastbourne next week to soothe the terrors of the English Seaside Resort and its disgustingly civilized trimmings!!

I hope you will like St. Francis de Sales. I had never read this one till a little while ago: when it pleased me well, so I hope it may suit you too. It is more advanced than the *Devout Life* and less sugary I think!

Have you read Miss Lowndes' *Nuns of Port Royal*? It is so interesting. . . . I think 17th century religion is extraordinarily interesting if one can get inside it. Port Royal, St. Vincent de Paul, St. Francis de Sales, St. Jeanne Françoise de Chantal, and the Quietists for contrast, make a fine group. Do you know Bougeaud's lives of Vincent de Paul and Jeanne Françoise? Rather fascinating though a little sanctimonious in places.

Hotel Bethell,
Rome.
Wednesday night.
[*London postmark*, 10 March, 1910.]
To Hubert Stuart Moore.

. . . We have had a splendid day in spite of a sharp hailstorm middle day; and have seen St. Péter's, and a wee bit of the

[1] *Scola Cordis, or the Heart of itself gone away from God, brought back again to Him, and instructed by Him, in XLVIII Emblems.* By Christopher Harvey, 1647 Often wrongly attributed to Francis Quarles.

Vatican, and two other churches. My private opinion about St. Peter's is that it is frankly hideous and not a bit more religious than St. Paul's Cathedral. It is perfectly impossible to realize that St. Peter is really buried under that dreadful conglomeration of fancy marbles. The Vatican felt much more like the real thing, when one was challenged on entering by a Swiss guard with a halberd. It's all extraordinarily light and airy, pale yellow and white-wash everywhere: in fact, all Rome seems mostly pale yellow. We went hunting for my Mr. Bannister, who wasn't there to-day, but I am to see him Friday: and incidentally we saw all the people arriving for an audience with the Pope. I don't know whether I shall get one, as it appears a personal introduction is required. Do you think your Sir Rennell Rodd would be any good for that?

The Vatican is built all uphill in the strangest way. You go in, and up a great state staircase, and then out through a gallery into a great courtyard, and cross that, and then up another staircase into the next wing. All the gallery I went down to the library was lined with early Christian inscriptions from the catacombs on one side, and Pagan ones on the other.

This afternoon we went to St. Maria Maggiore, such a splendid basilica, long and straight, with antique marble columns from some temple, and 4th century mosaics over them; and in the apse beautiful 12th century ones. It was really impressive and beautiful. After that we went to St. Pudenziana, at the foot of the Esquiline, and sunk right below the road to the level of old Rome. It is on the side of the house of Pudens where St. Peter stayed, and to whom Paul sent his love at the end of the Epistle to Timothy, and the old mosaic pavement of the house, which he may have trod on, forms the floor of one part still. It's quite a little church and rather mangy, but over the altar is one of the loveliest mosaics I have ever seen, done in 350, and pure classical. Not stiff and Byzantine a bit. Altogether it was a most thrilling place, and it seemed so odd to see it tucked away like that almost under a lively modern street.

All the different patterned monks and seminarists who swarm in the streets are a joy to behold, especially the Greek students who wear the most beautiful blue clothes with orange sashes.

I'm so sleepy I must leave off. Good night, darling. All my love.

Hotel Bethell,
Rome.
Friday afternoon [March, 1910].

To THE SAME.

I'm getting quite blasé about 7th and 8th century things; they seem quite modern here. To-day I've been down into the excavations underneath the church of St. Cecilia: and there are her 3rd century house, and two others, all the rooms and some of the mosaic pavements still intact, and even the little household shrine of the family before they became Christians, still there, with the figure of Minerva on it. Most of the churches have been dreadfully spoilt with awful 17th and 18th century decorations and additions; and you see appalling stucco and gilt ornaments side by side with the antique mosaics. I went into one, however, to-day which is a perfect little beauty: an early Christian basilica in full working order, with the raised "schola cantorum" in the middle, with its marble screens round it, and the two little pulpits and great marble and mosaic Easter candlestick, and the altar standing right out in the church under a canopy, and the presbyter's throne *behind* it in the extreme east of the apse. And the whole floor is of marble mosaic, purple, white and green. It's a little jewel, in a deserted square on the banks of the Tiber, and close to it two little temples, a round one and a square one, which have been turned into Christian shrines!

Robert Hugh [Benson] has sent me *via* Jack [Herbert] an introduction to the English church here, through whom I may get my audience with the Pope. Very magnanimous of him considering how little credit he has got out of me! It's very difficult to get an audience it seems and personal introduction by a Catholic is essential. They are rather weary at the Vatican of being made a sideshow for inquisitive Protestants, and I don't wonder at it! When one is here and has felt the atmosphere of the place one ceases to feel surprised at the fuss about the temporal power, and the Pope submitting to imprisonment in the Vatican rather than give it up. When you go about everywhere and see how completely Christian Rome is the Pope's city and how every great building and fountain is inscribed with the Pontifex Maximus who did it, you do feel it is absolutely a thing in itself, and they are the true heirs of the Pontifex Maximus who used to light the fire of Vesta every year; and that it is a mere farce to pretend that the place is simply the capital of modern Italy. All the modern part is so odiously shoddy too, so put on from outside.

My love to the Felis Florophagus—how has his appetite been lately?

Hotel Bethell,
Rome.
Friday afternoon [1910].

To THE SAME.

All yesterday morning we spent in the Forum as my card said. It really is fascinating, and most picturesque, as the Palatine Hill, with ilexes, edges one side of it, and old buildings and temples turned into churches the other, and you look right down it and the Arch of Titus and the Colosseum. The most fascinating part is the wee little round Temple of Vesta, just big enough for the sacred fire and the Vestal who was attending to it, and the house and garden where the Vestal Virgins lived. There were only 6 of them but their premises seem to have taken up half the forum. They had a big sort of cloister with three cisterns for rain water because they were not allowed to touch water out of any aqueduct; and all round it were statues of celebrated Vestals. The pedestals are there still and a few statues, rather smashed up. There are also the places where Virginia was killed, and where Julius Cæsar was cremated and his temple put up. What is most fascinating is, that right under the hill a complete 7th century Christian church which had been made out of the inside of the library of Augustus Cæsar has been dug out, all complete with its frescoes on its walls. No one seems to quite know how many centuries it has been buried, but there it is all intact except the roof; a temporary one has been put on, just to keep the weather off. There is one of the very early frescoes of the Crucifixion with Christ in a long blue robe, and a wonderful set of the early Popes all round the wall.

Hotel Bethell,
Rome.
Feast of St. Joseph, 19 March, 1910.

To J. A. HERBERT.

My dear Friend,

Indeed, far from "minding" I am deeply grateful to you and R.H.B.,[1] for I don't think I should have got an audience without you! As it is, I went down to St. Silvestro this morning and Robert Hugh's name acted like a charm; and this evening I am to present my letter of introduction at the Vatican. I have written to thank Robert Hugh this afternoon.

We have not seen any great ceremonies yet of course; I am going to see the palms blessed at the Lateran to-morrow, and the enthronement of the Grand Penitentiary in the afternoon. The shrines of the saints, I grieve to say, are highly unimpressive. That of St. Cecilia has been "adorned" by Cardinal Rampolla with Neo-Byzantine mosaics, mostly gold, white and pale blue, till it looks like a very cheap Christmas card—all the more distressing as it is actually in her 3rd century house, the rooms of which form the crypt. St. Peter's is even more hopelessly un-Petrine. He is about the last person one can think of in connection with that horrid monstrosity.

On Monday morning I am going round the Vatican Library with Mr. Bannister and am looking forward to it immensely. We have not met yet but have exchanged several letters. There is some very early Christian glass in the library museum which he is going to show me. Next week will be one violent effort to fit in as many ceremonies, exhibitions of relics, etc., as one can. I am torn between the attractions of the Latin, Byzantine and Armenian rites! I went to a Byzantine Mass this morning, and it was a most wonderful sight. One felt centuries away when one saw the deacon with his crossed stole, with one hand held up, standing before the iconostasis like a 10th century announcing angel. And there were extraordinary persons in long gold dalmatics who bowed down and touched the earth each time they crossed themselves. And it is so wonderful when every now and

---

[1] Robert Hugh Benson.

then the veil of the iconostasis is suddenly withdrawn, and you see the priest inside holding up the Host!

The streets are agreeably full of monks and nuns and seminarists but the "atmosphere" of the modern city is horrid. If I lived here I should become a violent partisan of the temporal power. It is horribly sad to see all the squares and fountains inscribed with the name of the Pontifex Maximus who made or beautified them, and know that Pius X will never be commemorated like that.

Hotel Bethell,
Rome.
Saturday in Easter Week [1910].

To HUBERT STUART MOORE.

. . . Now I must tell you about my audience. I went with a weird old female staying here who was having one the same day and we arrived at the Vatican pretty early and walked up I don't know how many hundred stairs. At all the corners there were lovely mediæval servants in crimson damask doublets and the Swiss Guard in their full dress at the entrance of the throne room. The throne room is immense, all hung with crimson silk, and with a frescoed ceiling, and at one end the gold throne Venice gave him when he was made Pope.[1] There were chairs all round the edge and we sat patiently and watched the people arrive— such a mixed lot, every country in the world I should think. There was a Canadian sitting next me and beyond two Greeks, and a French lady the other side. Presently an officer of the Noble Guard came in and picked out a few favoured people who were having private audiences. The room got fearfully full and we saw there would be no possibility of each person kissing the Pope's hand. Then some purple ecclesiastics came and made us all close up into a big semi-circle round the throne. Fortunately we were near the front or would have seen nothing. Then the Papal Guard came in and then the Pope in his white things and ascended the throne so quietly and simply that he was there

[1] Pius X.

before one had noticed him. He has a beautiful voice and gives one an intense impression of great holiness, kindness and simplicity. He made us a little speech in Italian saying he thanked everyone for their kindness in coming to see him, and that he blessed us, our families and friends, but we must remember that only those who were trying to live good and Christian lives, etc., were capable of receiving the blessing. Then he gave the full blessing, very elaborate, to all the rosaries, etc., which had been brought to receive it: made the sign of the Cross over us: and went quietly away. There was a rush when he descended the throne to try and kiss his hand but I was not quite near enough to manage it. . . .

I went out to St. Lorenzo yesterday morning where SS. Lawrence and Stephen are buried. Such a beautiful basilica, right away from everywhere, standing by the side of the road in a clump of cypresses and a flock of sheep feeding in front of it The choir is the 6th century church, and the nave the 13th century church tacked on. There was hardly anyone there but a nice brown Cistercian lay-brother who gave me pious cards; and it seemed so peaceful and far from the world.

Hotel Flora,
Rome.
9 April, 1910.

To the Same.

. . . Yesterday I had a rather nice solitary prowl on the Coelian Hill—in fact, very nice. It's a lovely solitary place, beyond the Colosseum, with nothing but a few old churches and convents and a farm-housey villa garden or two and steep paved roads with old archways over them and little views of the mountains here and there. I went into four old churches—one I'd seen before but not the others. I think I most enjoyed St. Gregorio; it has been rather rebuilt and done up, but there are a lot of nice things in it and as there was a sudden downpour of rain just then I was there some time and saw it at my ease. Tell Dickums [Richard, her cat] that it is built on the site of the house in which Gregory the Great retired from the world in the 6th century, taking with him nothing but his favourite cat: so I was very pleased to see, in one of the front chairs in the nave, a very nice black and white cat, sleeping soundly. The old woman who was bossing about told me it always slept there, and during Mass was often curled up in the sanctuary. As St. Gregory was a Benedictine and wore black and the church is now kept by Camaldolese monks who wear white, the cat was rather suitably coloured wasn't it? I felt I was stroking quite a reverend piece of church furniture.

I saw the "miraculous" picture of the Virgin which St. Gregory thought talked to him when he was meditating before it—it's very beautiful and alive, and I'm not surprised he thought it!—and the splendid marble table sitting on the backs of lions, where he used to have twelve beggars to dinner every day. One day a 13th came in and insisted on joining the party, and when Gregory looked at him attentively, he saw that he was an angel! What with that, and the cat, and Gregorian music, and the "Non angli sed angeli" I think he was a really nice saint. . . .

Good night, darling. I am all right and resigned without being mournful, and seeing some nice things, but I do wish you were here.

Rome.
April 12, 1910.

To M.R.

I am so sorry to have left you unanswered all these days but you see we are still here—and for no very pleasant reason. Mother fell ill when we had been in Rome quite a few days and is only this week beginning to go about again, so travelling has been an impossibility. We leave this day week for Como and shall get back to England towards the end of the month. Husband, work and garden all call for my presence, but there has been no help for it! Fortunately her illness was at no time dangerous though trying: and we had a most delightful Blue Sister of the English "Little Company of Mary" to nurse her. Being forcibly exiled from the sick-room in the mornings, I have rambled about and done a good deal of desultory sight-seeing and also managed, though with some difficulty, to get an audience of the Pope! It was enormously impressive, not on account of any state or ceremony, but entirely by reason of his personality. I never received such an impression of sanctity from anyone before. Whatever muddles he may make intellectually or politically, spiritually he is equal to his position. I do not think anyone who had been in his atmosphere could doubt it.

I also, quite by chance, saw three monks make their final vows and receive their cowls at the shrine of St. Paul, which was rather nice: and have made pilgrimages to almost all the spots connected with him and St. Peter, and gone up the Scala Santa on my knees (very painful) and seen more relics than there is time to tell of! I did not read Livy, but managed to appreciate the spring in the Forum where Castor and Pollux watered their horses before disappearing into heaven, all the same! But though the classical things are the most beautiful—the Forum and Palatine are a dream of loveliness now the trees are out and the roses and irises in flower—I still like the Christian things best.

It is marvellous to be in the very centre of the Western tradition and see it all spread before one from the earliest catacombs right through the basilica period—and oh! such marvellous mosaics, from the 4th century to the 15th—and up to the present day! I had rather a fortunate introduction to a learned Cistercian monk who lives at—and for—the Catacomb of St. Callistus: and he took me through it, and showed me the very beginnings of Eucharistic symbolism in the paintings of the primitive sacrament-chapels. The obvious deductions, particularly as to the sacrificial character of the earliest form, and the offering of Mass for the dead, must be "awkward facts" for Protestant theologians!

You have my deepest sympathy in your uncertainties about that question of kneeling down under the eyes of one's companions when visiting churches! The same problem perenially haunts me: and like you, I usually end in a compromise! I certainly would not in any company pass an altar of the Blessed Sacrament without kneeling: but apart from this, I really think there is something to be said in favour of varying one's practice according to one's company. After all, the object of kneeling down is to pray—and it is not easy to do this under the amazed eyes of one's fellow-creatures! I think there is a legitimate reserve and shyness in religion which is not cowardice any more than refusing to kiss anyone you love in public would be cowardice. Also, many people would really be made horribly uncomfortable and embarrassed if you *did* kneel down when you went into a church with them; and I don't know why you should upset them like that. Personally I detest seeing churches with people! But when it has to be, of two evils I think it is better to sink one's individuality and go quietly round rather than make a disconcerting exhibition of piety. But I fear this solution will not appeal to you!

Rome.
Thursday [1910].

To Hubert Stuart Moore.

I *do* hope you haven't been worried by this tiresome and idiotic upset of our plans! It really does seem as though bad luck pursued us all the time doesn't it? And over this particular delay I feel specially savage because I am certain it's not necessary. However it will only have made 5 days difference and it's practically certain that on Saturday you will see me once more! You see when my cold suddenly got bad (I got a chill hurrying after a cab in the sun I think) it exhibited itself as violent rheumatism and then went on my chest. The Sister after a day of this coaxed me to see a lady doctor she knew, as I cordially disliked the doctor the Missis[1] had. Unfortunately I consented and the tiresome creature though a very agreeable woman has turned out to be one of those terrible scientific hospital products who treat everything as an illness and by rule! Having found my bronchial tubes rather stuffy she at once called it bronchitis and I have now been kept 5 days in bed and simply *starved*—nothing to eat but milk and a little soup—all for a common cold! Can you imagine anything more utterly exasperating? Even the Missis thinks it absurd but these two women take not the slightest notice of either of us! Of course I suppose after an involuntary hunger

---

[1] Her mother.

strike like this I shall feel weak when I do get up to-morrow—
which is annoying just before a long journey! I can tell you I feel
very much off lady doctors. The poor Missis is bearing it well
though of course she is having a very dull time—no one to go
about with but Sister, and she may never drive in an open cab!
She goes out for little walks and buys post cards but cannot be
prevailed on to go far afield. She ought of course to be taken
each day for a drive outside the walls, and would be if I could go
about with her.

She came back from her shopping this morning triumphantly
bearing 6 postcard reproductions of "the Greek pugilist resting
in the ring" under the full impression that she had bought the
Moses of Michelangelo!

Savernake Forest Hotel,
Nr. Marlborough,
Wilts.
Thursday [May, 1910].

To J. A. HERBERT.

Your letter has just reached me here. I am so sorry but we
do not come home till Monday: or I would have liked so very
much to have been allowed to be present at Rose's First Communion and Confirmation. It is very kind of you indeed to
suggest it.

That fortnight's retreat in the convent does sound rather
drastic for one of her small size: I do hope it won't be too overpowering for her and is sufficiently tempered with fresh air.
Still, as you say, it must impress her with the supreme importance
of religion: I hope it will impress her with its beauty and lovable-
ness too. But the priest who received her struck me as belonging
to the "commercial law in the spiritual world" school of piety.

I am quite strong again thank you: am walking 10 to 12 miles
a day, and anxious to get back to the vast amount of work I have
got to do if my MS. is to be delivered according to contract in
September. . . .

As to *toties quoties* in this connection, it means, I was told, that
you as owner can lend the Cross, with its blessings, to the sick

and dying, but must not part with it or the blessing goes. You are *real* owner, as I took it to the Vatican with "intention" to have it done for you.

50 Campden Hill Square, W.
Sunday [12 June, 1910].

To the Same.

I am perfectly ashamed of myself for leaving your various kind postcards unanswered! My only excuse is that I am working very hard against time and everything else seems to get "left." However, I am on my last chapter now, glory be! and only the ghastly processes of revision and appendix-making will remain.

I was very glad to know about the book on liturgies. I had not heard of it. I shall try another paper for the Burlington when this book is off my hands and then it will be very useful. (I *think* I have got a "find" in connection with Van Eyck's Adoration of the Lamb; but this is a great secret!)

I wonder whether you have been to the show at the Antiquaries yet. We went yesterday and I thought it most fascinating. Hubert did not send you a card because he thought you would have more than you wanted. I wonder whether you noticed the lovely little panel of the *Fractio Panis* amongst the "additional objects." Not a very usual subject is it? I have seen it in Flemish art of course: and this exhibition seems to show pretty clearly the community of feeling between England and Flanders, don't you think? In St. Erasmus, for instance. I last saw him, and also the *Fractio Panis* oddly enough, in the Cathedral of Louvain.

Edmund Gardner has been giving some glorious lectures on Dante's mysticism at University College. They were highly stimulating but also extremely depressing in their goodness for anyone in the same line of business! A young ladies' school attended regularly, and sat open-mouthed with a bunny-rabbit expression whilst E.G. discoursed ecstatically about the ladder of contemplation, and the soul's ascent to the vision of Truth! !

Feb. 7, 1911.

To M.R.

If *really* what you want from the bottom of your heart is as you say "to do your part in an ordinary decent way," then you *can* do it; because this is wholly a matter of the will and has nothing at all to do with what you feel or do not feel, like or do not like. If you go on, in the teeth of reluctance and dreariness, with a rule of life which you know is right and which you have deliberately accepted: then you are doing what you can and no one asks more of you than that. But if you "go off on a pagan holiday"—well, that is deliberate disloyalty and practically a confession that you accepted Christ for what He could give you, not for what you could give Him.

I do not think you have ever made the Cross the centre of your life *really*. I do not quite know what you have made the centre, but it looks as though it cannot be that. And you have *got* to, you know. Nothing else will do. And if you do not accept it deliberately, why then it will be forced on you in some subtle and ingenious way, as it is at the present moment. And by struggling and tiring yourself out, you make it worse and add physical and mental fatigue to your spiritual troubles. *Accept* what you are having, quite simply and obediently. Take it as it comes. Do not "will" or "want" this or that; however virtuous and edifying your wishes may be. All such willings presuppose that you know better than the Spirit of God. And do not get into a despairing condition. These experiences are a perfectly normal part of the spiritual life: which is *not* designed on the lines of a "Pleasant Sunday Afternoon."

As to what you ought to do, it is very difficult to advise any-one else in this sort of condition. But I feel pretty sure you ought not to shirk church and your ordinary times of prayer. Only, do not on any account struggle *at all* to feel things or get into communion or anything like that. Surrender yourself altogether and be quite quiet. The thing is not in your hands at present. You are just to remain true to your colours. Leave off mental prayer and meditation. Stick to formal prayer. And it would be well to leave those you ordinarily use, and take for the time to quite fresh ones. I do not know how long you spend in prayer but very likely now you will *not* be able to spend so long. There is no object in exhausting yourself. You have been poring over the whole thing too much; instead of letting it happen, like a spell of bad weather.

I would rather you did some external good works, and thought less for the present about your soul. (I do not mean by this that I think grate-cleaning a proper substitute for church.) I wonder whether you have let your physical health run down and got nervous: because of course that accounts for a lot, and must not be confused with the other.

This sounds an odiously unsympathetic letter, and sort of easy and superior. But it is not meant to be really.

I know quite well what these states are like, and how dreary it is; and do not behave at all well under them. But I know too that surrender is the *only* way out of them. Humility and *willing* suffering have got to be learned if we want to be Christians, and some people learn them by boredom instead of by torture. But once you really surrender it is extraordinary how the nastiness goes and you perceive that it *was* "shade of His Hand outstretched caressingly."

50 Campden Hill Square, W.
19 March, 1911.

To Mrs. Meyrick Heath.

It was kind of you to make time to write me so nice a letter out of the midst of all your work—work that seems to me so wonderful and alive, though I can well believe that it brings that hopeless, helpless feeling sometimes. Isn't it strange how the people one really thought to do something with seem to dissolve on one's hands—and one's nearest approaches to success are those things one did almost inadvertently? I've noticed it over and over again and come to accept it as being mysteriously "part of one's job." Often enough, I suppose, you don't see your best results at all: they are swamped temporarily and do not really appear till the stress of life begins to be felt? This must be hard: but when I remember the atmosphere of my schooldays (when we were confirmed, we were given a dear little book beginning,

"My child, your life hitherto has been one continuous Sin, and you are now walking on the brink of Hell") I feel deeply thankful that you exist. Your girls have none of the usual excuses for youthful agnosticism—though I agree that the average modern home atmosphere makes it frightfully difficult.

. . . Ruysbroeck is my own favourite of all the mystics—even beyond Rolle and Julian of Norwich. Traherne is no use to me somehow: too meditative and not sufficiently contemplative. I want someone with a higher temperature, at whose fires I may re-enkindle my chilliness. Do you know Gertrude More? She is quite neglected now, but rather wonderful I think.

50 Campden Hill Square, W.
31 March, 1911.

To the Same.

. . . Please don't ever talk or think of "sitting at my feet (!)" or any nonsense like that. If you knew the real animal you would be provoked to either tears or laughter at the absurdity of the idea. I'm an utter beast in my inside as a matter of fact—and this is not said for "humility" or something—but because it is unfortunately true, and I want you to understand it and not have illusions. Little things I write merely represent what I know I ought to be but am not. I am not "far on" but at the very bottom. So there!

It is very interesting what you said about the "anæsthetic revelation." At one time of my life I used to have abrupt fainting fits, and in those I used to plunge into some wonderful peaceful, but quite "undifferentiated" plane of consciousness, in which everything was quite simple and comprehended. ， I always resented being restored to what is ordinarily called "consciousness" intensely. Now when I read Blood's descriptions—especially that bit about "my grey gull lifts her wing against the nightfall" and also the opening section of Stewart's "Myths of Plato," I recognized at once that they had had exactly the same experience. Stewart's "solemn sense of Timeless Being" is rather a good oblique description of it. I've never seen any chain of cause and effect as you say—but rather felt happily *within* a quiet peaceful Reality, like the "still desert" of the mystics—where there was no multiplicity and no need of explanations. Personally I doubt whether this is a very *high* way of apprehending reality, though no doubt it is *a* way. Last week a little girl of about 21, very clever and with some poetic imagination but not at *all* highly educated, was here: and becoming confidential, she told me that it made her restless and miserable to read *Mysticism* because I talked in it about "Reality," and she knew that she had seen and known once what it was and forgotten it since. That once, under an anæsthetic, she had been "shown" reality, and that she "came to" with a voice ringing in her ears, saying, "Don't forget what you have seen—try to remember—we are afraid you will forget." She did try, but it all slipped away from her except the voice and the knowledge that she *had* seen.

... It's very kind of you to like *The Path of the Eternal Wisdom*. It was really my own little attempts to "make something" of that particular devotion—which I used to find indigestible—and then a great friend suggested it might be worth while perhaps to print it.

April 12, 1911.

To M.R.

As far as I know—but I do not know much and apparently rather less every day!—what you now see about the Cross does seem to me right. It is the active and heroic and glad taking on of the painful and arduous, for the sake of love, and because it is the best on the whole of the poor little things we can offer.

And of course it does need "ascetic" training of some sort: and such training, if wisely chosen, is good, for all sorts of other and less exalted reasons. Soft comfiness is the soul's worst enemy, and those who have let it become necessary to them will probably find heaven uncommonly like hell! The question is, how and where in a normal, active life, to fit in the said discipline and I agree with you, it is *very* difficult!

The one great rule must be, you must not do anything which lowers your all-round efficiency for life—if the absent hot-water bottle means always bad nights and slackness next day, it is not a good thing to choose. Ditto about food.

Personally—in case the idea is of use to you—I have taken to knocking off all æsthetic pleasure in Lent; *all* poetry, fiction, theatres, music. This I find, at any rate at first, a real deprivation, and absolutely harmless! Also, doing rather dreary social duties one is inclined to shirk and giving up attractive ones. . . . All this sounds very little and is, alas: but it makes a sort of beginning, and there are constant choices turning up in daily life, when one can try to choose the harder side *pour le bon motif.* We all want bracing, as you say, nowadays: and certainly the fact that the idea of going without some external comfort worries one is a danger signal that should not be neglected. Only, always keep your eye fixed on the object in view and never let yourself think the self-denials you manage to perform important in themselves. The wildest austerities of the most ecstatic saints are hardly visible against "the glory that shall be revealed."

Hotel de Lille et d'Albion,
223 Rue St. Honoré,
Paris.
Thursday evening [1911].

To Hubert Stuart Moore.

A most mysterious thing happened here. A Dr. Colquhoun, of New Zealand, staying in this hotel, sent in his card to me, with my name written on it, saying he would like to see me! I looked out for him but we didn't meet and this morning he left for me a friendly letter, saying he was so sorry not to have caught me, but was leaving to-day, gives me his London address and says he hopes we shall soon meet on my return to England and I haven't the least idea who he is! ! The Horticultural plants sound quite a decent lot on the whole: I asked for the Prims and Campanulas I knew, and think you were quite right to pot 'em up, the weather being so uncertain. It's really quite cool here out of the sun to-day. It's rather nice that Methuen thinks it worth while to print a 2nd ed. of *Mysticism*, isn't it? I've written begging him to wait till I get home and send my corrections. Did you read the letter from Edmund[1] you sent on to me? Very amusing! To-night a review by —— in *The Record* has come—most generous in its language, "great book," "classic work," etc.: but with a beautiful characteristic little dab at my mystical saints whose "transcendental eroticism" he finds "nauseating." There's also a long and splendid review signed "C. E. Lawrence" from the *Daily Graphic*—so I'm purring!

50 Campden Hill Square, W.
14 May, 1911.

To Mrs. Meyrick Heath.

. . . I wonder whether you and I ought to talk about religion, any more than you and your Roman friends. It will be horrid if we can't because I know we are at one about the inside, though clearly about the outside we differ a good deal. Anyhow I am not going to argue—that is so dreadful, and spoils everything. But the honestest way is to be a bit autobiographical and explain, and then you can choose if you care to go on with me—so if the rest of this letter becomes a series of egoistical confidences you must forgive it.

You see, I wasn't brought up to religion really—except just in the formal way of course. So when the "youthful crash" arrived it caught me fair and square, and for 8 or 9 years I really believed myself to be an atheist. Philosophy brought me round to an intelligent and irresponsible sort of theism which I enjoyed thoroughly but which did not last long. Gradually the net closed in on me and I was driven nearer and nearer to Christianity— half of me wishing it were true and half resisting violently all the time. In those days I used to frequent both English and Roman churches and wish I knew *what* their secret was. Finally I went to stay for a few days at a Convent of Perpetual Adoration. The day after I came away, a good deal shaken but unconvinced, I was "converted" quite suddenly once and for all by an overpowering vision which had really no specific Christian elements, but yet convinced me that the Catholic Religion was true. It

Edmund Gardner.

was so tightly bound up with (Roman) Catholicism, that I had no doubt, and have had none since (this happened between 4 and 5 years ago only), that that Church was my ultimate home. So strong is this conviction that to have any personal dealings with Anglicanism seems for me a kind of treachery. Unfortunately I allowed myself to be persuaded to wait a year before being received; and meanwhile the Modernist storm broke, with the result that now, being myself "Modernist" on many points, I can't get in without suppressions and evasions to which I can't quite bring myself. But I can't accept Anglicanism instead: it seems an integrally different thing. So here I am, going to Mass and so on of course, but entirely deprived of sacraments.

I no more like the tone and temper of contemporary Romanism than you do: it is really horrible; but with all her muddles, she *has* kept her mysteries intact. There I can touch—see—feel Reality: and—speaking for myself only—nowhere else. Alas, you won't approve of all this, and I don't either—it is all wrong, but at present I don't know what else to do. The narrow exclusiveness of Rome is dreadful—I could never believe it, for I feel in sympathy with every Christian of every sort—except when they start hating one another. But to join any other communion is simply an impossible thought.

50 Campden Hill Square, W.
15 May, 1911.

To the Same.

. . . Oh, that dreadful limiting of salvation! How can anyone who does it dare to take Our Lord's name on their lips again. As if His presence had not been with thousands who knew not who it was they entertained. You are right—we are *all* too narrow for God—and yet, to steer a clean course between bigotry and indifferentism is none too easy sometimes—for me, anyhow. But I cling to St. Paul—and seem to find his inmost teaching over and over again in all one's experience, and in everyone who cares for Christ—Catholic or Protestant or whatsoever he may be. Is it not amazing when one can stand back from one's life and look back down it—or still more, peep into others' lives—

and see the action of the Spirit of God: so gentle, ceaseless, inexorable, pressing you bit by bit whether you like it or not towards your home? I feel this more and more as the dominating thing—it seems so odd that everyone does not feel and notice it happening, don't you think?

July 25, 1911.

To M.R.

I am sending you *Les Grâces d'Oraison* [Auguste Poulain] to read because I think its description of states of prayer and recollection and its general advice is so sane and practical—and in it if anywhere, you will be able to locate yourself. Of course I mean by this in the earlier chapters. When he gets on to visions and such like, he gets rather absurd!! . . .

As to making an act of recollection, I can only tell you what I do myself. I think I generally (1) make a definite act of the will to *attend* to it, (2) some short verbal prayer holding on tight to each word, (3) go on direct from that, or sometimes without finishing it to a sort of staring at God. Of course very often it does not come off at all; and when it does (3) may vary from a mere deliberate act of meditation to real passivity which is entirely outside our own control and should *never* be deliberately struggled for. If I were you, I should try to do this for 10 or 15 minutes every morning at first, not for longer whilst it is an effort. What is really best for you I believe when you are like this, is just to say, you will put aside that (or any other given point of time) for attending exclusively to God—and then spend it as seems natural when it comes, not in striving for states that do not come of themselves, but just being content to give yourself up to Him and "be as you are."

You will see that Poulain regards such fluctuations and loss of perception as you have had as absolutely normal and indeed to be expected.

If you want a more formal, but very simple and sensible account of how to meditate, there is an extraordinarily good one in No. 26 of Mowbray's Manuals for the Million (1d. I think), *A Plain Guide to Meditation*, by Rev. G. Longridge.

I am afraid all this is not much use! You see I think it is very likely that the point for you now is *not* to be going on to the next thing, but to accept loyally the place where you are now and stick to it, putting up with the dimness and aridity and holding on to the knowledge of what you have had in the past.

Yacht *Nepenthe*,
Poole, Dorset.
Feast of the Assumption, 1911.

To Mrs. Meyrick Heath.

. . . No, I hadn't spotted the fact that you are a craftswoman— and you, apparently, had not spotted that I am one too! In the days when I was still too timid and reverential to dare handle the English language I used to be an almost professional book-binder and even once had a pupil who used to put me into agonies of impatience by her finicky amateurish ways! I can do weaving and have a lace-maker's cushion on board here: and my husband does really nice jewellery and enamels on the rare occasions when he has any daylight time. So you see I can sympathize with that side of you all right though I don't actually do those things now so much as I used. Gardening takes up most of my play hours in London, and I do a little Health Society and Poor Law visiting, and seem to go out to tea a terrible lot and have lunch with my mother every day. So existence is fairly full—even though it be of nothing in particular!

I'm so glad your long fast was a success! When I heard how clear-headed and undistracted it made you I felt quite inclined to try one myself, feeling just the opposite at present! Only not having any surplus tissue to feed on I didn't quite know what would happen. . . .

You and I have rather got that *Seeker* to ourselves, haven't we? I thought your article splendid and only hope it will go to the hearts and brains of all its readers. What a good thing it has got in ahead of ——'s contribution on the subject! I think you make religion very "amiable"—but I suppose the Cross is for the mature, not for babes. My Ruysbroeck is as flat as a pancake and almost an insult to that transcendent genius. But it was written "to order" when I was at my dullest and dreariest. The second instalment is even worse!

Newbiggin Hall,
Westmorland.
16 Sept., 1911.

To J. A. HERBERT.

Thank you so very much for your letter and for the gift of the Book, which I am much looking forward to seeing when I get home. I am delighted to hear that G.F. thinks so well of it and only hope that is the beginning of a long series of just appreciations.

I did read R.H.B.'s book,[1] with pain and disgust. I wondered what you were thinking of it; it seems to me the most dangerous attack on Catholicism which has appeared for some time. Its mixture of childishness, intolerance and unspirituality is heart-rending and one cannot help having a feeling that its author knew that it would give pleasure in certain high places, and efface the "disagreeable impression" made by the *Lord of the World*.

As for me, I intend to try and be definite and outspoken, so far as the indefinable can be defined! but whether the result will be acceptable to you is another and very different question.

I forget whether I told you that I have become the friend (or rather, disciple and adorer) of Von Hügel. He is the most wonderful personality I have ever known—so saintly, so truthful, sane and tolerant. I feel very safe and happy sitting in his shadow, and he has been most awfully kind to me.

50 Campden Hill Square, W.
30 September, 1911.

To THE SAME.

We got home late last night, and I got *Illuminated MSS.* and am very delighted with it so far as a brief turn over entitles me to express an opinion. Thank you so very much for it. You ought to be very pleased with the production of such a fine and

[1] *The Dawn of All.*

E   129

authoritative piece of work—and the illustrations are *splendid*: a marvellous improvement on the proofs! I doubt whether I shall be able to come to the show on the 7th. I am going to Bristol on Tuesday for a few days and may not be back.

I have got the Rev. Dr. Harford's *Lady Julian*, amongst other things, for "special review." It is a most interesting text, but I consider his idea of editing truly beastly. "Reaction and Nightmare" is hardly a felicitous title for her chapter about the vision of the fiend, to my thinking! Nor is "littleness of the Kosmos" a likely phrase on the lips of a 14th century mystic. He seems rather a queer creature. The day after I had been asked to review the book, I had a letter from him saying he heard I was going to do it, and enclosing typewritten notes of points to which he wished me to draw attention, and things he had left out and would like said! They went back by return of post and I have heard no more!

All good wishes for luck with the reviewers of *Illuminated MSS*. Only a few of course will be worth bothering about.

50 Campden Hill Square, W.
16 November, 1911.

To Mrs. Meyrick Heath.

I wonder what you'll think of *The Everlasting Mercy*. I have never read Farrar (wonderful wide acquaintance with Protestant literature you seem to have!) but cannot imagine they had anything in common. I think the last twelve pages the most wonderfully exact and yet highly poetic description of that sort of vision that has ever been written. Every time I read it, it makes me live the "first fine careless rapture" over again.

I've had such a perfectly charming letter from the Abbot of Downside, whom I have never seen, but who is reading *Mysticism* and wrote to say how absolutely he agrees with it. Wasn't it sweet of him, and such a surprise. It came yesterday and made me feel so warm and comfy and readier to tolerate the ever-growing crowd of bores who have had visions and want to tell me what they are like!

I don't believe it matters a bit feeling as you do just now about

Prayer—I mean of course I know it is beastly—but it's not your fault and all that really matters is holding on with one's *will*. I'm sure hard difficult prayer is more worth giving than the easy nice sort—though it is one of the hardest things in the world, when one has been grinding out spiritual sawdust, to feel this really is so. Anyhow there can't be any merit in being sugar-fed!!

Feb. 6, 1912.

To M.R.

No, I am not going to scold a bit: and if you read any of "these here ensuing" in that sense, you will be twisting my meaning and attributing too much importance to the harshness of an unchastened style.

I do not think you are doing nearly as badly as you fancy: you have made great progress these last few years and there are bound to be flat times when nothing very spicy happens and you appear to yourself to be stuck or even to be going back, because you have leisure to observe the great difference which always exists and always must exist between your actions and your ideals and dreams. It is dreadfully difficult to estimate progress when there has been no opportunity for showing positive acts or any outstanding highly coloured fault to be eradicated: but there are more ways than one of growing, and you must not assume you have not developed merely because you do not observe your frocks getting too short!

Now about self-examination. These general vague examinations are very apt to be deceptive and featureless particularly with a life and character of your type. Drop that now, and take up the "particular examination." Pick out a fault or lack which you recognize in yourself, and which comes out, however subtly, in your daily life. Whatever you find yourself most "up against"— pride, lack of loving response (to life in general, as well as to God in particular), slackness, depression—whatever it is. Watch that, and that only. Try if you have time in the middle of the day to glance back over the morning and see if you have fallen into it. Pull yourself together and make an act of contrition as regards that. At night, count up how many times you have committed it. *Write down the number*: and look a little into the circumstances of each. You will not find this tends at all to self-glorification, at first at any rate. But it is solid work in character-building and very bracing, definite and wholesome.

If you find in your prayers that you really tend to dreaminess and talking to yourself, it will be better to use more vocal prayers until you get back more of your power. When one is really tired, it seems the only thing possible to do: and remember, it is the direction of your will that *counts*, not the amount that you have strength to accomplish. Prayer, when one is going through a blank time like this, is really exhausting work and you must be as reasonable in your use of it as in any other form of work. Try to make acts of faith and trust and to cultivate the power of resting in God, even in the darkness. Remember, grace is pouring in on you *all the time* and it is not conditioned by the fact that your eyes are shut.

About church-going I am quite of your opinion. I should never dream myself of going to a cheerful hearty Evensong, and shouting hymns by way of expressing my devotion! I do not feel that it is anyone's duty to do so unless that sort of thing is a natural act of worship to them. No doubt it is excellent for M . . .: but a quiet hour of meditation and reading at home is probably far better for you. I do think it is right and necessary to attend a Celebration every Sunday but anything beyond that seems to me a matter of individual piety which one is at liberty to settle for oneself. As to Festivals—other things being equal, I do think it desirable to observe them in some way; and unless one does observe them, they will never come to mean anything to one—just as it is impossible to understand intercession unless one practises it, and they all do or can mean something—have a definite place in the interior drama of faith.

Now as to your last theological difficulty. This is really simply a "bogey" and need not cause you any distress. *Everyone* tends to worship God more under one aspect than another. The Trinity is far too great to be apprehended "evenly all round" by any one consciousness. Tyrrell said that everyone was either a God-lover or a Christ-lover: and no one was both, at any rate in an equal degree. Why was God revealed in Christ, except that such a revelation was an absolute necessity for the majority of human souls?

All the saints have taught that it is far better and safer to approach the contemplation of God through the Humanity of Christ than in any other way. So I would not worry about this at all. At the same time, it is rather a strong measure to give up the Lord's Prayer—the one thing which sums up the attitude of the human Christ Whom you are to try to imitate. If you say it in union with His Spirit it *will* become real to you sooner or later. But so long as you go on trusting and doing what you ought without getting anything for it, you need not have any fear that you are on the wrong track; or that your inward life is not secure. I am certain, myself, that it *is* secure; and that you will discover it for yourself—probably in some wholly unexpected way.

50 Campden Hill Square, W.
10 February, 1912.

To Mrs. Meyrick Heath.

. . . I suppose you have received ——'s. What do you think of that? What with Adam and Eve, and that wild notion of his about the visible order being the inversion of the invisible (the impudence of making St. Paul responsible for it!) I felt as if I had got a nightmare of a distressing kind—the sort of thing that makes Richard mew suddenly in his sleep.

I'm immersed in my book which is very difficult but enthralling, and involves consulting what seems to be an absolutely endless number of authorities. I write all morning and read in the evening; at least as long as I can but I generally collapse with dimness of mind about nine o'clock! I wish Miss R. would teach me to cure that. Her second class was much better than her first and I felt rather contrite at having run her down to you. She is all right when she sticks to physiology, and simple psychological facts—often quite illuminating. But when she approaches metaphysics or theology the thin ice begins! It is all very well, but this teaching does leave out something which seems to me an essential of Christianity as I understand it. It aims at making a healthy all-round efficient even-tempered creature, a perfect machine for doing God's Will: but not a "God-intoxicated spirit," a *lover* of the Eternal Beauty. Miss R. said on Wednesday, à propos of the stigmata of the saints, that modern Christians would never think of meditating on the sufferings or crucifixion of Christ but would give all their attention to making the world the sort of place where "such an episode" would be impossible. Rather a tepid, remote impersonal kind of religion, don't you think? And wholly wanting in the great qualities of wildness and romance.

Haarlem.
Eve of Dominica in Albis
[Low Sunday], 1912.

To the Same.

... We had a truly divine week at Storrington; walked ten miles each day, mostly on the tops of the downs, and soaked our minds in all the trees and flowers and growing things. There was a monastery church for me, with four doddery old monks and one brisk one with a superb voice. He took the whole Good Friday and Holy Saturday services as *solos* and no one else seemed capable of so much as making the responses! On Good Friday he sang the Reproaches, choir parts and all, and the *Crux Fidelis*, and then carried the Blessed Sacrament to the altar of Repose singing the *Vexilla Regis* all by himself. It sounds weird, but really it was most impressive—much more so than the attempt at fluffy anthems on Easter Day. But as on many previous Easters, I found nature a great deal more spiritually suggestive than ecclesiasticism! *Everything* seems then to surge in on you with new life, doesn't it? It is too much to be pinned down at the moment into any rites and symbols however august, isn't it? It's only after the glory and the madness have worn off a bit that one can bear them.

We saw Father Tyrrell's grave. He is buried there in the corner of the Anglican churchyard with the chalice that was taken away from him engraved on his tomb.

I am over here now for a fortnight or three weeks—rather waste of time, for Storrington did me such a lot of good I could quite well have started work again at once, and wanted to. However, I'd promised to escort mother on her holiday so it had to be done! It is all very bright, clean, crisp, sunny and neat here, and the fields of flowers look like a kindergarten exercise in "flat tinting." At the corners of them are *rubbish heaps* of masses and masses of cut flowers, all lovely mixed fading tints, and more melancholy than a thousand cemeteries. There must be a streak of real beastliness in the Dutch—they use the cut flowers for *manure*. Nature in her harshest and most dreadful mood has never equalled that, has she? It has quite put me off the bulb gardens and I take refuge with the glorious Franz Hals pictures— a whole room just bursting with vitality and getting realer and realer the longer one sits with them. They offer all sorts of interesting problems to be meditated on, those pictures: as for instance, *why* should a view of humanity so obviously superficial be at the same time so deeply alive? And, why should this end by impressing one as more mysterious than the avowedly mysterious pictures of Rembrandt? Kindly tell me.

Hotel-Restaurant Bellevue,
Dordrecht.
22 April, 1912.

To HUBERT STUART MOORE.

Here we are, safely arrived at Dordrecht so I will begin your letter to-night: which is really *extremely* nice of me, as I haven't heard a thing from you—no letter here! I suppose the garden on Saturday made you miss the post?

We were dreadfully sorry to leave Volendam—it was such a friendly seductive little place and wonderful bright air too. We came away by "house-boat," a small boat with an open cabin in the middle, and a sail and push-pole, to Edam, where we got the light railway to Amsterdam. The ancient bargee who managed the house-boat had to get on the roof at one point and manœuvre the pole, so—really almost unconsciously—I took the helm—we were heading straight into the bank—and cleared the main sheet which was jammed in the block. Tremendous sensation on the part of Dutch passenger and bargee, who was understood to say I was "een trouer schipper"!

I have bought one of the Volendam fur hats, and also a nice boy's sleeved waistcoat: it fits rather well and will be a most nice little garment on the boat, I think. One of the girls at the inn took us shopping this morning, to the real general shop where the people buy their clothes, not the tourist place; and amongst other things we happened on two good old silver buckles, of which I secured one.

High Mass yesterday was really distracting—the whole population in church, 2,000 or more, and only about six not in costume. Men and women sit separately, so where I was it was a forest of entrancing caps! I was rather amused because at breakfast at the hotel a very Protestant English couple assured me that if I went to the church I should have to stand the whole time as no stranger ever got a seat. A friend of theirs the previous Sunday had "offered any money" for one and simply been turned away. I thought this odd, but went off prepared for the worst. Went into church in the usual way, and the old man who took Holy Water next after me at once seized my arm in a fatherly way, said "Heer ist een platz" and led me to an excellent seat! They are a very religious, serious sort of people, and I dare say *do* discourage visitors who come to the church merely to see the show—don't blame them! A thing happened there which I had never hoped to see in real life: during the sermon the beadle walked down the aisles stirring up the children who were going to sleep with his staff—and again at the Consecration, giving all those a whack who didn't kneel down!

In the evening one of the innkeeper's daughters, in a delightful ingenuous broken English, discoursed to us, more frankly than I think she knew, of the manners and customs of Volendam, and of various local scandals. The other English, I think, were much shocked. Personally I nearly died of suppressed laughter, especially when one matron said, à propos of the cupboard-beds where all the family sleep together: "But of course the boys and girls do not sleep in the *same* bed?" and our informant replied, "Oh yees, zey do: till zee boys begin to go after zee girls, zen they must go and sleep in the boats. But zee Volendam boys very slow. Sometimes 16, 17 before zey begin to think of zee girls!"

We are much pleased with our quarters here, which have reconciled us a little to leaving Volendam. The hotel is just at the point where the three big rivers meet, and we have rooms with balconies where we can sit and watch the shipping, which just streams past all the time. Every pattern of barge and schoot you can imagine. In the twilight they looked most lovely. What is funny is that they carry no side lights here, only a mast-head one even for sailing vessels. We hope to go all the way to Middelburg by water on Wednesday—seven hours of it.

50 Campden Hill Square, W.
12 May, 1912.

To Mrs. Meyrick Heath.

... We've been back ten days and now in another ten I've got to go away for Whitsuntide. This is really a terrible time of year! No settling in for really connected work—just sudden vivid scraps.

I am so glad you had a good time in Rome. *Isn't* the Pope (Pius X) impressive? I never saw the last one—but the simplicity and radiant devoutness of this simply left me grovelling. However unsuitable he may be politically and intellectually, I am convinced that inside he is a great Christian and would be an ideal Pope if a Pope's job were purely spiritual (as it ought to be).

I can't remember where I wrote to you from last, but I fancy it was Amsterdam. We went to Volendam after that, which I loved, though in parts it was smelly. But the marvellous cos-tumes—the dear creatures with mediæval faces, in huge baggy trousers laced up with green, and rose-coloured waistcoats and fur hats, were entrancing. We were there for Sunday, and High Mass was a terrible struggle between the delights of the inward and the outward eye. Then we went to Dort and Middelburg, then Brussels (I'd never seen the pictures there—and some of them are really rather good, aren't they?) and then three wild days of shopping in Paris! It was its very sweetest and greenest and blossomyest, but there were no nice little old books on the bookstalls, which was a great blow. ...

(At this point an interval has occurred during which the thunderstorm being over, we have descended into the garden and caught 300 slugs. How I love the mixture of the beautiful and the squalid in gardening. It makes it so lifelike.)

Did I tell you about a thing called the Religious Thought Society which has been started lately? It is supposed to be going to get hold of the modern mind and deepen its spiritual life. I don't know whether it will: it has considerably diminished its chances by co-opting me on to its Committee, where I feel very uncomfortable amidst earnest and orthodox females. There's one nice open-airy man though with the proper Christian twinkle in his eye. The Dean of St. Paul's [Dr. Inge] is the head of it, which is at any rate a guarantee that it will not vapour off in the direction of sentimentalism. We are going to have two conferences on the Doctrine of the Trinity in June and July, the various groups of members who study together reading and discussing around that subject at their own weekly meetings, and in the autumn we shall begin, I hope, a course taking in the different aspects of the spiritual life.

50 Campden Hill Square, W.
15 May, 1912.

To the Same.

No papers so far about the Religious Thought Society as everyone seems anxious not to make it formal but just a community of people caring about the things, and leaving different groups complete liberty to form and act as they think best. At bottom I feel much as you do about it, and for some months flatly refused to go on the Committee as I regarded it as a mere excuse for Religious Talk. However, I do see that whilst Theosophists, Higher Thoughtists and every other kind of heretic are having organized campaigns and "group meetings" and the rest and getting hold of those who think themselves intelligent by the score, it is idle for Christians to sit tight and talk about the merits of "wholesome Church discipline," etc. We must meet them on their own ground and show what the treasures of Christian philosophy *are*. Not one in a thousand, believers or unbelievers, knows anything about them. I look on it as a sort of educative and missionary work really worth doing if it can be done in the right sort of way.

Yacht *Nepenthe*,
Walton-on-the-Naze.
29 May, 1912.

To the Same.

... No, I'm not going to retort with remarks about lights under bushels to your observations on the Religious Thought thing. On the contrary, the people who wave their lights under your nose on the smallest provocation generally fry me brown with disgust. All the same, I think this policy of modest reticence *can* be carried too far! Really much of what our people want to do—so far as I can make out—is just the sort of thing you do for your girls now, because millions have grown up without having it done to them; and their need cannot be met by ecclesiastical ceremonies which they don't know how to use. To my mind, if only a few of these are put on the road to first-hand experience, the Society will have been a success. Of course, a lot of purposeless talk will go on and a lot of rope be given to the pious gabblers, but that's unavoidable. It is not so much a case of speculating, as of expounding what we have got. Nine-tenths of modern Christians are blissfully ignorant of their own theology, and intelligent young sceptics hardly ever know the outlines of the religion they are too clever to believe. If we educate intellects, surely we must take account of them in religion as in everything else? If we don't, I think we run a frightful risk. Better get them for God than leave them for the devil, even though it is the heart He chiefly wants. It's odd I should be arguing like this because really the whole of my instincts are on the other side! I feel the ideal thing—and for me, the only possible way—is to get people individually bit by bit, one by one, when a "door is opened" to one. The idea of talking generally about anything that really matters, makes one squirm. Still, a thing like this, purposely left very vague and unfettered by rules, may attract "seekers" who may thus get into touch with those who can help them. There's a lot of religious loneliness about, I think; and the mere fact of a corporate spirit amongst those interested ought—if we back each other up and pray for each other—to be good, oughtn't it?

What a screed! and there are lots of nice plover in the salt marsh all round us talking much better sense. We might be at the end of the world here, it's so desolate—a narrow creek running up into the marsh—not a house or a tree in sight; and a queer orange moon in the sky. It's like a bit out of "Childe Roland to the Dark Tower came" and pleases me immensely.

50 Campden Hill Square, W.
Monday in Easter Week, 1913.

To Miss Nancy Paul.

. . . Thank you so very very much for your beautiful and generous letter. How *could* you think such kindness an "impertinence"? It soothed and delighted me beyond measure: for so far the outstanding results of *The Mystic Way* have been a rather harrowing letter from Arthur Machen, making it obvious that he no longer considers me a Christian; some objectionable flattery from unbelievers, and the amazing deduction of *The Times* reviewer, that I have proved that mystics value the sacraments highly, as an elaborate sham. Between them I've been feeling rather dismal and outcast: and even began to fear I had achieved the impossible and shocked Scotty[1] herself (a triumph in its way, I admit!), and your lovely letter has had a most restorative effect. You have read into the book just what I tried so hard to put there but which will only be found by those who already possess a clearer vision than I have at *my* disposal. Yes, "reverent insulation" is no good, is it? In its way, as destructive of love as the worst excesses of "rationalism". But I am gradually finding out that most devout persons are Docetists without knowing it, and that nothing short of complete unreality will satisfy them. It is queer, isn't it? Logically their Scriptures ought to begin, "In the beginning the devil created. . . ."

[1] Mrs. Ernest Dowson (*William Scott Palmer*).

Thanking you again many times for your letter—and I haven't told you a bit properly what it has meant to me.

50 Campden Hill Square, W.
Low Sunday (March 30), 1913.

To J. A. HERBERT.

No, of course, I am not "vexed"; though I admit that your letter is very painful reading. I had not expected *you* to misinterpret my attitude and intentions quite so completely, or so promptly take it for granted that I meant the worst. Far from going further on the path of destruction, the last thing I wish is to destroy the one thing which gives life meaning and beauty to me: but what seems to you, to my great grief, to be blasphemy, seems to me to make the things I love best more real and more sacred.

As to the critical side of the book,[1] I simply took the least common measure of what seems to me to be practically established beyond reasonable doubt, and did not, in most particulars, even go so far as Baron von Hügel thought I should have done. (You are of course quite right about Mark as the source for Matthew and Luke, and I should have made that more clear.) I think that theologians *will have* to accept these positions sooner or later (an enormous number of course have already done so) and that a Christianity which cannot survive that process is in a parlous case.

As to the Magnificat, apart from the difficulty of supposing that Our Lady remembered exactly, and repeated to others, a long and yet absolutely spontaneous rhapsody of this kind, it surely tallies with all that we know about antique writers of history, that they felt quite at liberty to write speeches for the persons whom they described? The case here is clearly quite different from that of Our Lord Himself whose words were evidently felt from the first to be of supreme importance, and were moreover heard and treasured by a group of disciples. I don't one bit wish to jar on any one. At the same time a recogni-

---

[1] *The Mystic Way.*

141

tion of the plain fact that the Magnificat is simply a wonderfully beautiful linked series of O.T. texts does seem to reduce the importance of the question as to whether or no this form of words, rather than the pure and intense emotion which they represent, goes back to Our Lady herself.

Of course I would not suggest that incidents given by one source only are necessarily "non-historical." It is not this, but their "literary" character and incompatibility with Matthew, which causes suspicion to fall on the Nativity episodes in Luke.

As to your last suggestion that I make it appear that Our Lord was inferior to "the really tip-top" mystics I do feel it rather difficult to write coolly. I say over and over again that He represents the classic and perfect achievement of all that the greatest saints have aimed at but *never* wholly reached—that throughout His whole Ministry, He exhibited, as none other did, the characters of the Unitive Way in their highest perfection, that, in Him, for once life achieved freedom and touched the Divine. Does not this involve the Incarnation? And could I make my disclaimer of the idea that I "rank Him below His followers" *much* more plain?

I never dreamed for an instant that anyone could bring such a charge as that or I most certainly *would* have "disclaimed" in the most violent terms known to me. At the same time the post-resurrection life surely was (or rather *is*, for we cannot, can we, regard it as other than directly continuous with His presence in the Blessed Sacrament?) of a more "exalted" nature than the "earthly" life and so does represent the achievement of new levels by one who is *human* as well as divine.

I should like to ask you just two questions on the whole subject (you need not answer them).

(1) Does it strike you as more consonant with the dignity and glory of God that His supreme revelation should run counter to the normal processes of the life He creates and upholds, instead of emerging *through* that life?

(2) Does not the Incarnation involve *complete* humanity? And can we sever complete humanity from the laws and limitations (mental as well as bodily) which go with our psycho-physical framework? Do you think the Incarnation could achieve its

purpose for man if it had as its instrument a special nervous system, a special brain, and was exempt from the working of the laws of growth, etc.? It seems to me that all conceptions of Our Lord's person as something ready-made, must eventually land us in Docetism—and personally I find my own heresy, horrible though it be, better to live with than that.

[April, 1913.]

To the Same.

I was just going to answer your previous letter when its appendix came. The funny thing is, that in the said appendix, your attitude to miracle is exactly the same as my own: which makes the reason why I shock you so, more of a mystery (to me) than ever. Moreover, to revert to the letter itself, my question did *not* mean "Can you swallow the Virgin Birth?" because as far as the possibility is concerned (though I think, for technical reasons I won't bore you with, that the evidence is weak and full of special difficulties) I have no difficulty in swallowing it myself. In the M.W. [*Mystic Way*] I left it absolutely alone; and nothing said there is affected by it. All the same, were it disproved to-morrow, I should not have to follow your suggestion and fall back on good manners as a reason for kneeling at "incarnatus est." My question had to do with the whole general question of revelation: not with possible modifications of the "material" under pressure of the "spiritual" but with the "growth theory" as against the "conjuring-trick theory." Personally, if I didn't think the *whole* of life was the work of the Holy Spirit, I should give everything up. It is the centre of my creed: so vivid that the things which seem to us disgusting, cruel, unjust—and I don't deny them—can do nothing against it.

50 Campden Hill Square, W.
[? 1913.]

To the Same.

I am a wretch not to have answered your kind letter before. I would love to see the Sherborne Missal and if it is possible for

me to get to the B.M. before leaving home I will let you know—
but my life is highly complicated at present by my beloved
Indian Prophet,[1] who is convalescing from an operation and
likes me to go to him every afternoon if possible, to work out
some translations of old Indian mystical lyrics. It is fascinating
work and a real joy and education to be with him—but it does
not leave much spare time when my other various jobs are done.

I had a long talk with the Baron [von Hügel] before he left
for Italy—much about your letter, which had disturbed him
considerably—and a firm but gentle lecture on my own
Quakerish leanings! His main point seems to be that such
interior religion is all very well for our exalted moments, but
will fail us in the ordinary dull jog-trot of daily life, and is
therefore not a "whole religion" for men who are not "pure
spirit"; "a steady-going parish priest like a dear nice eider-
down"(!) he thinks a better standby for daily life than any
prophet. Hard and dreary doctrine, to my mind, but I am not
prepared to say it is wrong.

50 Campden Hill Square, W.
12 October, 1913.

To Mrs. Meyrick Heath.

We got back a week ago quite dismal at having to leave Italy,
and are slowly getting used to the frowsiness of our glorious
country. We had a really glorious time. The best holiday I've
had for years, Very little bad weather and the last 10 days in
particular quite ideal—hot sun and bright crisp air. I think
September a far nicer time for Tuscany than the spring: so
few tourists, plenty of room everywhere—and then the vineyards such a sight. We went to one vintage and cut grapes
madly to cast them into great baskets, feeling highly Bacchana-
lian, for the best part of a hot afternoon! We had a beautiful
week at and about Vallombrosa. I love those great forests full of
little shrines to mark the adventures of St. Giovanni Gualberto;

[1] Rabindranath Tagore. *One Hundred Poems of Kabir*, translated
by Rabindranath Tagore, assisted by Evelyn Underhill, 1914. Published by the India Society.

the penitential baths he took, and the encounters he was always having with the devil. We had one wonderful day in the Casentino. I was *determined* to get to Camaldoli because there are still Hermits there, so we drove there: right over the Consuma Pass, and by Poppi and lots of other Dante places. The whole day was rather like being inside the *Divina Commedia*, and the whole landscape absolutely mediæval. The hermits are at the top of a hill above Camaldoli—seven of them, and *so* charming. They would not let me into their enclosure (and Hubert flatly refused to go alone!) but one came out and talked and showed me St. Romuald's cell, which is exactly the pattern they have still, though our hermit assured us that *his* was much more comfortable! I think it is an ideal life. You keep the canonical hours, do a good deal of gardening, and may talk to each other every other day. Six feet of snow all the winter, which some of course might think a disadvantage, but they don't seem to mind it a bit. We drove back by moonlight—so wonderful. It was full moon, and the eve of the Feast of the Stigmata and we drove in full sight of La Verna. I felt as if the original night must have been like that. There were sheets of lightning too playing round the tops of the mountains. Do you remember how the peasants reported that on the night of the miracle they saw a mystical fire lighting up the summit of the Mount? If it was such a night as we saw, their statement was absolutely correct.

50 Campden Hill Square, W.
Sunday [1913].

To the Same.

I like Mr. Gamble. He is not up to date of course, but his ideas are nice. The other book I haven't tackled yet, but I fancy it is rather too high and dry for me! It seems to me that in theology one makes a series of forced choices between history and poetry. Both are necessary if one is to get an adequate symbol of truth, but it's imperative to take them separately. But the professional theologian often falsifies history without attaining poetry and that's an unforgivable sin against the light!

I liked the Miracle as a pageant very much indeed: it had to my mind nothing at all to do with religion, and I agree with Miss W. in very much resenting the use of the *Ave Maria*. We narrowly escaped something much worse—as the producers originally meant an imitation of the Blessed Sacrament to be carried in the procession, but were dissuaded at the last moment by Father Thurston whom they had consulted about the accuracy of various details! I thought the Madonna and the Spielmann both magnificent pieces of acting. We saw the English Spielmann, not the celebrated Viennese, who has broken down under the strain of having to walk 6 miles at each performance!

50 Campden Hill Square, W.
Sunday [? 1913].

To the Same.

. . . I've been that *driven* this week! Mother's Sale of Work, Monday to Wednesday—Bergson's lectures, for which I have been simply *living*, then a sudden demand for an article on him—ordered Thursday and printed Saturday!—then a note from Methuen asking me to revise *Mysticism* for its 3rd edition, which is wanted immediately! So no time for reading, or for preparing to write anything that matters! . . .

I don't feel in the mood for theology and am not going to argue with you about Sacraments. I'm still drunk with Bergson, who sharpened one's mind and swept one off one's feet both at once. Those lectures have been a real, great experience: direct contact with the personality of a profound intuitive thinker of the first rank! London isn't quite so silly as it seems. It provided him with a big, wildly enthusiastic audience which followed him with a deep attention that one could almost *feel*. After the first lecture when he was shy, he got on very friendly terms with us, and thanked us at the end for our sympathy, in a sweet little English speech.

It was rather strange, and gave me quite a shock last night, when he gave us his final conclusions on the nature of spirit (conclusions which sounded like a metaphysical version of the

Communion of Saints), to find that they were exactly the same as my mystic declares that she *saw*—her intellectual vision, and insists upon in the teeth of all arguments, as absolutely true! I've not see her again but we correspond. She is a most strange person, frightfully telepathic and over-sensitive. Two days after I'd seen her she wrote to me, and said, "I have lost my awful feeling of spiritual suffering, for the first time for months, and I know it is because you are praying for me." It was true that I had been, almost continuously—*but* I had never said or suggested that I intended to do it.

Nov. 9, 1917.

To M.R.

It was very nice to hear of you again: though I am grieved that writing is still such a painful matter for you.

I could not help being a little bit amused at your description of yourself as becoming "worldly." Somehow it seems a very unlikely thing to happen to you and it certainly has not happened yet: for your old scale of values is, by your own showing, still intact although like the majority of the human race, you are not perhaps living up to your own ideals.

What has happened to you is happening in a greater or less degree to everyone. The present abnormal conditions are as bad for the spiritual life as for every other kind of life. We are all finding it frightfully difficult and most of us are failing badly. The material world and its interests, uproars and perplexities are so insistent that detachment is almost impossible. Some are utterly overwhelmed: others, as you say of yourself, take refuge in interest in little things. Transcendence of the here and now demands at present a strength of will and a power of withdrawal which very few possess. I am certainly not going to scold you because you cannot manage it—only the saints on one hand, and the spiritual egoists on the other, can.

All the same of course it is essential to hold on as well as you can and make a resolute and regular act of willed attention to God at the times set apart for prayer—only do not fuss at the poor and unappetizing results. The *will* is what matters—so long as you have that, you are safe—and anything achieved now, when you are tossed back to this state, is worth far more than the enjoyable prayers you could not help.

I know well the condition in which spiritual things seem secondary and unreal—it is not pleasant—but you *cannot* force yourself into the mood in which they will seem real again—it will come back in its own time. Meanwhile your duty is to act on your inner knowledge and conviction and put all questions of feeling on one side. I do not mind your reluctance of "unwilling pertinacity" as long as you *are* pertinacious. You are like a person who gets into a fog in the mountains and can only see a few bits of moss in the immediate neighbourhood. The thing is to trust your compass, plod quietly on and avoid getting fussed. You will find it is all right in the long run.

50 Campden Hill Square, W.8.
7 January, 1919.

To Horace Hutchinson.

Thank you so much for your very kind letter and the gift of your beautiful little book. I had already seen it, and was very nearly speaking to you about it when we met—only, as you say, the occasion did not seem quite to arise, and I hate talking about these things in a "general way." I am delighted to hear it is going into a second edition. I have already given it to people whom I thought it would benefit.

Although I can't, of course, say I agree with you on *every* point—although the mystical experience is one, it is doubtful whether any two people feel absolutely the same about it—I think your statement is admirably clear and lucid. Without unduly stressing the Christian view, you have put the subject in a light which ought to prevent your readers from making any of the cruder mistakes, or rambling off into theosophy and such-like follies. Of course I thoroughly agree with you that Christianity was from the first essentially a mystical religion; to me, the doctrine of the New Testament is only intelligible from that standpoint.

The only thing I do a little regret is the fact that in one or two

148

cases you have put forward guides who seem to me rather doubtful—e.g. Molinos, as to whose aberrations I agree with Baron von Hügel—and (especially) Mrs. L.—a lady whose spiritual practices were doubtless better than her declarations on the subject. I can't help thinking it bad to encourage people to induce a quasi-contemplative state by means of mental associations—boundless oceans, sky, light, etc. This is a psychic trick, not the real thing. I think it is better, really, to teach at once the hard and wholesome doctrine that the attitude of adoration and humility is what matters and that spiritual realization is secondary to this, and can only be prepared for, not obtained, by our deliberate conscious efforts. But very likely you don't agree about this. I don't apologize for writing frankly because I am sure you would prefer it, and we both care about the subject too much for anything but candour to be possible.

II

O Master Christ!
Thou hast loved us with an everlasting love:
Thou hast forgiven us, trained us, disciplined us:
Thou hast broken us loose and laid Thy commands upon us:
Thou hast set us in the thick of things and deigned to use us:
Thou hast shown Thyself to us, fed us, guided us:
Be graciously pleased to accept and forgive our poor efforts,
And keep us Thy free bondslaves for ever.

6 Dec., 1923.

To L.M.

(To her friend's dog.)

As for your Engagement block it is perfect and will give a special flavour to the whole year. You can think of it more or less buried in the fragment of primeval chaos which is called my writing-table and emerging every now and then with a pleasant little bark. It all makes me feel more than ever that the Psalmist must have been a bit wrong in his psyche when he wanted his darling delivered from the power of the Dog (unless of course his darling was a cat).

50 Campden Hill Square, W.8.
Saturday [? 1924].

To Laura Rose.

. . . I have just been asked to conduct a three day retreat at my dear Pleshey in Lent. I forget if I told you I might do it—now it is decided. It seems a great responsibility, but I think I have to do it. Of course the Chaplain will say Mass each day but I shall take all the addresses, meditations and interviews. So you must pray for this too.

Last Thursday evening was such a joy—we had a great meeting at the Albert Hall for my "Christian Citizenship Conference"; and it was *splendid*. Packed right up to the roof with people and everyone so keen and such a lovely spirit every-where. The Archbishop of York [Dr. Lang] was in the Chair, and the Bishop of Manchester gave a very beautiful address—in fact all did. I think I best liked Miss Lena Ashwell, the actress who did such wonderful work for soldiers in the war. She spoke of bringing more beauty and happiness into everyone's lives: and suddenly she said, "There is one thing I wish to say, because I am the last sort of person you will expect to say it—we shall accomplish *nothing*, unless we love God. I mean real love, not saying sloppy and pious things—and that is a very hard thing to do really!" Wasn't that fine? And we had Romans and Nonconformists speaking too, and all sitting happily together on the platform and "treating each other's beliefs with rever-ence"—as our Confraternity says. I did really feel the whole thing was a triumph for the Spirit of Christ.

Feb. 6, 1924.

To L.M.

I've been having a lurid week-end going through proofs of 80 sheets of galley—mostly by my co-editor who has a talent for pouring forth floods of heliotrope prose and a special love for triads of abstract nouns: not only our dear old friends, Goodness, Truth and Beauty, but Anger and Scorn and Despair—Joy, Love and Peace—Shame and Penitence and Grief—etc. etc. My own contributions stick out of this with the stark austerity of quotations from the Stores List. The St. Andrew's Lectures are done: they are Flippant and Pious and Obscure: you see what a good thing it is that the Principal is going to be away. I'm getting so excited about coming!

March 2, 1924.

To the Same.

... Been working all the week at my Pleshey stuff; got four of the eight addresses ready. They are coming out a bit on the cheerful side but p'raps that is better than the opposite.

Have just been asked to be one of the three speakers on the opening day of Copec—a truly horrifying responsibility. Dr. Raven for Anglicans, Mr. Maltby for Free Churches and I (I suppose) for "Any other Colour" as they say at the Cat Shows. Meanwhile I'm going each night to *Back to Methuselah* and finding it most stimulating. Somehow the spiritual plot of it comes out far more vividly when acted than when reading the book. He's a marvellous creature with a real visionary touch, though so often exasperating!

50 Campden Hill Square, W.8.
March 19, 1924.

To W. Y., A STUDENT.

Thank you so much for your very kind and interesting letter. . . . I am indeed glad you have come to see so clearly how necessary it is that we should try humbly to accept and use religious institutions and not cut ourselves off from history and the common life, if we are to develop a really wholesome and Christian type of spirituality. The withdrawal of the "cultured" from Church life has two very bad results,

(*a*) it either shrivels or puffs up their souls,

(*b*) it deprives the institutional life of the contribution they ought to be making to it. And as a matter of fact, though the first return to these things is hard and dry, especially to the naturally meditative temperament, the more we consent to use them, the more they gradually give us.

I don't mean by this that I admire "Churchiness," but that a moderate, regular sharing, in the degree suited to each, in institutional practice will always in the end enrich, calm, de-individualize our inner life.

I am glad you like *Practical Mysticism*—but please consider what is said there to be incomplete and requiring to be taken in conjunction with the sections on Institutional and Social spirituality in *The Life of the Spirit and the Life of To-day*—or better still with Baron von Hügel's teaching in *Essays and Addresses on the Philosophy of Religion*. It is only when we grasp the redemptive and creative side of spiritual life and *our* obligation in respect of it, that we escape the evil of setting up an opposition between the peacefulness of communion with God and the apparently "unspiritual" aspects of practical life. I mean, enjoying Him and working with Him have got to be balanced parts of one full, rich and surrendered life.

If there are any points on which I can be of use to you, or you feel you would like to write to me again, I hope you will not hesitate to do so.

March, 1924.

To L.M.

Here's the little Dante. I'm awfully sorry I forgot to post it yesterday, my mind being rather upset! I got back home on Wednesday to find a letter saying the Baron was seriously ill, unconscious—and had received the last sacraments and we must not even wish him to live. However, by some miracle he has rallied and is now conscious and even talking a bit though very weak, and it seems he may recover. A nasty 24 hours! . . . I trust you have the big flask and an extra stock of prudence to take with you to Italy and are going to come back calm and well in all dimensions. . . .

March 28.

To the Same.

So glad you find the little Dante a comfortable pocket companion. He is an experienced traveller and has ascended Scottish and Welsh mountains and done a little yachting from time to time.

. . . I'm glad you like *O Master Christ!*; it's my best of all one, and I like to think of your using it too. It really is almost complete. . . .

The address on Prayer that wasn't so-called, went off all right; though it's very different shouting out things like that in a big room full of 200 people and saying them intimately in a Retreat. However, the result was a resolution to arrange for a two-day Retreat later so that's a good thing isn't it? Afterwards a delightful young creature came and asked whether his ears had deceived him or had he heard me use the phrase "our finite spirits"? I replied that he certainly had heard me use it—and he then said that he regarded his own spirit as both infinite and Divine! Father Baker's "I congratulate thee," etc., seems to come in as the only possible response, doesn't it?

Palm Sunday, 1924.

To the Same.

Thank you so much for your letters. I have so enjoyed them, especially your account of Maria. I felt sure she was wonderful but you have made me see her quite vividly and now I feel I know her much better than before.

I am going to read all those parts of your letter to Mrs. Rose to-morrow. She is already tremendously in touch with Maria and had got the idea of her quite right. . . . But what an appalling amount of nonsense you seem to have talked about me!! However it will be abruptly corrected when I turn up there in September. . . .

No! I don't know any of them except *via* prayers and paper; and haven't really done anything particular for the *Entente*—but it's becoming a curiously strong little organization and the members of its inner circle do seem to be in actual spiritual touch. Your whole account makes me simply long to get out to them and bathe in that atmosphere, being at present a bit tired and chivvied and having very much to do what St. Teresa calls "drawing it all up in one's own bucket!"

50 Campden Hill Square, W.8.
June 20, 1924.

To W.Y.

I was so pleased to hear from you again; for you have remained in my mind since your previous letter.

I think your "practical" difficulty is really a mental and spiritual difficulty. That is to say it arises out of the inadequacy of your present religious and philosophic outlook. You have arrived at a sort of pantheistic belief and experience and have discovered—as I think nearly every sincere person must discover sooner or later—that it provides no real incentive or sanction whatever for moral effort, and yet you can't get away from the feeling (I think) that moral effort is part of your job! What you are really short of is the conviction of *personal* responsibility to a *personal* God—and pantheism of course can never give you that. It *means genuine* theism and preferably Christian theism—the true co-ordinating factor of our æsthetic and ethical life. Of course such a realization of the Divine in and through nature, as you describe, is religious as far as it goes: but it isn't a *sufficient* religion for the human soul, which absolutely requires a relationship with a personal Object in which its own partial and imperfect personality is summed up and made complete. This does not mean scrapping your present outlook, but including it in Something deeper and greater.

And (as regards specifically Christian beliefs) it means getting beyond the idea of Christ as a "perfect example," "spiritual genius" and so forth, to a realization of the principle of incarnation (and as a derivative therefrom, of sacramentalism also) as involving the special self-expression and self-imparting of the Infinite God, in humanity and for humanity.

If you will as it were let such ideas as these dwell in your mind, regard them favourably, be willing for them to be true, I think it probable that your religious attitude will gradually develop in the theistic direction and you will then find the clue and incentive you feel you need. But it does seem to me that you ought to try to pray. Your spiritual sense won't develop unless you give it education. I think you ought to take a short, regular time for this every day—perhaps only 10 minutes in the morning at first. Even if it begins merely as you say with reading a Psalm and "feeling transported." That is not mere self-indulgence, but quite a good preparation for subsequent objectivity and hard work. Hold on to this sense of peace and beauty, and in and with that, consider the duties, etc., of the day: surround them with that atmosphere as much as you can—and don't expect any very startling results at first!

I wish you would read (if you have not already) Otto's *The*

Idea of the Holy and Baron von Hügel's *Essays and Addresses*—especially the one on the "Natural and Supernatural" for I think you would find them illuminating.

July 7, 1924.

To L.M.

I've got the new book on Blake to read; it is mighty ingenious, but the attempt to wedge Blake into the most rigidly conceived categories of mystical science, requires a spiritual shoe-horn. Still there are lots of interesting and suggestive things in it. . . .

The Baron is keeping pretty well and able now to do without a nurse, though he won't be able to go away this year. . . . He does not regain any *physical* strength. I do so trust he is happy in his soul through it all; but that of course, he would never let anyone know. . . .

Do hope you are beginning to sleep a bit. Meditate upon the Sacred Cow and strive with Ruysbroeck to "become that which you behold": it's the right ideal for convalescents which I do trust you will soon begin to be. . . .

July 26, 1924.

To the Same.

I've had a heavily worldly week with all the parties to the American lawyers, ending last night with a really splendid show, the Lord Chancellor's reception in Westminster Hall. It *was* a sight, that glorious architecture and roof brilliantly lit up, as one never sees it, and every one in their best, swords, orders and all. I went with my dear old papa, who looked very sweet in his black velvet and buckled shoes. The Americans overwhelmed with awe and joy. I heard one say, "My! I'm all Eyes and Ears to-night!"

Wednesday we had them at Lincoln's Inn and led them round and showed them the antiquities including the crooked little streets round Staples Inn, which struck them as "cunning." Altogether it was rather fun.

Macugnaga.
Sunday, 7 September, 1924.

To Clara Smith.

... We got here Thursday afternoon, a wonderful drive mostly on the edge of precipices and through tunnels in the rock, on emerging from which you were apt to find an unexpected mule blocking the way. This is a lovely valley, with Monte Rosa blocking its northern end and looking simply enormous, Everesty and unclimbable. A tablet on the church says that the present Pope started from here to make two pioneer climbs before he was "called to still higher altitudes." The Vatican must feel pretty awful after Monte Rosa, poor thing!

The flowers here are not much now—dianthus, several sorts of campanula, pansies and so forth—not *real* Alpines, we are hardly high enough. Still they make up quite an agreeable little bunch. We have had two lovely long days in the wilds: the first one going up to the glacier, a steep and warm affair, and the second rather milder, climbing only about 1,000 feet, much companioned and beset by goats, who had the salt out of our lunch, and ate the paper; swallowed half a yard of my scarf, which had to be pulled back to the external world not looking as nice as it did before, and chewed up the strap of Hubert's glasses. But they were charming goats, soft and glossy, with most sweet faces; and quite content when everything else was finished to lick one's hands.

This morning just after everyone had come out from Mass we saw a most strangely shaped object coming up the road, which turned out to be a young woman with a full-sized cradle on her back on the top of one of the local baskets. A white lace veil covered the whole cradle and over it the best family shawl, a marvellous magenta silk affair with long fringe. Inside though one could hardly believe it was a live three days' old baby coming to be christened. The *greatest* pains had been taken with the packing, to exclude all air! At the church door it emerged, tightly swaddled and lying on a lace cushion, and was carried in by its papa, looking as if it came straight from a 15th century picture. Interested ladies from the hotel tried to assist in repacking it as before; but were gently repelled by the godmother, a most sweet thing with a pensive little face, who now arranged it quite differently, and threw the white lace veil over the shawl and everything observing, "Bianca sopra, adesso che e cristiana!" The cradle was strapped on her back and off she went down the valley again.

. . . After living in a hotel full of Italians I fully understand why St. Catherine shut herself in one room for three years—but it wouldn't have been much good unless she had a soundproof door.

Perugia.
Feast of the Exaltation of the Cross, 1924.

To L.M.

This seems a nice moment to answer your letter. . . . It is 2.30 and most deliciously hot and I am sitting in my room waiting for the Umbrian Horse Show to begin its jumping competitions, as we look right down on the ground—a very superior form of grandstand!

At 5 there is to be a *Festa* at St. Angelo beginning with a confirmation, discourse by the Archbishop and Benediction, ending with the illumination of the Church front and *musica scelta* by *two* bands!

. . . We are having a simply lovely time and the weather is perfect. The whole landscape seems soaked in light; and all I can think of is Jacopone's *Splendor che dona a tutto'l mondo luce,* etc. He must have thought of that on a day like one of these!

We drove to Todi yesterday. *What* a place! The only snag was I couldn't get to see his tomb as the crypt was locked and not a soul about. The picture of him, very chubby and curly and holding his heart is simply detestable, I think. But it was something to be in the Church he must have used and see the actual Piazza where Monna Vanna fell.

In the morning we had been out to St. Francesco al Monte in search of B. Egidio. Found *his* tomb all right; admitted after a long wait by a very damp and rosy friar who had plainly executed a very vigorous clean-up after our bell rang! I loved St. Bernardino's little cell. Rather a desperate new picture of Egidio, painted by a "signorina gentillissima" of Perugia and looking it, every inch.

Assisi.

17 September, 1924.

To CLARA SMITH.

We are having a simply divine time here and I feel as if it is the only complete holiday I have had for years—*very* hot, but not too much so and the evenings and mornings are perfect. I got up at 5.30 this morning and arrived at St. Damiano just at sunrise for the sung Mass, to-day being the Feast of the Stigmata. The lay congregation consisted of half a dozen peasants, a few mosquitoes, and myself. The friars sang very nicely and the celebrant had lovely white vestments embroidered all over with stiff little roses, which I thought just right. I could just see into the tiny little choir of your patron saint, which with her little garden is one of the things I love best. After breakfast we went up to the Carceri. Did you talk to Fra Raffaele when you were there, and did he insist on playing his harmonium to you because St. Francis loved music? I found him *most* sympathetic and hard to get away from and he even gave me a few leaves of the tree on which the birds sat when St. Francis talked to them. I enclose one for you. He advises boiling them and drinking the water in case of sickness but I hope to preserve mine intact! : . . I enclose a few bits of wild thyme from the Carceri—the same that were found still scattered all over St. Clare when her coffin was opened. How nice it is for you to have an Assisan name. I am carrying round a rosary for Rosa to all the shrines and collecting powerful incantations—it will be very fully charged before we have finished.

Spoleto.

Tuesday [1924].

To LAURA ROSE.

. . . Maria is all we felt. I got to the little station at 5 yesterday evening: it was just getting lovely after the heat; and then drove in the little village cab through the most beautiful country, olive woods and vineyards to the hills beyond: and just as we neared the Rifugio Miss Turton and Maria met me and I walked up with them. Maria and the Sisters have white cotton frocks, grey linen aprons, the cord of St. Francis and sandals on their bare feet. In chapel they have white aprons and white veils. Maria has the most beautiful expression, strong and humble, and a low gentle voice. I got quite a good deal of talk with her; it was wonderful to find how exactly she and my Old Man[1] agree, in spite of great differences in mind and language, in all the deep things of the spiritual life. We talked a lot about X. . . . Maria said her soul was "always very present to her." I told her X. had been asking me to increase the time she might give to prayer and asked her whether she would give her more. She said at once with surprising decision and authority, that instead of giving her more time, *she* would rather make her reduce the time—that X. was "an immoderate soul" though very good and humble, and had to "learn the way of simplicity" and make her whole life a prayer instead of wanting long special times for it. I said I felt less and less competent to direct her, and was afraid of holding her back— but Maria said my holding her back was "not only useful but necessary to X." It was just the same bracing treatment that I have long been used to! though coming with such gentleness. After we'd said a good deal more I asked her for something for myself and she said, "In torment and effort, to serve the brethren."

They have a little shrine of Our Lady on the staircase and yesterday evening we all said the Rosary there. Maria used your rosary as I felt sure you would like that and Miss Turton mine and I hers. There was an Italian priest there too, who came to meet me because he knew my Old Man and years ago had been helped by him and owed him everything, and so wanted to hear his latest news, and this morning he said Mass in their tiny chapel, and Maria served, and she and the little Sisters made their Communions. It was *lovely* and they sang sweet little Italian hymns. They put in "Our Father St. Francis" in the Confession, etc. and have special Franciscan collects, and the Mass was for the unity of the whole Church.

My husband fetched me at lunch time and we motored here: a wonderful old city built up the side of the mountain and full of old buildings and Roman remains, but quite without the atmosphere of Assisi, which it was very hard to leave!

[1] Baron von Hügel.

Your rosary has been to every possible place I think, and ended by being laid on the shrine of St. Clare, where she lies behind a glass, in her Abbess's dress, looking hardly changed from what she was in life.

To-morrow we shall be in Rome, and in less than a fortnight home again.

. . . Maria loves Ruysbroeck too and was so delighted to hear how much you cared for him, and for Dante—both of them her dearest friends.

Dec. 26, 1924.
To L.M.

The Baron has been awfully bad again and again rallied but not to the point where he was before and can do very little now. However I hear he is full of joy and peace—and that is what really matters one feels.

How would you like to receive "from the . . . University, U.S.A." a thickly typed *questionnaire* which you are requested to answer, on religious experience for the benefit of "one of our choice students who projects a work on mysticism?"

Some would make even a clergyman blush ("Do you feel God's presence in prayer? If so, please give description and instance") and others make a philosopher feel poorly ("Do you conceive the Cosmic Spirit as an individual? If so, how? Give detailed illustrations"). I'm keeping it for your entertainment when you come to London.

Holy Innocents' Day, 1924.
(From bed.)
To the Same.

Yesterday was much enlightened by a letter and Christmas parcel from my darling little Fra Raffaele at the Carceri. I'd sent him a tiny offering from notes left over from our Italian trip. . . . "Most illustrious and beloved benefactress" seems a bit strong for what works out at about 15/2 at the present exchange! I get also his prayer that I may receive "all the true riches of Paradise" and his "affectionate and paternal blessing" as a wind up! Accompanying this was a night-light box containing a very nice silver medallion in a case of the Crucifix and St. Francis embracing Our Lord; a silver Cross with the benediction of St. Francis which Julie (Rose) will wear at her 1st Communion; various other medals and crosses, a wee rosary, a rich collection of cards and the dear man's own photograph! You can imagine the excitement of unpacking them; they seemed to bring a breath of Umbria right into the room. . . .

Jan 29, 1925.

To the Same.

Just a hurried line to thank you for your note. Yes! we are so glad the Baron has gone to God as he craved to do. It was "very peaceful" and his last talk to G. at the end of the week, which she wrote down and sent me, was so lovely and utterly himself—how delighted he was to give himself to God and so grateful for being clear in mind and without pain. How God was so generous to us and we ought not to be niggardly in self-offering. . . .

The Requiem is to-morrow, Friday, 11 o'clock. I feel he is awfully strong and happy and very much with us.

Feb. 1, 1925.

To the Same.

I loved what you said about the Baron—it *has* been a bit hard now it has come, in spite of one's rejoicing for him. Lady Mary wrote me such a kind and beautiful letter and said "nothing could have been more tranquil and perfect than his death." There were lots at his Requiem . . . the singing of the *In Paradisum* when they carried him away, was almost too much. . . .

I'm trying, with my heart in my mouth, to write a bit about the side of him I knew for next week's *Guardian*, but quite anonymously: so please know nothing if you should happen to be asked about it.[1] I hear Professor Kemp Smith, his great

---

[1] This was reprinted in *Mixed Pastures*, p. 229.

friend, did the *Scotsman*. . . . I did see about Sir James Mackenzie and feared much it was your friend. I'm so sorry; it is hard when these supporting kind of people are withdrawn. But they are *there*—so safe—and their influence goes on radiating.

Feb. 15, 1925.

To THE SAME.

We went to Kew this morning and the Alpine house was a dream of loveliness; wee cyclamen, primulas, blue anemones. And a sort of American Mrs. . . . came to tea and examined me about Trance and the Laws of the Universe and what not: and I said I knew nothing about them: and *she* said, "But you have Concentrated along these Lines!" The first I've heard of it anyhow. . . .

May 13, 1925.

To THE SAME.

Pleshey was heavenly; though there was some rain, it was possible to be a lot in the garden, which was full all day of the song of birds: and at Compline a nightingale sang just outside the Chapel window. . . . I stayed an extra day—a great luxury—and came away feeling much better in body for it all. . . .

I'm glad you like Grou; the Baron thought great things of him, and belongs quite to his school. I *love* the ones on Spiritual Childhood, Abandonment, the Use of our Imperfections and Communion: but they are *all* the real stuff, aren't they? One can't go far wrong with him. The Baron's very first published writing (when he was 39) was an article on Grou's Spiritual Teaching. I was given a copy of it the other day. . . .

May 15, 1925.

To THE SAME.

I'm just off to address . . . the Central House of the Mothers' Union on the "value of Retreats"—*one* value being that once you are inside a Retreat no one can speak to you! (At Pleshey, the last morning some one said to me, "I've been so interested watching you"!)

I'm going to Appledore next week and I think to Devonshire for Whitsuntide, a restless but agreeable life. Good-bye. Keep very quiet and good. The only aspiration I can think of at the moment is one you probably already have,

"Thou art in me and I in Thee: and thus assembled make us ever to dwell together I pray Thee."

Yacht *Wulfruna*,
Salcombe, S. Devon.
Aug. 10, 1925.

To the Same.

We are ambling down the coast, delayed by head winds and fogs—are just returned from an adventurous effort to leave this place which is neatly entrenched behind a bar and two reefs. When we got out the fog descended on us like a blanket and as we felt our way back again, abruptly lifted to show us a ledge of particularly nasty rocks just in front of the bowsprit. The helm went hard down and we *just* paid off in time and cleared them. Otherwise it would have been the end of this poor old craft, as the tide was falling and there was a nasty roll coming in. Our ancient skipper, who was responsible for this error in pilotage, is now wearing what is called his "stuffed monkey" expression!...

Don't be in a hurry with your convert! it isn't everyone who is equal to "giving themselves freely" at the beginning. Let her go along gently, following her own *attrait*. She will probably do best on a sugar diet for a little while and in due course find out for herself that it isn't adequate.

... I've not put much in my Andrewes lately: but am thinking of the prayer on p. 187 of Grou's *Méditations sur l'Amour de Dieu*. Miss Small gave me the suppressed verse of Bishop Ken's Evening Hymn—rather sweet for ending night prayers—

The faster sleep the sense doth bind
The more unfettered is the mind;
O may my soul from matter free,
Thy Loveliness unclouded see!

50 Campden Hill Square, W.8.
Aug. 14, 1925.

To W.Y.

I was so very glad to hear from you and to know all that you tell me in your letter.

Of course no "apology" was needed: but, when I saw you in London I realized that there was, at the moment, nothing I could do for you further until you had quieted down. Yes!—I am quite satisfied that you *did* have a genuine experience of God and surrendered to Him and that whatever He may demand of you in the future, you must never go back on that.

I would like to advise you at the moment, not to dwell too much on theological difficulties, Christology, and so forth. Your intellectual side is already sufficiently alert and does not need stimulating! Feed your soul quietly on those things that are already clear to you, but don't make theories etc. excluding the doctrines which at present seem to you difficult or absurd. It is perfectly right that your conception of God should be wider than your conception of Christ. Surely He reveals to us not *only* God incarnate in the time series, but God Eternal and unincarnate too? And so long as you preserve your sense of the distinctness of God and don't wash it all down into mere pantheism, it is all to the good that you should be sensitive to His self-revelation in Nature. I think that what you need here to get hold of more firmly, is the idea that this revelation is not of the "all-or-none" sort, but graded; and that it is one and the same living *personal* and loving Spirit whom we feel dimly in nature, more vividly as the inspirer of human goodness and heroism of all sorts, and perfectly (so far as our little souls can bear it) in Christ.

All this will grow in you as you humanize and spiritualize your experience; practising together prayer and the service of others, especially children and the poor. I could wish your "institutional connections" were with a sacramental type of religion, as this would help you a great deal. Don't take it for granted that "lonely prayers under the sky" will always mean much more to you. They will doubtless always mean a great deal, but when corporate religion gives you what it has to give you and you badly need—and this must take time—you will find your private devotional life enriched and steadied in a way you don't dream of now! !

Grand Hotel Lido,
Lido, Venice.
14 September, 1925.

To CLARA SMITH.

. . . Cortina was exquisitely beautiful but terribly cold with a piercing wind off the snow, so I'm rather glad to get down to sea level again. There was a most horrible English church, so I had to go to it: all the rigours of Continental Anglicanism—the parson virile . . . with a bushy moustache—points which a rather nice R.C. woman who had made friends with me, took pleasure in emphasizing! *She* went to Mass at the parish church with lots of nice creatures in Tyrolese dress, with broad ribbon streamers to their hats and bright little fringed shawls.

The drive up from Bolzano was of course intensely exciting, nearly all in curves and whirls along the edge of precipices. First climbing up along narrow gorges lined with forest and then with great Dolomites all round one, and then more and more barren till at 9,000 ft. we came to the snow. So sweet to find nearly the whole distance marked with wayside shrines—mostly crucifixes with the little roofs on them, but sometimes the Madonna in a little house with a door. I saw one woman on a very lonely hill, with a big basket on her back, who had opened the door and was leaning inside, just talking, and quite absorbed. I suppose the rational description of this would be Gross Superstition of an Unenlightened Peasantry.

Venice.
Saturday [19 September, 1925].

To THE SAME.

. . . Our French pilgrimage has left, and a German one, 90 strong, arrived to-day. I've discovered that the modern pilgrimage combines the advantages of a Cook's Tour with those of an Ambulatory Retreat. The French ones were rather sweet— when I went into my little church on Thursday, it was full of them, priests saying Mass at all its five little altars at once. I got a corner at one and found with some pleasure that it was the same as that to which we gave our candles at Mawnan Smith. Afterwards they all sang *cantiques* unaccompanied and with much vigour, the favourite being a long affair with the refrain "Nous voulons Dieu, c'est notre Roi." This morning at 6 they all went away in 2 steamers side by side, singing.

There *is* an English church in Venice and by catching the 7.20 steamer to-morrow morning I can manage it, so must. Its Programme suggests that it is more of our way of thinking than the usual continental Chaplaincy effort: and anyhow there's High Mass at St. Marco at 11.30 to finish up. St. Marco is a real, live church, and a joy to be in—or would be if one could just stay put a bit and leave off examining the works of art. In fact *all* the churches are nice. We went to the Dominican one this afternoon and a dear little friar, who somehow seemed to detect a sympathetic heart, lamented to me about the decay of all taste for the mortified life—"Our old friars are dying, and young ones do not come—they seem to *prefer* the world. . . ."

Did you know St. Athanasius was buried here? I never did till now—no guide-book lets it out. And to celebrate the Nicene Creed Festival here, they took him out, and carried him with great ceremony to St. Marco, and showed him to St. Mark! And the Armenians, who are the most primitive type of Christians here and have a little island and monastery of their own, carried him, and said the Mass.

Sunday. I've just come back from Venice and had breakfast— rather a lovely expedition really—we started in thick mist— Venice very faintly looming up in rosy and golden haze as we crossed the lagoon. The Grand Canal was like a Turner painting exactly and the Chiesa Anglicana, hidden in a wee campo approached by a bridge over a tiny canal, took some finding. Coming back the sun was out and all the bells ringing and the great banners outside St. Marco had been hung out, and carpets over the balconies of the Palaces. Now I'm going back again to High Mass. It's very hot again to-day; I think we must spend the afternoon on the water.

50 Campden Hill Square, W.8.

Oct. 11, 1925.

To W.Y.

Well! I think that you are, so to speak, getting on all right: and the chief thing I desire for you is, that you should think about it as little as possible! Your tendency is to be self-occupied and self-analytical: but attending to God means above all self-oblivion, doesn't it? Lose yourself in work for and interest in other people and above all in thoughts of Him, of the humblest kind. I am so glad you have taken up some work among children and are living a family life—both excellent.

Yes—ambition and forecasting the future are certainly both bad for you: just try day by day to respond to God, pray quite simply and peacefully for light and support from Him, and *don't* be in a hurry.

Now as to institutionalism. When I said I desired for you a more sacramental type of religion, the *last* thing I meant was "music, beauty and liturgy." By all means have a taste of these from time to time if they appeal to you—but please recognize them clearly for what they are, the chocolate-creams of religion.

By sacramentalism I mean the humble acceptance of grace through the medium of *things*—God coming into our souls by means of humblest accidents—the intermingling of spirit and sense. This is the corrective—one of the correctives—needed by your tendency to "loftiness"!

I sympathize with your determination to remain in your own Church at present: but would you please make a rule, from now onwards, of going to Communion at frequent and regular intervals? . . . at least once a month, if once a fortnight, all the better. By this balanced régime of sacramental acts, mental prayer, and love and service of others, you will nourish and deepen your spiritual life better than in any other way. If you want a book to use in connection with your Communions I think there is nothing better than Book IV of the *Imitation of Christ*—especially lovely in the old English translation published in the *Everyman* series. Much of the *Cloud* is beyond most of us! it is one of the books that keep on and on revealing new depths.

Reading and meditating on the N.T. as you have been doing

is of course excellent—and it is well as far as possible to do this at the same time each day. For purely devotional reading you might like St. Teresa's *Way of Perfection*. The best edition of the *Purgatorio* for ordinary reading is, I think, the one in Dent's *Temple Classics*, with Italian and English texts: or Anderson's verse translation of the whole *Divine Comedy* is wonderfully good—I could lend you this if you like, or other books? . . .

50 Campden Hill Square, W.8.
All Souls' Day, 1925

To the Same.

I have liked your last two letters so much: the first I left unanswered according to your orders, but should like to say something about the one that came to-day.

(1) Please at once check the habit of getting the bulb out of the dark to see how it is getting on! It is impossible, and also undesirable for you to judge your own progress. Just go along simply, humbly, naturally, and when tempted to self-occupation of this or any other sort, make a quiet act of trust in God. So long as you care to go along under my advice, it is my job and not yours to watch your soul and you may be quite sure I shall speak promptly when I am dissatisfied! Your faults and old fixations are going to give you lots of trouble for quite a long time and it's part of your job *not* to get discouraged. You will be much stronger and more useful to God in the end, for having had something to contend with.

(2) But do please distinguish between faults and temperamental bias. There's nothing *wicked* in disliking current institutional religion (except Holy Communion). You aren't and never will be a real "institutional soul" and are not required by God to behave like one. Your religion must of course have *some* institutional element, but it is particularly important that this element should not be overdone; and it certainly is not to be used as a penance. Therefore dismiss all ideas of forcing yourself to go to the weekly prayer meeting—it's not your *attrait*. I think a sufficient institutional rule for *you*, is to go to Church always once on Sunday, and this should be to Holy Communion by preference

when obtainable. You have family worship at home; and let that, and perhaps some occasional service you may care to attend, suffice. I'd *rather* you gave, at present, the time to your work with children and not the prayer meeting. The (quite natural) horror of seeming pious will wear off gradually as you settle down into the joy and peace of your new life.

I wonder whether you realize the extraordinary support and grace you have been given in your home atmosphere? The bulb has been put in the dark in a room with central heating so to speak, instead of the usual cold shed. I did so love all you said about your mother and wish I could know her. She must be the greatest of helps to you and of course can solve all your tangles if you talk to her freely—she no doubt knows all about them all the while. There's nothing more lovely is there than such a perfect Christian old age.

I'm glad you liked Baron von Hügel's *Essays. He* was the most wonderful example of wisdom, sanctity and depth of soul that I suppose our generation is likely to see and had faced all the difficulties of a highly trained and uncompromising intellect and vehement nature. You *can't* have better spiritual reading of the intellectual sort than his works: for the heart, though not on the surface, is there as well as the head—and no one I should think ever sought more persistently for the perfect humility you long for.

Dec. 22, 1925.

To V.W.

I do so hope that Christmas will bring peace and healing in its wings. . . . I know you are willing to accept everything, which takes away the worst of the sting—what the Baron used to call "being cross with our Crosses." He has one lovely bit about "Gentle attempts gently to will whatever suffering God may kindly send us: the grand practice of at once meeting suffering with joy. God alone can help us to succeed in this: but what is Christianity if it be not something like this?"

Folkestone.

Jan. 4 [1926].

To W.Y.

My own idea about Prayer is, that it is far more rich and complex and far more of a "force" than either Heiler or Cairns suggests. And because it *is* a spiritual force implanted by God, it is a duty to use it in prayer for others, as well as in direct Communion with Him.

Whether in so doing we pray for material benefits for others depends really on the importance we attach to material things. So too with illness (Prayer for the King, etc.): where sincere and generous and not just a formula, such prayer will be an agent of God, a co-operation with Him for the King's good whatever that good may be; and will be a support to His merely human forces in their fight with disease.

I think that we are partially free and that our freedom includes a spiritual freedom and power over circumstance, though always of course penetrated and overruled by God. Therefore prayer asking God to intervene, is a real and free act; extending the area within which His intervention can take place. I more or less agree with Cairns in this; though personally I shouldn't use this power much in respect of material goods and events. But then different people are called to quite different sorts of prayer. It's one more case of the fact that in religion our exclusions are nearly always wrong, and our inclusions, however inconsistent, nearly always right.

50 Campden Hill Square, W.8.

Sep. 17 [1926].

To the Same.

I'm so sorry for you. Yes—of course it is a Cross, but calling things by a special name does not make them any less hard at the moment, does it? The thing is, that blows of this sort—or indeed any sort—that are partly directed at our self-esteem, can be taken either in a way that embitters us or a way that purifies us. It is up to us to decide which! And the way to make them purifying so that they help our ultimate growth as few other things can, is so far as we *can*, willingly to accept them as sent to us and then *not* to let ourselves brood on them or suck the last drop of disappointment, etc., out of them, but to turn right away from the subject towards God. This is a really difficult prescription I know—but do try to do it—then you will preserve your sense of proportion and get tranquillity and strength in the only way we really can get them—and there will be no fear of this temporary set-back making you ill.

> 50 Campden Hill Square, W.8.
> 25 Oct., 1926.

To A.B.

I have read your letter and considered it carefully. It is of course always very difficult to advise anyone whom one has not seen. But it certainly does seem to me that the reason why you remain as you say frustrated and without peace, is exactly because of that doubleness in yourself which you describe. You alternate between your "dream" and the "muddy stream of doubt and fear." And when the "dream" isn't actually present to consciousness, as it never is continuously even to the most advanced, you lose hold of it, and let yourself be swamped in the current of lower life. To be able to pray "in spirit" in the way you wish is, after all, a great grace from God and is the continuous lot of very few. We all have to go through plenty of blank and dreary times —it is part of the discipline of the spiritual life, isn't it? I think what is asked of you is (1) a definite act of faith, a refusal of the temptations to doubt, etc.—a willed confidence in God, and (2) a gentle acquiescence in the way that He leads you, altogether apart from what *you* want.

You speak in your last letter of "church," and I am wondering what your ecclesiastical position is, and, e.g., whether you are a Communicant and the sacraments mean much to you. Because this, in which we can do little or nothing and much is done to us, is exactly the sort of spiritual practice which should feed and help you. It puts the emphasis on God, not on our awareness; and reminds us that the "lover and keeper of the soul" has us quite safely whether we realize Him or not, and *in sua voluntate e nostra pace.* Do try to drop, or turn away from thoughts of your blindness and dumbness, and all agitated striving; be content, till God gives you another kind of prayer, to practise the sort you *can* do, and do it quietly and steadily, by rule, at the same time each day. If you act thus, I think you will gradually find the dream will grow steadier, the fear and the doubt will fade. Do not expect quick results. It is a wholly new attitude which you have to form. And remember always, the initiative is not with you, but with God. It is for you to follow bit by bit where He guides.

50 Campden Hill Square, W.8.
21 November, 1926.

To THE SAME.

I am very sorry you find the idea of humility depressing! because really you know it is perfect freedom, and no more depressing than playing on the nursery floor. What is really depressing you, I think, is that you are straining, perhaps unconsciously, after something which is not in God's purpose for you yet. After all there are many stages in the spiritual life, aren't there? And it is for Him not you to decide on the time you remain in each. I am sure God has something to teach us in every situation in which we are put, and through every person we meet: and once we grasp that, we cease to be restless, and settle down to learn where we are.

50 Campden Hill Square, W.8.
March 8 [1927].

To W.Y.

Thank you so much for the beautiful tulips . . . that lovely mauve shade with very pale green leaves and looking their best in a dark blue jar. They were particularly comforting as I am imprisoned with "flu" not bad luckily as I have to go to Pleshey on Friday to conduct a Retreat. I will be very grateful if you and your mother and sister will pray for it.

As to what you say about the difficulties the Cross presents to you—the simple explanation is, that you are not yet grown up enough spiritually to understand it. Leave it alone and be content with the truths God *has* shown you—there is plenty of food there for your soul, without risking ghostly indigestion by trying mysteries which are at present too big for you. It is only disguised pride which makes us fret over what we can't understand! You see it is true; and that is already a grace: so be content, and go on quietly! cf. the meditation in Père Charles about the soul that will keep starting up and bounding into the air and never keeps quiet enough to make a resting-place for God. . . .

Yacht *Wulfruna.*
1 August, 1927.

To A.B.

. . . You have made me understand your whole position ever so much more clearly by what you have told me; and I do thank you for your frankness and confidence. Very often one feels one is floundering in the dark when trying to help people, because there is some vital situation in the background which has not been disclosed. Now I know just where you are and also that you have (or have been *given* rather) the courage to do the right thing, in cutting this friendship out of your life. I know in such cases it seems a hard and even cruel thing to do or advise. But the fact remains that a competing emotional interest though technically "innocent" can't be kept in one's life once one has given oneself to God. This very friendship may, later, return to you in the tranquil and purified form in which all one's human loves can be woven into the substance of the spiritual life. But as things are now, I am sure you are right in feeling that a clean cut is the only way. The fruit of all you experienced at Pleshey really hangs on your willingness to make the first definite sacrifice asked: and that you *have* made it, is the best of guarantees for your future steadiness. Moreover the pain you quite naturally dread won't be, in the event, so hard as it looks now. It is the *willingness* to suffer God asks. When we accept that, His grace comes with the pain and mysteriously takes away the real bitterness. Once the thing is done, you will know a new serenity, far better worth having than what you have given up:

and all that is true and pure in this friendship will live on as a spiritual and unbreakable link and influence even through many years of silence and separation.

Now as to your future course:

(1) I don't think you should, at present anyhow, try to "go on alone." You must expect ups and downs, difficulties, etc.—and it is much better you should have someone to whom you can tell them and who can look at your situation in a detached way. So I hope you will continue to write when you feel it is necessary.

(2) Yes, I am sure your feeling that you should do some kind of spiritual work is sound and there is no reason to think that what you are most drawn to (Intercession and Healing) is unsuitable. On the contrary, other things being equal, one should always first try to follow one's spiritual *attrait*; though moderately and gradually, *not* exclusively and vehemently! So go gently in this direction, in the way and degree in which God suggests and opens ways for you, but balance it by your personal communion with Our Lord, in prayer, sacraments and reasonable voluntary renunciations.

(3) (Of great importance.) Develop and expand the whole-some, natural and intellectual interests of your life—don't allow yourself to concentrate on the religious side only. Remember *all* life comes to you from God, and is to be used for Him—so live in it all, and so get the necessary variety and refreshment without which religious intensity soon becomes stale and hard. . . . You will in this way retain, in the long run, far more of the sense of God's Presence than you would get from feverish concentration on it. Religious fervour eludes us when we chase it; but creeps back unawares. It is crucial that you should get these truths firmly fixed in your mind *now*, as they will have to govern your conduct (and so your growth) for years to come.

God bless you.

50 Campden Hill Square, W.8.
Tuesday [? 1927].

To LAURA ROSE.

. . . As to what you say about prayer—the Baron always taught that "very delightful prayer" was far more exhausting than one realized and must be dealt with carefully; and it was usually wise to do rather less of it than one felt drawn to. With your health I am almost certain he would say, obey the instinct which warns you not to let yourself go—and this discipline will really be better for your soul than any experience you may miss through self-restraint. I do not think this is at all want of trust in God. He expects us to behave with common-sense even in regard to His graces doesn't He? On the other hand my Bishop [Dr. Frere] says, "if our Lord calls you to Bethany, go to Bethany and never be afraid of His closer visiting." But that I think is rather different from what you mean.

Plymouth.

Thursday, August 13th [? 1927].

To the Same.

I loved your letter, and always love it when you talk about the real things—there are so very few to whom one can speak of them, and I feel that is one of the most precious parts of our friendship when you do say those things, though I should never press you, or anyone else, to do so. Your Sister Helen must be a most beautiful soul; I should love to know her—it is nice, isn't it? that you and she have found each other. And although she has the sorrow of not being accepted as a Sister, in such a case as hers it can't make very much difference, for she will always lead a consecrated life.

Did I ever tell you about a Brother, who, although a most wonderful scholar, was refused as a priest and choir-monk because he is too small to celebrate at the altar—almost a dwarf. It nearly broke his heart. But he became a lay brother instead and does all the hardest and most menial work he can find, and is "the servant of all."

Z. . . . has quieted down, and got far far more gentle and humble-minded and as a consequence is beginning to find things out. She says now she has been desperately unhappy for over two years because she wanted God so much and couldn't find Him; and realizes it was her own pride that shut her off. That she used to *hate* the text "Blessed are the meek"! and now the one she loves best of all is "Learn of me; for I am meek and lowly of heart." Isn't that lovely? I feel so happy about it, for she is difficult and I had been wondering very much what was happening in her soul. She has been re-reading St. John's Gospel and that has cleared up her difficulties about Our Lord, she says. Isn't it wonderful the quick progress souls make when once God lays His hand on them?

50 Campden Hill Square, W.8.
22 October, 1927.

To A.B.

You have made your choice and a brave sacrifice, which I do not under-estimate: and now, when the natural pain of the wound subsides a little, God will gently and firmly build you up in your new life. As Huvelin said: "We are detached in order to be attached to something better, not to fall into a hole!" And the suffering you have faced can all be offered to God, can't it? It is of the very stuff of prayer—there is no such thing for a Christian as a vain sacrifice. I think you are at present too disturbed to see your "light"—but hold on—and peace will return and will find you stronger than before.

Dec. 6, 1927.

To L.M.

Your wonderful box came this afternoon and was unpacked with great excitement! How can I school the Rebellious Flesh to Sackcloth and Ash ideals when I'm given things like this?

Very glad there's happier news of you and that you are resigned to lying quite still and practising patience in the 3rd degree. When I have had to do it, among other dodges to pass time, I've made Alphabets of Saints and had a look at each one in turn and asked each for a "grace." It makes a picturesque sort of litany to live with.

I go for my whole day at Lloyd Square convent on Friday. . . . My last reviewer (Quaker) says I "share the biased views of my friend von Hügel"!—an accusation I feel I can bear!

Tony sends his love to G. He is getting quite a Cat and is very sinful but no one seems to mind. Next Thursday afternoon I have to be formally received as a Fellow of King's College, it being Commemoration Day—awful occasion! and a Dinner afterwards!

Friday night.

To THE SAME.

The show at King's College came off yesterday and was even more alarming than I had thought, as I was the first Fellow to be admitted and after running the gauntlet of the great Hall and intense curiosity of the undergraduates, had to walk up alone to the platform and stand in the open while the Dean who presented me expatiated on my career and qualifications—ending, to the joy of all present, by saying that I enlivened my leisure by talking to cats!

The Principal received me as "exponent of mysticism and poet" which surprised me a good deal. The college dinner that evening was however great fun, nearly 200 there. I sat at the theology table, between X. and Y. and managed to be quite polite when they talked of "superstition." But oh! how completely these intellectualists miss the bus!

50 Campden Hill Square, W.8.
January, 1928.

To A.B.

Be careful and don't attempt early Celebrations when it means risk and over-fatigue. I am sure it is more pleasing to God that we should be reasonably prudent in such things and treat the bodies He has given us with respect, than follow at the risk of illness our own devotional inclinations. So there! ! I would like you to get to look at the Sacraments in as objective a way as you can; and realize that the gift is always made to you, whether you feel it or not. I allow the early morning is far best from our point of view, but after all God is outside time, isn't He, and never refuses His grace if we are faithful? And in the same way about prayer—I would not feel troubled, or strain

178

after more comprehension because it seems to you that you know very little yet. We all know very little, but the way to know more is to practise very gently what we have. So I'm not going to tell you anything special to *do* during the next seven weeks: only to exercise quite a simple, loving trust as towards God, and realize He is moulding and leading you and it is His job far more than yours! Try and see your ordinary daily life as the medium through which He is teaching your soul, and respond as well as you can. Then you won't need, in order to receive His lessons, to go outside your normal experience. So too the type of prayer best for you is that to which you feel drawn in your best and quietest times and in which it is easiest to you to remain with God. Whether you do or don't use words or books is not very important. But there should be confidence and self-surrender in it, and of course prayer and self-offering for those you love and who need you.

Avila.
Sep. 11, 1928.

To L.M.

I must write you a line from here in the interval between our very late dinner and crawling to bed!

We have had such a wonderful day and not yet seen St. Joseph's which we shall to-morrow morning. Got here late last night and owing to the unspeakable noisiness of Spanish nights I overslept myself and did not get to Mass which was very sad.

But we went down to the Encarnacion directly after breakfast and luckily fell in with a young American Jesuit, speaking perfect Spanish, who helped us a lot. It is a pale, rosy-brown place, very Italian externally with flat tiled roofs and a big walled garden with trees. You go into a little court with a splendid old vine which must have been there in Teresa's day and then into the actual parlours she used, with the original grilles from behind which she talked to St. Peter of Alcantara and St. John of the Cross. The Church has been much enlarged, the site of the old Dormitory, including her cell, having been thrown into it and of course horribly decorated—but the west end is still as in her day. I think perhaps the most affecting thing is the little grille at which

St. John of the Cross sat to hear her confessions, she being of course within enclosure.

The door into the choir through which the nuns receive communion is the one she used and where she had the vision of the Spiritual Betrothal. A very bad picture commemorates this—in fact, a good deal has to be passed over lightly!

Then we went up into another series of parlours and saw a selection of relics; and two Carmelites came to the grille and talked to our Jesuit and asked if C. and I would not like to become nuns as they had "plenty of room." They were by no means closely veiled! and seemed very pleased to have some conversation and drew a curtain which allowed us to see into the cloister where large stuffed figures of the Saint and the Holy Child marks the scene of the episode "I am Jesus of Teresa."

13th. I went to Mass at the Encarnacion this morning; such a divine walk down from the walls, with early morning light on the mountains. There were two other women in the big, bare church and of course the nuns behind the grille. They sang the *O Salutaris* and then the priest walked down to the west end and gave each Communion through the little gold door Teresa used. Then they sang the *Tantum ergo* and we had Mass. It was really lovely.

After breakfast we went to St. Joseph and spoke to a very gay Carmelite through the turn-table, who again suggested we had better become nuns, and then asked if we were Catholic or Protestant. On C.'s struggling to describe herself as Anglo-Catholic the nun said she only understood Catolica! Catolica!

We were then shown the original Chapel of St. Joseph where the first Mass was said and the first nuns took their vows and then the relics, including Teresa's little drums and pipes in perfect preservation, her leather belt, one of her letters *and* one of her bones! At the *Casa Santa* where the room she was born in is turned into a Chapel, the friar who showed us round let me hold her rosary in my hand.

The whole town seems almost what it must have been in her time. You see the covered mule carts in which she travelled at every turn; the peasants are still mostly in old costume, the mules in paniers and the ox waggons quite unchanged.

All water is still carried from the public fountains in great Roman jars balanced on the women's hips. Altogether it is a dream of a place and ranks next after Assisi. You *must* come here. The accommodation is quite decent and we like the Spanish food. The weather keeps splendid; a real southern sun but a bright air. We have put in an extra day so will not get to Toledo till Saturday I think.

St. Jean de Luz.
Sept. 24, 1928.

TO THE SAME.

We are having a few days' complete sloth before returning home, sea and sun and nothing to do . . . very reviving after Spain which was rather too much for H. and me. . . .

Toledo is *marvellous*. Nothing Teresian there but her convent (Church rebuilt) and one tooth which I refused to see! also the great fortress-like house of Carmelite Friars, grim enough to make prisons for a dozen inconvenient saints. But the Moorish things—the two mosques they turned into churches but now are kept empty and mosquey again, and the exquisite synagogue built by Moorish workmen for a Jewish merchant whom the Inquisition polished off later on—are simply lovely and so are the Mozarabic towers and the mediæval walls and gates. The streets, with very few exceptions are Oriental alleys between high walls and have donkey traffic only—the paniers touching the houses and sweeping all before them.

Everywhere one finds lovely little courts with *azulejo* and old pillars and galleries quite unchanged.

We went to the Mozarabic Mass. I had not been able to get a description of it so could not follow all the eleven points of difference though some were obvious, e.g. the Epiklesis, loudly and distinctly repeated *after* the words of Consecration, the offering up of the elements at the very beginning of the service, the Pax given all round, a quite different arrangement of the Canon in short bits, a highly ceremonial washing of hands with a big jug and basin and above all, a startling savage *howl* uttered by the choir at the end! they did it again at Vespers! most peculiar!

50 Campden Hill Square, W.8.
Nov. 6 [1928].

To W.Y.

Yes, I agree with you, that Christ gives Himself eternally—that is, through His self-giving God comes into the soul whether we know it or not. Holy Communion is one of the great ways we actualize this and also give *ourselves* in our turn, to be used in the Divine work of redeeming the world.

These modernists are very useful in translating religious truth into current language, broadening the basis of faith, etc., but they are curiously deficient it seems to me in simplicity.

I think the old woman who could in the Sacrament realize "my Jesus" was spiritually far in advance of the theologians who argue about it.

I do hope you are better again and back with your children. I had to address a big meeting of S.S. teachers the other day! such nice young things. I talked mostly about sheep-dogs!

50 Campden Hill Square, W.8.
Aug. 4, 1929.

To Z.A.

... I am very glad indeed that the Psalms and St. Augustine suited you so well and I hope you will go on using those for "daily food" while extending your reading in other directions. One never, I find, exhausts them, in fact the more familiar one gets with them, the more spiritual treasures they reveal. I was interested in what you said about St. Augustine's "cosmic experience" because it shows so well just where you are and the direction in which you want to expand.

Of course it was the *insufficiency* of this experience—true enough as far as it goes—which compelled him to become Christian. It lacked the personal love and obligation to a personal God, the real, heart-breaking penitence and longing for a costly perfection that comes with the recognition that Christ is not just "perfect man," but the very character of God self-revealed in human ways and appealing to the free love and will of man.

When Augustine said of Neo-platonism. "How could these books have taught me Charity?" he put it in a nutshell. At his conversion, he didn't just sanctify, but went clean beyond the "higher pantheism" to a personal relationship that taught him humility and love.

I think without at present struggling with dogmas of atonement, meditation, etc., which won't mean anything to you yet, you *should* face the fact that "Christ as the ideal which in the course of evolution man may become"—is not Christianity. Christianity says that in Christ God *comes to man*—enters the time process. As von Hügel says somewhere "the essence of religion is *not* development from below, but a golden shower from above."

I can't remember now whether you told me you'd read von Hügel or not. If not, do try his little *Life of Prayer* and his volume of *Letters* and see how you feel about them. There's a new book just out, *Dogma in History and Thought*, edited by W. R. Matthews, which I think will clear your mind about actual doctrines, especially Professor Relton's article at the end. And I think, if you don't know them, Bishop Gore's *Belief in God* and *Belief in Christ*. All these are by first-rate scholars but of course definitely Christian. My own idea is that it is really better to face up at once to what a genuinely Catholic religious philosophy teaches, than to temporize with half-Christian pantheistic-immanentist books. . . .

By all means report on what you think of any of the above you do read. In fact I think that is essential at present if I am to be of any use to you. You are perfectly right in thinking that you have got to make the transition from "God in everything" to "Everything in God"—If "Christ gave Himself for *me*" is difficult—perhaps Christ as a Bridge between the Divine and the Natural (and this is St. Catherine of Siena's image) isn't so difficult? Don't be troubled because you do not feel these things emotionally—the focus of religion is will, not feeling, isn't it? Try, gently without strain, to turn your Psalms and your own thoughts and desires into prayers. Simple acts of communion with God—and if and when that experience of silent peace you describe returns, accept and remain in it gratefully, but *don't* deliberately force it. Remember God is acting on your soul all the time, whether you have spiritual sensations or not. I hope you will write again as soon as you feel inclined and have the opportunity.

Yacht *Wulfruna*.
Aug. 26, 1929.

To the Same.

I am so sorry to be late in answering your last letter. . . . There are just one or two points I would like to say something about now.

(1) It isn't a bit surprising that you find the Psalms and even your own attempts to develop personal prayer, an "exercise" rather than an "experience." One has to make up one's mind to submit to training, including the drudgery of training; nor is one's spiritual state ever to be measured in terms of feeling and conscious experience. This is where the corporate religious life comes in as such a support. You *will* find concentration difficult, and prayer and the things of the spirit will often seem unreal. Nevertheless, if persevered in, all those things will gradually train and expand your soul, as certainly as gymnastics train the body.

(2) *Books*. By von Hügel's *Letters* I did mean the big volume if you can get hold of it. I think some of the more philosophical ones will interest you and help you and make a preparation for his *Eternal Life*. Other useful books I think I didn't mention are Temple's *Mens Creatrix* and *Christus Veritas* and Otto's *Idea of the Holy*. If you like my *Life of the Spirit* perhaps you would find its successor *Man and the Supernatural* a help. Anyhow I have said what I could there about the relation of Christ to God and the soul's life to both. Christianity would surely not be "nullified" but victorious by the coming of the Kingdom?—the mystical body of the Incarnation "would then be conterminous with humanity"—redemption would then be an achieved fact? . . . The time is hardly come for giving up your work in order to think things out. It seems to me God is arousing and working on your soul—and it is better to go quietly on, working, thinking and praying as much as you can manage

without strain and remaining very docile in His hands. But if you *could* somewhat reduce your work so as to have more leisure of mind and heart that would be a very great help.

Langeais.
Sunday, 15 September, 1929.

To CLARA SMITH.

We had a wonderful day at Chinon yesterday—started with a white autumn fog over the river, and ghosts of poplars standing up in it—and through a hazy forest, till just as we reached Chinon it cleared, and we had a lovely afternoon: walked up St. Joan's old paved track to the Castle, saw the tower she stayed in and the ruins of the chapel she used, and—in the church where she received the sacraments before seeing the King—lighted two candles at her altar. It's quite a nice district for saints. We went to St. Martin's tomb at Tours (more candles) and at a tiny old dead place called Candes, at the confluence of the Vienne and Loire, found a *miraculously* beautiful Angevin church, built over the cell in which he died. To-day we went to Fontevrault over a villainous road which nearly made us seasick! Recovered we had a wonderfully good lunch at the village drinkshop, which looked impossible but where the gendarme insisted, rightly, that we should "eat very well"; and then saw the abbey and cloisters and the tombs of the Plantagenets, all mixed up now with a large prison and entered via the police station: but a glorious piece of architecture. The abbey did have three floors of cells in it but everything has been cleared out. It has one of the most lovely Romanesque apses I ever saw but it looks unhappy without an altar in it. Very few people seem to go and see it compared with the other places, though it is *really* far more lovely and interesting than these Renaissance châteaux created by kings for the use of bad lots. I could not get any photographs or postcards of it, or of the "lanterne des morts" near the parish church—the only one we have seen. The whole district is stuffed with wonderful old things, ignored by the guidebooks, so that one never knows what one is going to find: most exciting.

Rather a nice little hotel here, with a half yard, half garden (described as *Jardin énorme avec boscage*) in which we have all our meals. Last night a French couple arrived in a motor, travelling with two charming *cats*, one aged 15 and one 9, whom they had trained to motoring and always took everywhere with them! Of course we made great friends and I had all the cats' domestic arrangements explained to me in fullest detail!

Nice inscription found in the church at Chinon: "Que les chrétiennes aient le bon goût de s'approcher à l'autel avec les lèvres *au naturel* s.v.p."!

Étampes.
Sunday night [23 Sept., 1929].

To the Same.

We came here to-day from Beaugency; having lunch at Orleans which is a dull hole, except for the Cathedral and its associations with St. Joan. A great statue of her stands behind the High Altar now, and at her feet is buried the Cardinal Archbishop who got her canonized—and quite a nice figure of him kneeling at her feet. The whole place is full of memories of her and makes up for a surfeit of altars trimmed with paper roses for the Little Flower, who meets one in every church.

Nice little hotel here with 5 cats and a lovely fluffy white rabbit, who has a day hutch in the *cour* and a night hutch in the kitchen, which glows with burnished copper and provides very good food, of the normal French kind. Some of our food has been *far* from normal. I think our most startling meal was at the Hotel of the Fairy Melusine at Lusignan: Radishes—large dish of mussels (refused and exchanged for 2 fresh sardines!)—fried pigs' trotters (one each)—pork chops and saucissons—cheese—grapes. The Fairy Melusine's view of knives and forks was of course very economical—and as to her ideas of sanitation! ! ! She was run hard by St. Savin, where déjeuner began with two little baked potatoes each, and went on to ham and gherkins.

But St. Savin had the most miraculous Romanesque Abbey Church, still full of its original 11th and 12th century frescoes. I don't suppose anything so exciting as that will happen now, as we are on beaten tracks. We think of going to Les Andelys to-morrow and thence to Beauvais.

Feb. 21, 1930.

To Z.A.

Thank you very much for your letter. I gather from it that you are still much too concerned with the question of your own "progress" (I wish you could forget for quite a year that this word exists!) too anxious, too impatient. It is quite impossible for any of us to measure ourselves and estimate our progress. Our job, having found the path we honestly believe God wishes us to follow, is to go quietly on with it and leave the results to Him! This may seem a hard saying but it's the only way to keep self-occupation out.

I don't think during this period of transition you can reasonably expect to be creative or constructive in your work. You will have to wait for that till things settle themselves a bit. Of course it is to the good that you have ceased, as you say, protesting against life—so long as one does that, there can be no question of spiritual growth. Don't *strain* yourself in the effort to formulate and understand things, as a result of your reading. Very likely X. . . . is too advanced for you at present—if so, quietly leave on one side the things in which you can't follow without floundering. The same applies to formal meditation, though the gentle effort to apply your mind to some New Testament scene or saying of Our Lord, etc., is probably a good discipline. In all you do, think, or pray about, throw the whole emphasis on God—*His* work in your soul, *His* call to you—the fact that you only exist, from moment to moment, by His Act and your whole *raison d'être* is to praise, reverence and serve Him.

5 May, 1930.

To A.B.

. . . I am so glad your retreat this time brought you sunshine and peace. Those "times of consolation" are lovely, and refreshing—but in the nature of things they cannot be continuous. That you should have a reaction is not a proof that you "go wrong"—but if you "go to bits" as it were when the light is withdrawn, then that shows you relied on it too much, and that your spiritual life is still based too much on feeling and not enough on *will*. It is your natural temperament, I think, to fly backwards and forwards between depths and heights! Try gently and gradually to get into the centre of your picture not your experiences, needs, aspirations—but just God's Will for you, whatever it is; and make your chief practice a quiet self-offering to Him, to be used His way, and if He pleases without any "experience" at all. To be a tool, a channel for His work on ... all you touch. And just leave yourself out. You can perfectly well trust Him to attend to your interests if you are faithful in attending to His. So your chief prayer must not be to "*see* Him first and always" but to be *useful* to Him first and always! I think you will find this practice tends to steadiness and peace—and it is only in steadiness and peace we really draw nearer God. The emotional cravings for Him you describe in your letter are perfectly natural—but not necessarily spiritual! And they actually operate like the "law of reversed effort" against the realization of the Presence of God.

at The Quillet,
Appledore.
May 14, 1930.

To Z.A.

It has been in my mind for some little time to write to you and say how much I hope you are getting on all right and *not* concentrating too fiercely on religious problems! I feel with you, especially just at present, that it is most necessary to keep your human, non-theological contacts and interests supple and alive. Kindly acts of service, firm discipline of your tendency to judge other people, to look at them and their views critically, etc., and all kinds of humble work in which you can forget yourself, are all things which will do most to make your soul fit to realize Christ. So do keep up all your general interests, mix with people, love them, but don't try to "do them good" or discuss religion with them! All this will make a better preparation for your Retreat than reading religious books and thinking of your soul. If any of your work is uncongenial, seize on that and do it with special zest as something you can offer to God, and act on the same lines with people. The Retreat is only a fortnight off now, and then I shall look forward to seeing you.

50 Campden Hill Square, W.8.
May 20, 1930.

To THE SAME.

Thank you very much for your letter. . . . This is only to say that the last thing I wish for you is that you should be badgered or hustled into the Church. As to whether "I shall make you a thorough-going Catholic"—I hope I shall never try to make you any particular thing! My job is simply to try and help you to find out what *God* wants you to be, and what will help and support your particular type of soul in His service. I certainly hope you will be confirmed and become a regular communicant—as to Confession it may or may not be for you. Wait and see. And meanwhile be as humble, peaceful and interested in your daily jobs and surroundings as you can!

Presteign.
June 12, 1930.

To Y.L.

Last night we were out till nearly 10 (it was quite light with a glorious sky) driving slowly along the lanes looking for creatures. We found a charming adolescent plover, like a miniature ostrich, taking his first walk and very nervous and of course many kitten-rabbits bent on suicide. . . .

Now to business.

(1) *Anyone* can "lead a prayer-life," i.e. the sort of reasonable devotional life to which each is called by God. This only involves making a suitable rule and making up your mind to keep it however boring this may be.

(2) If dryness and distractions have you in their clutches just now, fall back on the Divine Office. Say Prime or Terce in the morning, Vespers or Compline at night, with the *intention* of joining the great corporate prayer of the Church. You will then

be making acts of Adoration, Penitence, etc., though probably not *feeling* them, which is another story and much less important. You can also offer your prayers, obedience and endurance of dryness to Our Lord, for the good of other souls—and then you have practised intercession. Never mind if it all seems for the time very second-hand. The less *you* get out of it, the nearer it approaches to being something worth offering—and the humiliation of not being able to feel as devout as we want to be, is excellent for most of us. Use vocal prayer and use it very slowly trying to realize the meaning with which it is charged and remember that anyhow you are only a unit in the Chorus of the Church and not responsible for a solo part so that the others will make good the shortcomings you cannot help.

> Helford Passage,
> Mawnan Smith,
> Cornwall.
> Aug. 21, 1930.

To Z.A.

. . . Thank you so much for your letter. . . . I send this book, which seems to me *very* good,[1] and I think may interest you, especially the parts towards the end, bearing on the Eucharist. It really is *religious*, which so few theological books are! . . .

I am so glad you feel you are now getting more hold of the power of prayer.—No! I don't mind your continued lack of emotional feeling. This is a pleasant stimulus but not the real foundation and there is always a risk at the beginning of mistaking fervour for faith. You are building more solidly without it and will be the better able to use it when it comes. God knows His job better than we do and will give you what you need at the right time. Your will and perseverance are already proofs of love—all the more worth offering because you are not getting any pleasure out of it! Keep calm and all will be well. Let me know where you are going to be for your confirmation, won't you? and when you intend to make your First Communion?

[1] Hicks, E. C., *The Fullness of Sacrifice.*

Hartland,
N. Devon.
Sep. 2, 1930.

To the Same.

Thank you so much for your letter. I *do* wish I could be with you on Sunday in the flesh as I shall be in the spirit: but Francis will take care of you [her confirmation]—and it will be I hope the beginning of much and ever-increasing strength, peace and happiness. I am glad you go straight to the Convent. You realize they are very advanced Anglo-Catholics and the whole routine is monastic. . . . They keep silence in the mornings and at meals; so you will have as much quiet as you like. But I do beg you not to attempt to spend all the time in prayer and devotional reading! Just be quiet and grateful—don't strain yourself or try to whip-up emotion. . . .

As to devotional preparation, Psalms viii and cxvi, St. John vi and xv, the Fourth Book of the *Imitation*, especially chaps. 7, 8, and 9 . . . will give you enough to choose from. Don't be disappointed if you don't feel anything—no one can tell you beforehand whether you will or not—but even though you *should* feel cold or dry or baffled, this does not affect the main point: which is that Our Lord comes to your soul to *feed* you, not to give you sensations and you come to offer Him your *whole self*, not just your emotional life.

I like to think of the Sacraments as points where the supernatural penetrates and transforms the natural world—and truly gives itself to us, under an apparently natural form, so that we can receive It as we could not do in Its spiritual essence alone. So that humble receptivity and faithfulness is the main thing asked of *us*—and however imperfect our dispositions, that does not diminish the fullness and beauty of the divine gift, or the reality of the Presence which is there just thé same, whether we feel it or not. . . .

I'm glad you like Dr. Hicks' book. It impressed me very much. I am sure you will find his teaching on the Eucharist a help: partly because he doesn't try to explain too much but leaves the fringe of mystery intact.

I do so hope those coming days will be full of great blessings and the deepest kind of joy.

This little Franciscan Cross was blessed at Assisi and had the benediction of St. Francis on it. I thought perhaps you would like it.

Sept. 10, 1930.

To THE SAME.

... The Sacrament of penance in its reality *is* an awful and sacred thing. I think myself, as von Hügel thought, that it should be kept as it was in the primitive Church for healing the results of grave sin, or seriously sinful states of mind, etc., and not be a routine discipline. ...

But anyhow, as long as it means nothing to you the only right and wholesome course is to let it alone I think. ... You *must* relax, and just be as quiet, child-like and confident as possible and take all the interest you can in the non-religious side of your life.

Indeed I *never* taught you that "the flesh doesn't matter"! ! —it is quite un-Christian to think that—and I hope you are eating your meals properly and sleeping well at night? Both can be done to the Glory of God, can't they?

The Christian life is something so rich, deep, supple and altogether lovely—so naturally supernatural as it were—and not anything which asks more than we can do, or in any way strings one up. So keep calm like a good child, won't you? You now have the support of the whole family you have joined, including the Saints: God *never* badgers souls who surrender to Him—but lets them grow gently, feeding on what suits them and leaving the rest. And that is what you are to do.

50 Campden Hill Square, W.8.
All Saints, 1930.

To THE SAME.

I think these notes (from that wise old saint Augustine Baker and arranged for your use!) will answer your questions about mortification. The austerities of the saints must be left to the saints: we are not to presume to attempt them, unless distinctly called by God. The only result of sampling strong tea when our proper diet is milk and water is a severe spiritual tummy-ache. Go slow.

I'm actually up and dressed and am going to Canterbury to do the Wives' Fellowship Retreat on Monday. So please think of us and of your veil beginning its new life. . . . Then I'm going to Moreton for a short Retreat (for myself) . . . and then shall have another shot at my hermit-like London life, until the plan now on foot to export me to the South of France matures. . . .

NOTES ON MORTIFICATION FROM AUGUSTINE BAKER

(1) Quietly to suffer all crosses, difficulties and contradictions to self-will whether internal or external, including temptations and dryness. This is the very essence of a mortified life.

(2) Never to do or omit things on account of one's likes or dislikes, but refer all to God's will.

(3) Those mortifications are right for us which increase humility and power of prayer and are performed with cheerful resolution. They are wrong, if deliberately undertaken instead of the obvious difficulties of life and if they produce depression and strain.

(4) Habitual quietness of mind is essential to true mortification. All impetuosity and unquietness has in it some self-love but the Holy Spirit is stillness, serenity and peace.

(5) In general, the mortifications sent by God and the ordinary friction of existence are enough to discipline our souls. Voluntary mortifications are *never* to be assumed till the necessary difficulties and contradictions of life are cheerfully and fully accepted.

Rosemullion Hotel,
Budleigh Salterton.
Feb. 7, 1931.

To THE SAME.

Thank you so much for your letter. You were just in time to get a place in the March Retreat at Pleshey, so that's all right.

I am awfully pleased with this place—such beautiful air and

wonderful sun whenever it is fine, as at present! and even the two weeks here have done me far more good than the six at Sidmouth.

Now about your letter. You are not required to have a "prayer policy." Do you have a policy about intercourse with your friends or any other of the deepest relations of life? Your "policy" must simply be to respond to what God gives and do your best, as you can, in the circumstances. And don't be too proud to acknowledge that what He does is infinitely more important than what you can feel or do.

Resting quietly in the Divine Presence *is* a prayer and often a far better one than our deliberate efforts can manage: and more humbling, because we can't produce it at will. Our part, when it is like that, is very grateful acceptance. Please don't increase your Communions at present. I would rather you observed a very moderate rule and put obedience before spiritual experiences. When you feel your prayer is blank and poor and deficient in love, say how sorry you are. And when you are quite left dry, use formal prayers and try honestly to enter into them and mean them as your little contribution to the total prayer and praise of the Church!

The more you think of *that* and the less of your own condition the better!

Romsey.
Wednesday in Easter Week, 1931.

To X.Y.

This is by way of being an answer, probably most inadequate, to your last letter. I think the *general* answer to it is that you fuss *far* too much—and haven't nearly enough assimilated the priceless art of letting God make the first move. Thus, as to "mortifications"—having fully, generously, gratefully accepted *all* the conditions in which you are placed and dealt with them to the best of your ability, *ignoring* as much as you can your personal likes and dislikes (*not* deliberately acting contrary to the said likes and dislikes) you will surely have done a good bit to mortify self-love, comfiness, fastidiousness, slackness, inordinate affection, etc. If you haven't, anyhow you can! The string of imperfections you mention are nearly all things that are in your own hands. You just needn't do them!—that's the truth. And your right course surely (as regards the ones which really are faults and not fuss) is to give your whole will to ceasing to do them— just that, and not fossick round for "extraordinary mortifications." Quietly dealing with one's own uncontrolled thoughts and desires is infinitely more humbling than any sort of deliberate austerity; which only makes one feel one has done something! But don't have hand-to-hand tussles with distractions and wanderings of mind—that intensifies the disease. Try and drop all that and hold some thought or word that does mean something to you, before your soul. Remember that in the Sacraments you get actual energy, enough to do and be what God requires of you at your present stage. If vocal prayer helps you most at the moment, use it by all means and be quiet and humble about that too, and don't expect to "realize" all the time.

But don't load the dice against yourself by *assuming* that you are "sure to get slack again." That is unfair to God, isn't it? and merely asking for failure. Assume rather that if you are quiet and faithful and correspond as well as you can to what He gives, He will produce in you what He wants.

9 June, 1931.

To Dom John Chapman.

This is really an answer to the last bit of your letter, because I feel I owe you an explanation of my "position" which must seem to you a very inconsistent one. I have been for years now a practising Anglo-Catholic . . . and solidly believe in the Catholic status of the Anglican Church, as to orders and sacraments, little as I appreciate many of the things done among us. It seems to me a respectable suburb of the city of God—but all the same, part of "greater London." I appreciate the superior food, etc., to be had nearer the centre of things. But the *whole* point to me is in the fact that our Lord has put me *here*, keeps on giving me more and more jobs to do for souls here, and has never given me orders to move. In fact, when I have been inclined to think of this, something has always stopped me: and if I did it, it

would be purely an act of spiritual self-interest and self-will.
I know what the push of God is like, and should obey it if it
came—at least I trust and believe so. When . . . I put myself
under Baron von Hügel's direction, five years before his death,
he went into all this, and said I must never think of moving on
account of my own religious preferences, comforts or advantages
—but only if so decisively called by God that I felt it wrong to
resist—and he was satisfied that up to date I had not received this
call. Nor have I done so since. I promised him that if ever I did
receive it I should obey. Under God, I owe him my whole
spiritual life, and there would be much more of it than there is,
if I had been more courageous and stern with myself and followed
his directions more thoroughly. And it seems to me a sort of
secondary evidence that God means me to be where I am, that
He gave me that immense and transforming help, and yet with
a quite clear light that I am to stay here and not "down tools."
Of course I know I might get other orders at any moment, but
so far that is not so. After all He has lots of terribly hungry sheep
in Wimbledon, and if it is my job to try and help with them a bit
it is no use saying I should rather fancy a flat in Mayfair, is it?

Please do not think this cheek. It is not meant so, but it is so
much easier to write quite straight and simply.

Aug. 5, 1931.

To X.Y.

On our way up, we went round by Kelham and saw their new
Chapel. Everyone was away of course but a charming novice,
who was acting Sacristan, showed us round. It's awfully impressive—intensely austere and all done by line and plain surfaces—
not a statue, not even of our Lady—no stations—the Blessed
Sacrament reserved in a tiny Oratory we were not allowed to see.

The whole Church is dominated by Jagger's wonderful Rood.
One gets no idea of this from the small photos. Our Lord
bound to the Cross with cords; a living figure, full of intense
power and looking straight into the eyes of whoever looks up at
Him—and Mary looking up in an ecstasy of worship; and John
crushed by penitence and grief. The effect, against the deep

purple apse-wall, is simply marvellous. The few things they have are all perfect works of art. . . . There was perhaps a certain lack of homeliness—but a very great sense of the numinous.

We drove through Sherwood Forest, where I once saw a fox having a quiet evening stroll and rabbits watching him. But saw nothing better this time than a young wagtail that had not got a tail to wag.

S.S. *Venus*,
North Sea.
September, 1931.

To L.M.

This will be posted in England, to which we are gently rolling our way—not such a smooth passage as when we came but so far quite comfy. . . .

Stalheim was a marvellous place—the hotel perched at the top of a 1,000-foot cliff and looking right down the Naerodal— one of those solemn rock valleys which seem like an approach to the Inferno. Our arrival was adventurous: as when we reached the foot of the cliff the car stopped and the driver said calmly: "I go no further. From here you walk." He then pointed to Heaven and said, "There is the Hotel!" It was 9 p.m. and pretty dark but light enough to make it obvious that the climb was far beyond me! and not alluring to any but the young and strong.

In the end we got a horse from a farm which scrambled slowly up the 13 steep zig-zags. The high valleys and hills at the top were splendid and I would like to stay there for days. We got one very good walk among the summer pastures and saw the cows and goats being called down from the tops for milking.

as from
50 Campden Hill Square, W.8.
17 September, 1931.

To Dr. Margaret Smith.

C. tells me that you have very kindly sent me a copy of your new book,[1] now waiting for me at home. Thank you so *very*

[1] *Studies in Early Mysticism in the Near and Middle East.*

much for it—I shall most specially value possessing it from you, as well as for its own sake. Meanwhile the *Spectator* sent me a copy here to review, so I have had an opportunity of reading it. I have been more than interested—really excited. You seem to me to have made a contribution of first-class importance to the history of mysticism and to have completely proved your point about the doctrinal origins of Sufi-ism. Of course, as always, when a historical problem is cleared up, one promptly thinks, "Why on earth did no one think of this before!"—the answer being of course that they didn't have the requisite combination of knowledge, sympathy and common sense.

I was also rather struck (perhaps more than you intended!) by the very slightly Christian character of much of the Eastern mystical writings—they were really ready to the hand of the Sufis, weren't they? and had hardly anything in them to vex the most sensitive monotheist. Your quotations are lovely both of the Christians and Muslims.

24 Sept., 1931.

TO DOM JOHN CHAPMAN.

I sometimes wonder whether (*a*) at certain points or stages the soul must suffer; and then an apparently inadequate cause may be the occasion of the maximum pain it can endure . . . or (*b*) it may be allowed to pay some of the price of the happiness of another soul.

Nov. 27, 1931.

TO A YOUNG MOTHER.

Yes, I am sure you find the C.S.S. rule of Poverty very difficult to square with married life. When you told me what you intended, I could not imagine how you were going to manage it! How *can* a husband and wife adopt different scales of living without tension? it must become very acute in relation with the children and their clothes, education, amusements, etc. Married tertiaries in the past presumably both embraced poverty or else, like Jacopone's wife, wore the hair-shirt secretly under their nice clothes! I do hope you will find a solution that really simplifies life instead of just making it complex in a fresh way....

Dec. 2, 1931.

To Z.A.

Thank you very much for your letter. I think you deserve full marks for taking mine so well!! The unfortunate part of trying to communicate (our spiritual) experiences is that we never manage it and at best only interest and at worst amuse or repel. Hence the deep wisdom of St. Bernard's "My secret to myself." ... "Let us keep our heads," as the Baron was so fond of saying!

50 Campden Hill Square, W.8.
7 February, 1932.

To E. I. WATKIN.

... The last thing (years ago!) my friend told me of the Golden Fountain lady was that she said she had been "told inwardly" not to write and publish any more. I own I did not feel wholly satisfied that her experiences *were* supernatural. (*a*) The extreme emotionalism, (*b*) the lack of reticence, (*c*) the note of spiritual self-assurance, all seemed to contrast rather vividly with the undoubted mystics. I agree with you that ecstatic phenomena do seem to be related to the physiological rhythm (e.g. St. Teresa) and like conversion tend to appear about the end of adolescence and again at full maturity—30 or so—and at the close of middle age. This doesn't bother me because I think them a by-product and not the essence; and often better away! The development at its best seems to be towards depth and steadiness—the "theopathetic state"—rather than raptures. This, surely, would agree with St. John of the Cross, a safer guide than all the fervent females put together! The St. Teresa of the *Foundations* seems to me a nobler figure, more deeply and fundamentally united to God, than she is in the ecstatic period described in the *Life*. I suppose Charity, as an infused grace, is given in the "ground of the soul" and it is there that the abiding union with God takes place; and that the divine

199

love then spreads more and more throughout the whole psychic life—like Ruysbroeck's "fountain with three rivulets"; the contemplative life, therefore, which first appears to the soul as a contrast, and is realized by way of vision, audition, ecstasy, etc., becomes as it matures more deep, still and universal. But I don't feel sure you will agree with this!

50 Campden Hill Square, W.8.
12 February, 1932.

To THE SAME.

Thank you very much for your very interesting letter. I expect you are right, and that the Golden Fountain lady's trying way of expressing herself is partly due to the lack of a good tradition; but I still feel that, even if her experiences were all that they seem to her to be, the normal movement of the soul to a much quieter, deeper and less emotional type of realization *is* an advance and not a loss.

As to St. John of the Cross, I think that return to an almost physical description of ecstatic joy in the end of the *Living Flame* becomes explicable when we remember that he died before he was 50; therefore, presumably, it describes not the final but the intermediate stage of a mystic's development, and tallies with St. Teresa's ecstatic period, not with her last state. It comes, too, at a moment in the physiological life when ecstatic or emotional experience of an intense type often seems to occur, doesn't it? . . .

No! I can't feel the fact that ecstatic experience is so sporadic and has a close relation to "age and condition" is disturbing. It's real when it happens, and mediates the Absolute just as the passion of Romeo and Juliet mediates something of an absolute sort. And anyhow "nude faith" is surely the really solid, splendid and convincing thing? I have an idea heaven will be both absolutely happy and absolutely dark, to protect us from the blaze of God.

50 Campden Hill Square, W.8.
16 February, 1932.

To F.H.

. . . I think that restlessness and feeling of dissatisfaction with life is partly physical in origin, and should be met on the natural level of cultivating wholesome interests as much as one possibly can, facing (as you realize) the true facts and accepting them, trying to find happiness in interesting yourself in children and so forth. *All* lives can seem futile and unfulfilled without God but *no* life is futile with Him, is it? It is a question of centring yourself on Him more utterly, and abandoning your will to His. *That* is the string for your beads. If there are great sides of life withheld from you, it is your opportunity, isn't it? to dedicate to God all the love, energy and service which would have gone into them, and be ready and alert to see what He wants of you, perhaps something that seems on the surface quite inconspicuous and humble, but which can be irradiated by the intention which directs it to Him. The "drive," the "roots" are all *there* and not in the particulai thing you do, aren't they?

As to writing, I don't think anyone else can definitely advise you—but if it really is a strong impulse, then I should try—but with the full knowledge that you *may* fail and that you will vanquish the mere vanity which is afraid to fail. No creative urge which can't conquer that demon is going to be any good. You must be prepared to stand on your own feet, do the work as well as you know how, and leave the results.

19 February, 1932.

To M.C.

Did M. tell you of my darling Italian Saint (head of a tiny group of Italian Primitives) whom I asked to join the Disarmament Prayer Group and who replied she could not promise a fixed period because:

"Agli uccelli non si puo chiedere in dato canto in un dato tempo. E noi vogliamo essere nella nostra espressione di religiosita come gli uccelli—pregare, cantare, perche amiamo, in tutta liberta e semplicita. Senza nulla d'imposto e di stabilito."[1]

May 30, 1932.

TO THE SAME.

I'm so glad the Passion Play is done and long to see it. My thing is done too, except for the last read-through, and will, I think, go to Methuen's next week. I know I'm doing an awful thing but I'm sending in this a bit of MS. and asking, would you read just the piece from half down p. 3 to beginning of p. 5? It seemed to me to express a patent truth, which I am certain does happen . . . if you are busy, don't dream of bothering with it.

I was awfully interested in what you said about having an image-making mind. I think on the whole mine is the other kind and of course it would make a great deal of difference to one's devotional framework. I don't a bit want to break the 2nd Commandment! but I *wallow* in the Athanasian Creed! all the same I agree, one must watch and listen to our Lord all one can, and the more one does, the deeper the wonder grows.

We had an icy day (physically) for the W.F. Quiet Day, but M. arrived with some of her prayer group, like a troop of dynamos; and after that it gave me no trouble at all. It *is* amazing what a difference a few real praying people can make.

Good-bye. It's lovely to feel you will be with us at L.C. We shall end on the Feast of the Sacred Heart which, in spite of the terrible pictures, I do most dearly love. Do you know that bit of St. John Eudes?—"The Sacred Heart of Jesus is the Holy Spirit."

[1] Birds are not expected to sing a particular song at a particular time. And we wish our religion to express itself like the birds: to pray and sing in perfect liberty and simplicity because we love—without rules and regulations.

[1932.]

To J.K.[1]

Thank you so much for your letter and for giving me your confidence.

I can guess very well what the position is like and that there is much in it that you must find very hard, painful and disappointing.

It *is* heartbreaking to think that lives given to God should, by bad training, be prevented from developing their best. But still, the story is not finished yet, is it? God's training goes on to the very end; and in the present phase *you* are part of the material He can make use of in the deepening and sensitizing of other souls. That gives you a very great responsibility and incentive to keep your faith and hope alert in the very difficult conditions which surround you. Yours is a missionary job and missionaries always have to bear loneliness for Christ; and the effect, if they take it rightly, is to throw them back on Him and develop more and more their hidden life with God. He comes to us in and with all circumstances, however adverse they may seem to us.

This hard bit of the way has in it much that can purify your love and strengthen your soul. . . . Have patience! Remember how St. Augustine said, "One loving spirit sets another loving spirit on fire"—sooner or later the thirst for God will awake in some soul and you will be there to make the link. Meanwhile go on quietly, don't let your own devotional life drop below normal and don't let yourself be critical or hostile about others.

[1932.]

To the Same.

It is lovely to think of you steadily gaining ground with your group of women[2]—very difficult work I am sure, but how supremely worth while. It seems so hard to make modern people see the distinction between Christianity and *all* other

[1] These two letters (and that on p. 219) were written to a friend who was disappointed in the spiritual life of a church and parish in U.S.A.
[2] A class of "modern" mothers.

systems, doesn't it? Some people say "Life" and "Spirit" seem more real than God; and they "need contemplation," but don't bother about *what* they contemplate!

June, 1932.

To L.M.

Thank you so much for letter and MS. safely received. . . .

Someone was much upset at the bit in *Action*[1] saying a self-willed prayer of demand, not submitted to God, might be effective and even do harm as an exercise of psychic energy disguised as prayer. She thought it would frighten people and that prayer could never do harm. But personally I think this sort of spurious prayer does happen, and as you do not protest, shall leave it. . . .

As to what you say about Peace, Yes! I think too it is possible to be used as a channel without feeling peace, indeed, while often feeling on the surface in a tornado! Nevertheless, the essential ground of the soul *is* held in tranquillity, even through the uproar and every now and then the soul perceives this. The real equation is not Peace = satisfied feeling, but Peace = willed abandonment.

June 15, 1932.

To M.C.

I don't think I can write to you about the Passion Play, because it simply overwhelmed me—I don't know whether you have done much textually to it (I don't think you have) or if it's the result of quiet reading straight through—but the effect is *tremendous*. Of course, it seems to me by far the deepest thing you have done. That sense running right through it, of infinite mysteries accomplished almost unknowingly, in a finite scene, and the awful and creative grief and love—it really is shattering, you know, as well as so intensely beautiful. . . .

Something very strange happened about L.C.[2] and its experiences. Last week I got a letter from Sorella Maria, my Italian

[1] *The Golden Sequence*, Methuen, 1932.
[2] A retreat she had conducted.

Saint, asking specially how it had gone, as those three days, and especially the last evening she had suffered so greatly—"far more than usual" and how deeply thankful she would be if this suffering had "availed for a blessing."

Good-bye till the 22nd. I am looking forward to it more than a mortified person should.

Trinity II, 1932.

To THE SAME.

I am no intercessor myself—when I have the feel of God at all, I can think of nothing else—and when I haven't, I mostly fidget. I'm very relieved to hear the way you do it, because that is, when I manage it, my way too!

L.C. was nice. . . . And, for the first time in a Retreat of mine we had the Blessed Sacrament on the altar all the time. I thought, poor fool that I am, how lovely it would be! But as it went on, the awful power of that white eternity seemed more and more overwhelming: it seemed to make noisy nonsense of everything I was trying to say; and I ended feeling like a cross between a monkey and a parrot. Everyone else seemed quite calm and happy, so it was evidently all right for them. But I felt like Angela when she kept saying to her Secretary, "Brother, I blaspheme, I blaspheme."

July 5, 1932.

To THE SAME.

This will be an incoherent letter because I have just been given a very engaging Persian kitten, named after St. Philip Neri (who was very sound on cats) and his opinion is that *I* have been given to *him*.

Blakeney.
Tues., p.m. [1932].

To THE SAME.

You see, I come to Christ through God, whereas quite obviously lots of people come to God through Christ. But I can't show them how to do that—all I know about is the reverse route. The final result, when you have the two terms united, is much the same—"the figure and the mountain are one"—but the process quite different.

I've never in any of my phases been a "good Evangelical" and I expect you have—but on the other hand I'm not sure you have ever been a white-hot Neo-Platonist! so I should feel awfully shy and awkward expounding the personal side; whereas I'll go to any length to try and make people "feel God."

Still, I expect I *must* try to develop that section a bit more. So pleased you like the bit about primitive adoration beginning with the childhood of the race. I do feel that so much; and that we ought not to be ashamed of the humble origin of many of our religious acts and ideas. Have you read Marett's *Faith, Hope and Charity* yet, I wonder. There's a lot of that sort of thing in it—most thrilling.

You would love this place—the immense salt marshes looking like sheets of greenish-mauvish opal—and the white clouds of terns, and the larks always shouting alleluia. . . .

And now I've nearly finished without saying how *lovely* I think your Prayer Pamphlet is—and why ever did I not know about it before? . . . That's a wonderful thought, about watching His daily Crucifixion in, out, and so forth (and, alas! in much "organized" religion!). But what I feel most (when not deep in the metaphysical dumps) is the triumphing life in the Saints in spite of all appearances—something like St. Clement's "The Christian life is a perpetual spring-time."

Oh yes! I'm sure we must adore the Purpose before we can even see it really.

Sep. 12, 1932.

To U.N.

You are very often in my thoughts for I know what a desperately hard time you must be having and how much prudence as well as courage you will need to get really on your feet again and recover your hold on life. In a way, the fact that you accepted the sacrifice so fully in the first instance may possibly make the inevitable psychological reaction specially severe. I hope that may not be so—but if it is, my dear, and you are troubled by uprushes of bitter or violent feeling, rebellious thoughts, exasperated nerves, lack of interest or any of the other miseries by which our unstable psyche makes us pay for great strain—do not blame yourself too much, do not get frightened, but reckon this in as the result of the heavy blow which has, as it were, left a bruise on the subconscious that may work out in one of these humiliating ways. Consider that this too is suffering and therefore can humbly be offered to God. Do not try to struggle with the situation and its difficulties but so far as is in your power turn from it to other things, in this case obviously a special love and interest in your other children. . . . Fill your mind with them and every detail of their time. . . . If you do go away for a bit, let it be to a place where your interest and attention is filled with active work and you have no time for silence and meditation and living through it all in thought.

When it all seems unbearable, talk about it—do not brood or practise suppression. . . . When you find in your prayers that you are moving away from thoughts of God to thoughts of your own unhappiness, *Stop!* Get up, read if you can, if not, do not scruple to turn to some active occupation. Short aspirations, constant thoughts of and appeals to God will be better than long prayers just now. . . .

St. Francis, 1932.

To G.F.

. . . it is one of the advantages of being a scamp, that one is unable to crystallize into the official shape, and so retains touch with other free lances and realizes how awful the ecclesiastical attitude and atmosphere often makes them feel. As to feeling rather dismayed by the appearance of the Church Visible at the moment—that is inevitable I'm afraid to some extent. But keep your inner eye on the Church Invisible—what the Baron used to call "the great centralities of religion." That is what really takes one up into itself "with angels and archangels and all the company of Heaven," not only the Vicar and the curate and the

Mothers' Union Committee. But there is something entrancing, don't you think, in a supernatural society, so wide and generous and really Catholic, that it can mop up all these—even the most depressing—and still remain the Bride of Christ? The Church is an "essential service" like the Post Office, but there will always be some narrow, irritating and inadequate officials behind the counter and you will always be tempted to exasperation by them.

III

Divine things are not named by the intellect as they really are in themselves, for in that way the intellect knows them not, but they are named in a way that is borrowed from created things.

ST. THOMAS AQUINAS.

March 1, 1933.

To CONRAD NOEL.

Thank you so much for your letter. I am terribly sorry that I am entirely snowed under with work at present; and could not write anything for your Crusade, as you so kindly ask me to do. Also, to do this would rather conflict with my fixed policy of not identifying myself with any particular parties or movements within the Church: more especially those of a religious-political character. You see I do feel that my particular call, such as it is, concerns the interior problems of individuals of all sorts and all opinions: and therefore any deliberate labelling of myself, beyond the general label of the Church, reduces the area within which I can operate and my help is likely to be accepted: but telling *you* what I think is quite another matter!

So far as I can see, the sense of "absorption" with nature and with other beings is far more characteristic of the nature-mystics and the pantheists than of the real Christian mystics. The deep love and sympathy with mankind, and often with all life, which one finds in them seems to be the direct result of their sense of union with the Divine Charity. They aim at that first, and thence flow out, as Ruysbroeck said, in a "wide-spreading love to all in common." The saints whom I have known in the flesh have often been quite unable to keep anything for themselves, and have agonized deeply for the world's suffering; but I don't think they felt any mystical absorption in life in general. They just loved all things with God's love. That is why I always feel that the best way to teach the Second Commandment is to concentrate on the First!

March 21, 1933.

To U.N.

How lovely it will be to have you at Pleshey. . . . The new Chapel is most beautiful and simple and seems to have been born full of the spirit of prayer. Everyone loves it. We had a perfect day for the Dedication last Friday week (March 10).

If you ever see the *Church Times* you will find in last Saturday's number an account of it all by me. NO! ours won't be the first Retreat in it. They are beginning this week. . . .

50 Campden Hill Square, W.8.
20 March [? 1933].

To F.H.

. . . As to that restless feeling that the Roman Church is drawing you (*a*) mere nature makes us all a bit restless in the spring, and is likely to rouse our dominant interest; (*b*) the Church of Rome must always have a sort of attraction for those who love prayer because it *does* understand and emphasize worship. *But* the whole question of course is, not "What attracts and would help Me?" but "Where can I serve God best?"—and usually the answer to that is, "Where He has put me." Von Hügel used to say that only a definite and continuous feeling, that it would be a sin not to move, could justify anyone changing. It is obvious that people who can pray and help others to, are desperately needed in the C. of E. And to leave that job because the devotional atmosphere of Rome is attractive, is simply to abandon the trenches and go back to Barracks. If all the Tractarians had imitated Newman's spiritual selfishness English religion to-day (unless God had raised up other reformers) would be as dead as mutton! There is a great deal still to be done and a great deal to put up with, and the diet is often none too good—but we are here to feed His sheep where we find them, not to look for comfy quarters! At least, that is my firm belief! And the life of prayer can be developed in the C. of E as well as anywhere else if we really mean it.

as from
50 Campden Hill Square, W.8.
20th April, 1933.

To A.B.

Those feelings of bitterness, resentment, etc., you speak of come bubbling up from the animal levels of our being and can so easily taint our whole lives. The only cure is the frank acknowledgment of them for what they are and an absolute trust in the power of God to help to transcend them. When we receive absolution it is God Who enters our soul and frees us from the crippling fetters of sin and gives us a fresh start. It is for us to co-operate and use the fresh start! Remember the boundless pity and gentleness in Christ's attitude to those who must often have jarred on Him; and come back to that, quite quietly and humbly if or when you catch yourself falling into these faults again. Your beautiful Good Friday was a seal set on your absolution. When we get fresh lights of that kind it is a sign that our act has been pleasing to God. So I feel that with you all is very well. Go gently, however, don't concentrate on "Catholic" practices, keep your Christianity wide as well as deep.

50 Campden Hill Square, W.8.
11 May, 1933.

To F.H.

... I'm so glad you've lost the unsettled feeling about the R.C. Church. I know just what you mean about using their books and things and so on. But after all many of them are the spiritual treasure of the Church Universal which our forebears tossed aside at the Reformation and bit by bit the Spirit is giving back to English Christianity in our times. I feel a great call to help on that renewal of sane Catholicism in England and am sure it is a work of God. My Italian saint, Maria (R.C.), says, "The Venerable Roman Church does but preside at the Universal Agape"—not, alas, their usual view, but full, I am sure, of deep truth.

50 Campden Hill Square, W.8.
12 July, 1933.

To E. I. WATKIN.

I have just received the *Dublin* with your terribly generous review of *The Golden Sequence*. I really can't thank you properly for all you say; or—most particularly for the fact that you do seem to like the book personally! I am particularly interested in the points you pick out and am rather pleased you think I go too far on the anti-emotion, anti-audition-and-vision tack! It is because I am so dreadfully afraid of the opposite excess! The sterner view seems on the whole the safer, don't you think? because we may be quite sure *in practice* that valid "auditions," etc., will carry their own guarantees and no one who gets them will be frightened out of believing in their worth—the same with emotion: whatever its theoretical views may be, the soul touched by love will feel and express love! As to the "universal and personal," I agree that "almost" *is* quite wrong and I don't know why I put it. But I think the purely *intellectual* combination *is* beyond us—we manage it in intuition (or dim contemplation if you prefer that) and the intellect accepts the result, without having done the work.

50 Campden Hill Square, W.8.
July 20, 1933.

To L.K.

. . . Here is *The Cloud of Unknowing: Abandonment* is out at the moment, so that must wait till the autumn, but I am sending de Caussade's other one, on Prayer. You will find Part II the most interesting. I am also sending you, as a little present, my last book. If it does not agree with you, throw it away and don't force yourself to read it. But I think you may like the last part.

As to your question: yes, surely all generous, self-giving love, with no claimfulness, *is* part of God's love—"who dwelleth in love dwelleth in God"—any kind of real love! That is surely what St. John is always trying to say. "God is greater than our heart."

As to all the rest, be content with this. God is enlightening you and teaching you direct, bit by bit as you can bear it. It *will* feel uncomfortable, you often *will* feel lost, ashamed and contrite. But all that is a great grace for which you must be very grateful, because it comes from the contrast between the great God deigning to touch you, and your small soul. It is for Him to choose what He shall show you, for you just to accept His lights and *gently* purify your love. It is natural and right that the soul should desire Him in Himself *and also* to be used by Him. Both these phases are part of a full spiritual life. But our longing for Him must be the kind that longs first for His will to be done, even though it means darkness for ourselves—at least that is how it seems to me.

Don't strain after more light than you've got yet: just wait quietly. God holds you when you cannot hold Him, and when the time comes to jump He will see to it that you *do* jump—and you will find you are not frightened then. But probably all that is a long way ahead still. So just be supple in His hands and let Him mould you (as He is doing) for His own purposes, responding with very simple acts of trust and love.

50 Campden Hill Square, W.8.
Oct. 27, 1933.

To the Same.
. . . I'm glad you feel you begin to like St. John of the Cross—because I think he will be a lifelong friend to you. He *does* help with the bare, painful, self-stripping side—which is only *one* side of course—but must be there. . . .

St. James's Day, 1933.

To M.C.
The Leiston Abbey Retreat was quite lovely from the Conductor's point of view. A marvellous place, exquisitely beautiful and well inhabited! The 14th century Lady Chapel of the Abbey to give the Addresses in and a real cell in the cloister (but with H. and C. and fitted bath!) to live in. And the general

feeling of the spirits of kind and devout white monks helping us along. It was all so peaceful, miles from everywhere, and the birds' songs all mixed up with the hymns. A dear old crippled priest, a perfect saint, as Chaplain, almost going on all fours to give thanks after his Communion, 'cos he couldn't very neatly kneel down. A friend of yours there . . . also a Russian and a blind girl and 2 missionaries and a rebel. . . . Also a spiritual healer who came into my cell late the last night, saying she had been guided to the Retreat and after a little talk, suddenly asked if she might lay her hands on me as she felt I was completely tired out (not that I felt so!). So she did and it was a most strange experience. She put one on my head and one between the shoulders and a stream of warm energy seemed to pour through from them. Then she made one startlingly apropos remark, made the Sign of the Cross on my forehead and walked away. . . .

Lesjaskog.
16 August, 1933.

To G.F.

I knew you'd like Barth, but I hope the eager dog won't get a displaced heart from too much following of the bicycle! To change the image, Barth is rather like a bottle of champagne . . . too intoxicating to be taken neat but excellent with a few dry biscuits! He is not "the only real religion": I can't allow you to simplify like that. He is a neglected and splendid *part* of the whole rich complex of religion. Consider what Barthian religion *alone* would have to give to the poor, the miserable, the lonely, the childlike, and all in fact to whom Christianity is specially addressed. You must have the gentle and penetrating intimacy to balance the over-againstness surely, to get the total need and experience of the soul expressed? Von Hügel is far better, saner and more complete. Barth and Eckhart are interesting, stimulating excessives—too exclusively transcendent and abstract, carrying the revolt from naturalism too far. But splendid if kept in their place.

Lesjaskog.
25 August, 1933.

To THE SAME.

After all even he [Barth] in his milder moments, acknowledges that what he is offering is a "theology of correction." And it is worth while to reflect on what happens when the whole emphasis of religion is thrown on the transcendental and eschatological. The majority of people must have something to lay hold of, and if it isn't given them by the Incarnational and Sacramental path, uniting supernature with homeliness, they just vulgarize supernature, and claim familiarity with it. The result is seen in the paradoxical fact that now Brunner is one of the pillars of Buchmanism and Barth's "breaking in of God" becomes "guidance," and once more the deep spiritual sanity of the Christian-Catholic scheme is vindicated.

as from
50 Campden Hill Square, W.8.
4 Sept., 1933.

To F.H.

. . . Mother X. has written to tell me you are going to them, and evidently hopes that it may turn out your vocation is to Community Life. As to that I would not dare to express an opinion—God will guide you and show you your path, so long as you are *absolutely* straightforward with Him and do not try to persuade yourself you feel an attraction where none truly exists! The fact that you have been pushed bit by bit into this situation, without definite choice on your own part, is doubtless important—but all the same do please be careful to avoid being biased by it. I should think from what you say there has been a secret pressure on your soul through your whole life, to give yourself to God—and it may be that this is the place where He wants you to be. Anyhow He can and will accept, transform and use your self-surrender—and with the C.H.F. you will see one form of the Religious Life (*not* the contemplative, however, except incidentally) at its best.

Mother X. is a most remarkable personality, both intellectually

215

and religiously, but her Order exists at least as much for horizontal as for vertical activities, indeed for what the Baron calls "the interweaving of the two movements." You may find at B . . . the opportunity for the steady practice of the upward look you are craving for now—but being a postulant, if it really comes to that, will involve a lot of drill, much of which you may find very irksome! Those stiff collars and cuffs are symbolic. But I hope and pray God has much for you in all this and whatever happens it will bring you fresh knowledge of His love. I don't think any of it silly—not even Sister M.'s kiss, though that, of course, should not seriously weigh in such a decision, as you know very well.

There will be young things at B . . . too—and I do feel the active side of your call, whatever it may be, should include a teaching office towards the young. But *don't* hurry a decision, *don't* be influenced by the real love and generosity and holiness you will meet unless a steady and insistent pressure urges you to this life.

9 September, 1933.

To G.F.

He [Karl Barth] does key it up too much for average use. . . . So glad you like the *Dark Night*. I love it, but not better than *Mount Carmel* I think. The *Flame* I have never got on with very well, but perhaps shall some day. It is really only during the last few years that St. John X. has become one of my most intimate friends! . . .

. . . At one stage and for a long time I found them [the Gospels] just as baffling as you do. But since—though the meadow is God—they include all His best grass, one cannot of course here apply the Baron's rule to the extent of leaving them out. And since . . . something in you far deeper than your brain and critical sense insists on finding God very specially through Holy Communion and the Eucharist, it seems likely, doesn't it, that a long and very docile patience and a faithful response to the bits of light you do see, will gradually resolve this difficulty for you and gradually disclose, as far as you can bear it, what "the Word made Flesh" means in actual fact? It must mean something quite downright, factual, concrete; something that comes the whole way into our human world. And a career staged truly in our human world will look thoroughly matter-of-fact and concrete. It is quite an old difficulty—"is not this the carpenter's son?" The Resurrection and the prompt formation of the Church out of a body of frightened and disillusioned men, and that revealing scrap at the end of St. Mark: "the Lord working with them" give the real clue. I think also the fact that St. Paul's Epistles, with their view of the transcendental character of that concrete life, were in circulation before those matter-of-fact Gospels (except possibly St. Mark) were written at all. But one only gets the feel of it by working from the here-and-now living experience back to the historical embodiment. Of course, the "good and heroic man" is no good at all, and makes nonsense of the history of the Church. When criticism has done its worst, the words and acts of Our Lord which remain are *not* those of "a good and heroic man," but of one deliberately claiming unique authority and insight, and conscious of a unique destiny.

as from
50 Campden Hill Square, W.8.
15 Sept., 1933.

To A.B.

. . . The most important of these suggestions to you I take to be, trying anyhow to refuse to consider and regret the past. It is done, it has happened—you only weaken yourself by dwelling on mistakes, frustration, etc. (which happen in some form in all lives!). Take the present situation as it is and try to deal with what it brings you, in a spirit of generosity and love. God is as much in the difficult home problems as in the times of quiet and prayer, isn't He? Try specially to do His Will there, deliberately seek opportunities for kindness, sympathy and patience—don't "open up" your bitterness, etc., deliberately but bring your whole situation *en bloc* into your Godward life. Knock down the partition between living-room and oratory, even if it does mean tobacco smoke and incense get a bit mixed up. I think it a wholesome sign even, though painful, that you feel and see so acutely the disharmony between your attitude to home problems and your love of God. Quietly and humbly acknowledge you have not yet got this right and ask God's grace that you may do it in His way. If you go to Confession now, don't rake over details but make a general statement of repentance for lack of love, tolerance, etc., etc.

Oct. 16, 1933.

To M.C.

I've got a wonderful new edition of the Sayings of St. John of the Cross—his Spanish text, with crib opposite which shows how terse and deep and splendidly unpious his real voice was and how amazingly daring his spiritual declarations—a wonderful example of how to be a Quaker without being a Quaker, if you know what I mean.

Nov. 18, 1933.

To L.K.

I'm writing this in the train on my way home from Lincoln, where I have been giving the Ordinands Retreat. There were 36, of all imaginable types, all longing to know more about prayer but with the queerest sort of notions about it. . . .

Here is another St. John of the Cross. I think possibly it may clear up the situation for you a bit. Yes, I do understand about the fog that keeps lifting a bit but never clears and shows you what you want so dreadfully. But that is exactly the form, you see, that your probation is to take, completely cleansing you of all spiritual self-seeking and utterly subordinating you to the Will of God. It is the willingness to go on in the fog, not frightened, because God is both on the road and off the road too, "if thou could'st but see Him," which is, after all, of the essence of faith, isn't it?

It is the *Cloud of Unknowing* over again. And also, how humbling and therefore how good for us, when we are obliged to realize as you say, that we *can't* honestly say we want to serve

God without limit and at whatever cost. Wait quietly a bit and pray without fuss, for such a steadying of your love and such a quieting of the dithers, that you are able to feel through and through, even though with pain that "His will is our peace."

Don't attempt to force a complete surrender while it raises a tornado. Just acknowledge very humbly that you cannot get past the tornado without His grace but that underneath it all, you *do* desire to give yourself, or rather to be taken from yourself, into His love. In our natural selves we can't help being afraid of the cost when we catch a glimpse of what it may mean—and this makes the gift, when the moment strikes for it, a real and total offering we're ready to pay for—not merely something of which we haven't reckoned the price and can't go through with.

Dec., 1933.

To J.K.

The letter you sent me is clever, absurd and pathetic all at once, isn't it? The writer is obsessed by jargon and by her swollen sense of the importance of human individuals and the final character of "psychological" advice. But after all it is those who have a deep and real inner life who are best able to deal with the "irritating details of outer life." I think at her present stage, Self (her own or others) is all-important to her. I would begin at that end with psychology!

As far as her letter goes there is no indication that she has at present any idea at all of what religion *is*. And indeed the more I see of the psychological point of view, the more I feel its distance from the Christian point of view! Still, God can do anything; and at any moment her soul may wake up. Keep on friendly terms; pray for her; avoid arguing with her; trust the "catching force" of your faith! She is quite right I think in saying that it is more important to know *what* we are, than *why*; but then the *what* is Children of the Eternal God and inheritors of heaven! Only when we have achieved recognition of that can we see any "psychological situation" in a true light.

I can well believe that the greater part of what you achieve will be unseen by you now and will bear fruit later. It needs much faith and love to accept that and carry on all the same in a spirit of loving confidence. But that is the way, I fancy, that God's hardest jobs are done.

50 Campden Hill Square, W.8.
20 June.

To D.E.[1]

I'm so glad you wrote, and hope you always will when you feel the need of a paw in the dark. Anyhow this time the paw gives you a very pleased squeeze, and says, "All's well!" Every word you say in your letter goes to prove that. It is a tough noviciate but a real one; and all the dark and humiliation (but what a lot of light and love there is with it too) is the shadow and tension which must come with God's direct dealing with the soul. He is showing you things very quickly now and opening new paths and opportunities of self-oblation. Don't be discouraged if you get a bit breathless or even fall flat on your face now and then. Far better, more alive, more demanding, and more utterly purifying from self-love than that "blissful era of peace" you thought might come. You have so much to bring to the altar in the way of love, sympathy, compassion, all of which can be used by God through your intercessions. But while things are moving at this pace, please be careful not to overstrain. If your rule of life merely irks you—stick it out; but if it really strains (and perhaps it may) then modify it a bit. And above all, proper recreation, a day off if possible from taxing jobs, and ample sleep!

No—we can *never* become un-selfed on our own—it is God's work in us. We can only open the door and say, "Do what You like." Stick to your Chapman—he is a safe guide—and if you want another book, Grou's *Spiritual Maxims* will do well.

[1] This and the next eleven letters are undated; they are grouped here as preceding that of New Year's Day, 1934.

50 Campden Hill Square, W.8.

19 November.

To the Same.

. . . I am sorry to hear of you in bed—though I expect it is far the best place for you to be for a few days; and am not awfully surprised that the strain has been too much for you. It's all part of the game, I'm afraid, that one should *feel* as if one had failed God and taken it all badly. This adds to the unhappiness but also (and that's the one point that really matters) to the humbling effect. If we felt how very nicely we were taking our troubles, so brave! so patient! so devoted! they wouldn't have a particularly purifying effect. If you *had* by some miracle (not of grace) "accepted and wanted this bit of darkness as part of His will," you might have felt quite a fine little fellow—and *that* couldn't conceivably be part of His Will! ! We *have* to feel utterly helpless, weak, unable to stand up to it, if we are ever to learn real trust and abandonment. After all, Our Lord Himself didn't say, "I accept this darkness peacefully," etc. *He* said, in the first instance, "Why hast thou forsaken me?"—pain, bewilderment, and all that you reckon in yourself as "failure"—but it isn't, my lamb—it's the "other side" of love.

Don't struggle to "find proofs of God's existence" when He seems to vanish. Throw your hand in and wait, as quietly as you are able. Do you remember von Hügel in his little book on Prayer compares this experience to meeting a sandstorm in the desert—and says the Arab, then, doesn't struggle with the situation but accepts it, lies down in the sand, covers his head with his mantle, and just waits. That is what you are asked to do. God can't be clear to us all the time—if He were, He would not be great enough to worship. But the more we care, the more we suffer in the cloudy bits. It must be so; and desperate as it seems at the time, it does great things for us. I, certainly, am not one scrap disappointed in you! . . . But I'm very sorry for you; for I know how impossible it is for you to realize that it is, as a matter of fact, All Right. Please stay in bed till you are really rested, and after that, don't force yourself to any special religious practices except your Communions, and don't be fierce in preparing for these but go, quite without scruple, however impossible you may be feeling. Otherwise be dormy on the pious side for a bit.

Alexandra Hotel,
Lyme Regis.
December 1st.

TO THE SAME.

. . . I always meant to answer your remarks about the Kingdom of God and forgot. I suppose "Kingdom" is really a misleading word, and Reign of God is nearer the sense of the Greek: in which case it means, not merely a neat, benevolent and hygienic social order (the Baron used to say "the Holy Spirit is *not* a Sanitary Inspector") but that transfiguration of the world and of life into something consistent with God's Will, which is the aim of redemption. And in that case, it is both now *and* hereafter, isn't it? But can't be managed by social workers as such, but by the self-abandonment in love of all souls. So that it *is* within and comes without observation, but will have noticeable results on all levels, and, ideally, is identical with the Church and based on the Cross.

as from
50 Campden Hill Square, W.8.
14 March.

TO THE SAME.

I think there's a great stir going on in the invisible world, bringing people to such thoughts as yours; and that presently perhaps if we keep our doors and windows open and our wills alert, we shall be shown what to do. The Church, I'm sure, holds the pattern on which the new world should be built, but no one will believe it till she becomes much more sacrificial than she is yet. No, I should think it unlikely that the convent is your solution; if it is, God will make it quite plain to you so don't worry. But at the moment, except for the special cases of intense vocation to prayer, I think the need is for keen and alert and practising Christians in the world, showing in action (public as well as private) what being a cell in the Corpus Christi can mean.

50 Campden Hill Square, W.8.

Lent II.

To the Same.

. . . No, I don't think Truth for us (after a rather elementary stage) can be a static, dogmatically defined "This Is It" sort of thing. It is a flash from the Absolute, never complete, always suggesting further depths and further splendour as, in and through the particular truth concerned, God more and more reveals Himself. You'll find, of course, lots of pious persons think this nonsense—never mind. It is the way you will be led and is all right. Von Hügel somewhere speaks of Truth as we know it, as a blazing light fading off into the darkness of the unknown—or something like that.

50 Campden Hill Square, W.8.

Monday, p.m.

To the Same.

I am so sorry things are being hard. . . . Just lie down as quietly as you can in the dust and *wait* for the Lord; don't struggle—it is perfectly useless at such times, and merely exhausting. This "oppression of sins" is one of the Devil's pet dodges. Point out to him and to yourself that we *all* have them—very little difference between us! There is nothing very interesting or unusual about it. And in spite of it all, God loves us and holds on to us. Is there anything special which has caused this hurly-burly beyond the uncertainty about your future—which of course *is* very unsettling? But I have a feeling perhaps there is something else which is troubling you, and against which you are struggling. If so, leave off fighting it; that only means strain, not "getting free." Accept this fresh suffering as your bit of the Cross, and offer it—even though you have to offer it in darkness—for the world.

50 Campden Hill Square, W.8.
21 October.

To the Same.

... It is not waste of my time when you come! Please don't ever think that, or that the "spiritually interesting" are particularly interesting. Those who think themselves so are usually pretty awful. Yes—I realize these last three months have been tough—but the thing is, that you weathered them and I hope will soon feel able to relax a bit. For you won't be happy or stable until you are able to have in your life people whom you *can* love without fear of disaster. This keeping them at arm's length must only be a temporary measure until you really have yourself in hand; and already the improvement is so great that it's only a question of time. Meanwhile God is using you, and also supporting you with the power of His love, in and through struggle and pain.

50 Campden Hill Square, W.8.
25 October.

To the Same.

My poor lamb, I am so terribly sorry for you. I know it is horrible, but it is really all right; and was bound to happen sooner or later. After all, if you choose Christ you start on a route that goes over Calvary, and that means the apparent loss of God as a bit of it. There is no by-pass. But as long as you were getting the assurance of God, your offering wasn't *absolute*, was it? This means total sacrifice. So face up to it, and thank Him (for He *is* there all the time—you must trust your fellow Christians for that) for the privilege of being allowed to taste a little bit of Christ's suffering and offer it for all those you long to help. Apart from this attempt at acceptance, don't do anything. It isn't your fault—it is just part of the route—and God will again show Himself when you are through this bit. Don't struggle with prayer you can't do—just say "Into thy hands I commend my spirit." Continue your Communions quite steadily but don't pull yourself to bits over them. Remember it is you who are temporarily blinded, not the world that has gone black. Early bed, novels, the flicks and so on are all good and help to minimize the nervous strain. Do not be too ferocious in your exercises in detachment at the moment, and try not to be discouraged, though I know this is hard. Your grief at God's absence is the best of all proofs of your love. If you have Dom Chapman's *Letters* by you, read them again. Lots are addressed to people in this state. It is a normal experience in spiritual growth.

> 50 Campden Hill Square, W.8.
> 29 October.

To the Same.

... I had a dreadful feeling that I was no real good to you this time, but still, if you only feel you can hang on to me, and say whatever you like—that, I know, is some use! I'm sure the great thing is to remember, so far as one can, God's Ocean of Peace, and the way it abides and holds us safe, right through all our little storms, which can purify us even while they humble and hurt us. As von Hügel says, "it is so much more He who must hold us, than we who must hold Him." And that being so, it is He who must ordain what we are to do for Him; and if He wants bad tools like us, we must not object, but just gratefully get on with it. He knows that the storms in your nature are much more temperamental sufferings than sins—and, being sufferings, you can accept them and add them to the Cross. The root principle I think is (*a*) since God is all that matters in religion there is never anything to be afraid of in spite of our illusions to the contrary; (*b*) a Christian can always do something with suffering. Stay as quiet as you can when it happens, and wait till it blows over—then get up and go on.

> 50 Campden Hill Square, W.8.
> Michaelmas.

To the Same.

As to C ..., I don't feel clear that you should give this up. It may be the bit of relief in your life you positively need; and if, as you say, the children are "pure joy and a real part of you," it may be that the extra space in your life and reduction of strain which would result from giving it up, would be too dearly bought. I'm not therefore going to say you should give it up at the moment; and I could not possibly promise that doing so would bring you nearer God. But be reasonable. Remember you hold your body and nervous system in trust from God and must treat His property well. So carry on for the present, as quietly as you can, obeying His pressures when you discern them. The great task for you, as you see, is cleansing love of possessiveness, and that you are doing, and I know it is a big job which asks for real heroism. It will get easier, as more and more God takes the central place and you gradually find yourself loving others in and for and with Him.

I think it would be better really if you felt able to take up a moderate and disciplined attitude to those you love—seeing them and writing to them less than you would like, but to a reasonable extent, and for their sakes rather than your own. Your plan of entire separation seems to me too drastic; and likely to react in over-strain, depression, etc. But this is a question you must solve for yourself. You know what is possible to you and what is not. But keep an eye on the fact that you are temperamentally inclined to go to extremes! and this will show itself in your spiritual plans as well as in your emotional life. I feel it is likely that God's Will for you just now will be that you shall take things quietly, as they come, doing what turns up to and for Him and being content to offer just that. After all the oblation which becomes the matter of consecration is ordinary daily bread, isn't it? "I look not for thy gifts but for *thee*." You do not seem to me at all a useless person—on the contrary, I think you have a great deal to offer, and should be happy in spite of the Cloud.

50 Campden Hill Square, W.8.
23 October.

To the Same.

As to confession, I very much hope you will come to feel it is a good plan and will find the right person for it. If so, and I can help you with the technique, let me know. You are sure to have many ups and downs, and indeed real tumbles—but these don't

THE LETTERS OF EVELYN UNDERHILL

in the end matter, however agonizing the bruises, if one carries on! And it helps to that, to have the definite process of going and telling God's delegate, on your knees, about it all, and receiving help and the sacrament of forgiveness. I am sure you would find this deeply tranquillizing and strengthening and it would help you to realize that the important thing is your whole Christian life and intention, not your very real difficulties and falls. No—it would not in the least mean that I gave you up and handed you over. There is plenty of room both for a father-in-God, to whom you go to make your confession, and, so to speak, an aunt-in-God in the background!

I think all this readjustment of life must be a hard patch for you and make great demands on patience and long-suffering and self-oblivion. Also that you are really getting on with it whatever you may think to the contrary. The one point of real importance is to have enough trust and humbleness not to be discouraged even by really spectacular falls! In the sight of God a few somersaults aren't nearly as bad as going into the garden to eat worms.

50 Campden Hill Square, W.8.
Advent II.

To the Same.

... I'm glad you wrote, for I was just tuning-up to write to you! One of my many defects as a physician is that I remember several items for the prescription after the patient has left.

(1) Realize quite definitely that your storms are to be classified as psychic illness and *not* as sin. It is true you are responsible for doing your best to cure them—as any other malady—but, when in spite of yourself, they occur, you are *not* to regard yourself as "guilty." Your emotional life has got out of gear, and you have to bear the resultant suffering and humiliation, just as if your tummy had got out of gear, and let you down for a time. Accepting this as the reality of the situation will take out the worst of the sting, and also be a real help towards getting yourself in hand. When anything does happen to touch you off, say to your self *at once* if you can, "This situation is perfectly all

right really; my horrible feelings are merely my possessiveness getting inflamed—a tummy-ache of the soul." Slight attacks can sometimes be stopped this way—and each one defeated is a long step towards ultimate victory.

(2) I think you would be wise to use bodily as well as spiritual helps. I don't advise a psychologist but I *do* advise a decent and sensible nerve-specialist to whom you could frankly describe the situation. For I am sure a suitably compounded sedative would help you a lot, quiet you, and so heighten your control. This is not a cowardly resource or a second-class ticket. Our bodies and nerves enter into all our mental states. In default, when you feel a real storm brewing, at once take two luminols, or similar harmless sedatives, and lie down. Yours is a case for circumventing the enemy—that excellent dream showed you the results of direct attack.

(3) Confession. Prepare somewhat like this. First, consider, quite generally, your life from childhood to (say) 18 or 20. If any known wrong act, habit, relationship, etc.—anything you are ashamed of—emerges, note it down. Then take your adult life in five-year chunks, and consider it in the same way, specially observing your chief faults and temptations and when you fell into them or failed to resist. Don't do this with a tooth-comb but quite generally. The final few years you will take in greater detail, especially as regards your chief faults and difficulties, sins of omission and of thought as well as of act. The things that *matter* are all forms of misdirected or insufficient or self-regarding love, you will find; and 1 Cor. xiii forms a very good examination paper. The easiest plan is to write down one's findings and take the paper with one to Confession. Say (if you have not made an appointment before), "This is my first Confession," and then the Confession we have in Compline up to "by my own fault," and then add "especially I confess——" and give the contents of your notes. If you get stuck, the priest will probably help you out; and at the end will talk to you a little before giving absolution and a "penance," usually a prayer to say as an act of penitence. Finally, he blesses you or says, "Go in peace, your sin is done away," and you just get up and go away to another part of the church and say your "penance" and thanksgiving. . . .

But one confession won't work a miracle; though I am sure it will release and help, and also [show], that you *have* made a start in the direction of victory.

50 Campden Hill Square, W.8.
New Year's Day, 1934.

To the Same.

. . . This seems just the right forward-looking day to write to you: even though at the moment we are wrapped in a thick fog!

I am sorry for all the apparent bad luck, and not getting to Confession when you had primed yourself for it. Never mind. The outward act is the least part, and the "awful list" of sins, etc., is got rid of, the moment you have offered it to God with gratitude for His patience and love. Wait a minute now, as next week I shall be seeing someone whom I can ask about the sort of priest I would like you to go to. Meanwhile resist the inclination to re-examine the collection! It is out of your charge now.

I'm glad the sedative stopped minor storms—each time that happens it means a trench won, and though I don't deny there are a good many of them, still "Are we downhearted? NO." As to the doctor—I just think that all this is a severe strain on nerves and body, and part of what you suffer is psycho-physical and should be dealt with from that end. You need all the help you can get on all levels, and some wise medical advice might be such help. But if you feel strongly against this leave it for a bit, treating yourself sensibly, not scolding yourself and when you do come a cropper saying, to God, "This is my weakness and knowledge of it can purify me and make me more dependent on You. Give me your strength, and help me to go on again as if nothing had happened." When your desire and love are truly centred on God and His purposes, not in a fiery way but in a gentle self-abandoned way, the demon of possessiveness will get one of the worst snubs he ever had in his life. I am glad you have identified that tendency to collect material and brood over it, as the first stage in storm-production. The *first minute* you notice that, say, "No, you don't! this is just the dog hunting in the dust-bin.

Come away and attend to the things God wants done *now*."
There is a saying of von Hügel's you should keep for such
moments—"The best thing we can do for those we love is to
help them to escape from us." Very hard, but true—and moreover the best way to keep all the pure and noble and enduring
part of love. I want you to accept all the events and deprivations
of your life because God is in them; and all the pains and
struggles connected with your great power of loving and longing
to give yourself, because these are the very disciplines and puri-
fications that power of loving needs if it is to be useful to Him.

You *are* winning the war, even though some of the engage-
ments go wrong.

Eve of the Epiphany, 1934.

To U.V.

The Christmas roses and violets arrived in absolute perfection.
I have never seen such lovely ones. They are a perfect joy and
have made a lovely vase to stand before my Donatello Madonna,[1]
and also a little bowl in my own room. Thank you so very very
much.

[? January, 1934.]

To G.F.

I look forward with childish pleasure to our holiday. I hope
it will be like Origen's description of the first hermits: "They
dwelt in the desert where the air was more pure and the heaven
more open and God more familiar."

Jan. 10, 1934.

To L.K.

I'm glad you wrote and I think you have managed to express
the situation on paper quite clearly. It is a perfectly usual situation and one that anyone being led by God along your path is

[1] This Donatello plaque presented by her husband is now E.U.'s
Memorial in the Chapel at Pleshey.

bound to have to face, sooner or later. I know how horrible it is but it is a fine test of loyalty and courage. All you are required to do about it is to keep as calm as you can and go through with it, making your chief prayer to God deliberate acts of acceptance of the discipline He has sent you. That scrupulous fear that, after all, you did not love God for Himself alone but there was an element of self-seeking in it, is part of the experience and shows too what it is meant to do for you—namely, purify your love.

We all need that. He draws us first by our own needs and longing and then afterwards, when we can stand it, to a pure love which does not even secretly desire reward. The transition, when the jam-jar is removed from the nursery table and only the loaf is left—is very bitter to our babyish spirits but *must* happen if we are to grow up. It is St. John of the Cross's *Night of the Senses* you have come to. Face the fact, and trust God and not your own miserable sensations. You are being made to dissociate love from feeling and centre it on the *will*, the only place where it is safe! This does not mean feeling has gone for ever, or ardour, or joy. They are to come back, at God's moment not yours, in a far better, deeper form. It is rather like one of the long stuffy tunnels in a mountain railway—they seem to go on and on, and then suddenly we come out, one stage higher up the mountain than we went in. . . .

I know the distaste for Holy Communion does seem the last straw. But again, it can remove the emphasis from what He gives, to the total, abandoned giving of yourself. Do not reduce your Communions, but do not try to beat yourself up into a "suitable" stage of mind and soul. Take them as an act of loving obedience.

Do not add to your prayer—even reduce mental prayer a little if it is a great strain—and replace by Offices or vocal prayer, offered, however dryly and coldly, as an act of service. Keep quiet inwardly and let God act. Don't dash about trying to get out of the fog and do not be frightened. He is in it, and is working on your soul through it. You will find it a help to put as much of yourself as you can in the active side just now— practical work for others, etc., and offer that. Don't be worried. —all is well. It is God you want and God Who wants you.

50 Campden Hill Square, W.8.
Shrove Tuesday [? 1934].

To D.E.

. . . I don't know when anything has made me so happy as your letter. I've always felt that if only you could be protected from discouragement and persuaded to carry on, God would show Himself to you—and then you would know it was, in spite of all the difficulties and sufferings, more than worth while. I'm not surprised you "get excited," for it is so wonderful and over-whelming. But all the same, please keep as calm as you can! It all makes a considerable strain on the emotional apparatus, and yours has to be treated with care. The "tiresome desire to be alone" is an inevitable part of it; and I'm very sorry that con-ditions at present make it so difficult for you. All you can do at the moment, I think, is (a) to take such opportunities as you reasonably can without neglecting either duties or health, and (b) humbly offer up to God this unsatisfied desire as your "reasonable sacrifice." You have to reckon with the fact that the intensity of your nature is now turned into this channel; and it may be a very useful, indeed essential, bit of training for you, that your desire for communion with God is checked for the time being by circumstance. Do you remember the letter on packing in von Hügel's *Letters to a Niece?* That just fits your case! All the same, I hope a little time to yourself may soon be possible. You don't say whether you have managed anything about confession . . . don't scrape yourself raw in preparing the confession!

Feb. 16, 1934.

To L.K.

What a wonderfully unsuitable beginning to Lent; to have your lovely box of spring bits to unpack and play about with. There's no present I enjoy so much as that. And to have real country violets and tall snowdrops to sniff at is a perfect joy.

Non-liturgically it came at a very good moment, as we had a mild motor smash on Monday (our first!) and I'm in bed with a face like a prize fighter and (supposed) slight concussion . . . nothing really but awfully inconvenient. . . .

1st Sunday in Lent, 1934.

To M.C.

. . . Except for the mess made of work, etc., concussion is a lovely disease, I think. You just lie in a "sleepy device" as the *Cloud of Unknowing* says, like a particularly contented baby in the arms of God, and don't care a straw about anything. However, this blissful state is rapidly passing and I hope to get to Holy Trinity, Sloane Street, for my address on Thursday. So you might think of that.

50 Campden Hill Square, W.8.

11 June, 1934.

To E. I. WATKIN.

. . . The new St. John of the Cross [Allison Peers' translation] seems to me *very* good, as far as it has gone: but of course the Spiritual Canticle volume will be the real test. I have been spelling out the Spanish in Dom Chevallier's edition—marvellous, isn't it? No one could have guessed from *any* of the translations what an experience the encounter with the original is—the short version I mean, of course. I'm quite in agreement with those who think St. John did *not* write the other. It seems to me incredible that, considering what the short one is like, how deeply and passionately personal, he could have sat down and made a nice neat treatise on the mystic way out of it!

I am so pleased to hear your book is nearly ready—I wish I could hope to review it for *Spectator* but, alas, under the present (strong Nonconformist and Modernist) editor, I get practically nothing from them and the sort of books which interest me are seldom noticed at all. I have just begun, however, a very interesting new job—to write the volume on Christian Worship for the Library of Constructive Theology. It is to include individual as well as liturgic and corporate prayer, and I am given a fairly free hand—so am quite looking forward to it. . . .

Philip Neri and Antony Puss send respectful purrs to Tinker and tell him to Stick to It and Never say Die. They hope he saw the photos of England's largest cat in the papers—weight 35 lbs. and waist 33 inches!

50 Campden Hill Square, W.8.
12 June, 1934.

To F.H.

. . . I loved all you said about your new insights, and the Divine light on the dishcloths and the dirty water. But I did not at all like that failure to carry out orders in the matter of eating eggs. You know as well as I do that it is a direct obligation to God to keep your body as healthy as you can. I hope and trust you have confessed it all to Rev. Mother now and *are* having the food you need, even though it does make you different from others and is difficult and so forth. Tabloids may be a temporary help, but you *must* have your proper meals. So if it has not yet been done, please "pluck up your courage," and tell Rev. Mother you have not been carrying out her instructions and why. I am perfectly sure the Community do not think you an "object of charitable hospitality." Mother X. called you "a blessing to them." So there! But if you get run down and really ill, they will be terribly worried and distressed.

21 June, 1934.

To L.K.

I loved your letter and am quite glad you do feel a bit stirred up about the Christo-centric, incarnational side of religion. I expect I rubbed it in rather, because I am temperamentally like you in that, and left to myself would just go off on God alone. And Baron von Hügel made me see that it simply *won't do* and does lead to a sort of arrogance (as you discovered!) as well as missing some of the loveliest, deepest and most touching parts of Christianity. You will always, I think, be mainly theocentric. But just keep an eye on the other side, without fussing! . . .

It is hard not being able to be alone when you are longing for it. Still, this apparently is what God asks of you at the moment and so is all right, and the renunciation of your own will can just be offered to Him *as* your adoring prayer, can't it? After all, even were you in a contemplative order, you'd have to carry on and put up with it if you had to give out the groceries just when you felt inclined for prayer! Things usually *are* like that I find.

July 19, 1934.

TO THE SAME.

No, one can't like St. Teresa as much as St. John of the Cross—at least some people do much better, but I do not think you and I ever will. Still, I am glad you feel friends with her. Suso perhaps was a mistake! Too personal and romantic. Still, he has some fine bits about God, and doubtless for him, his kind of prayer was right. It's like Tribal Lays—there are Nine and Ninety Ways and Every Single One of them is Right.

I hope you will have time again for your "real" prayer soon: because I am sure you will get to feel very starved without it. But the summer is a difficult time.

I had 100 Clergy Wives at X. No one told me there was Mass at the Cathedral, and the bell rang while I was in my bath, but I arrived, damp, just after the Gospel and found NO one connected with the Quiet Day there. . . . Well then, I had them from 11 to 5 in a frowsty little church, and we had ham-sandwiches for lunch being Friday; and all felt it was a Wonderful and Devotional Day. And I got back to London 10.30 p.m. feeling that was that. Still, they did like it, and I had talks with a few and they were nice creatures.

I forgot to say, it seems to me, though sending R. your precious book *seemed* a wash out, it has probably stirred her up. . . . So perhaps like Ornan your heap of corn was used in another way than you thought! It generally *is*.

13 September, 1934.

TO G.F.

. . . All suffering involves some imperfection, disharmony, wrong relation or decay—and all this is quite unthinkable in connection with the Being of God who is Perfection and Harmony and eternal Joy. What's more, I don't understand how anyone who loves God can bear the idea that He suffers. And though in Christ God reveals Himself right down in human nature and in closest communion with human suffering—which indeed has to endure the utmost as the vehicle of such revelation —that does not mean that God *qua* God suffers. Suffering

235

belongs altogether to the temporal and successive, not to the eternal sphere. The "torments of the lost" are the torments of knowing they have failed to achieve eternal life = God.

Eve of St. Francis, 1934.

To M.C.

Thank you so much for reading "Sacrifice"[1] so quick and kindly and all you say. . . . As to why man conceives that God requires the death of the victim, the most recent and reputable books on Sacrifice say the essential point is the total gift, *not* the death which is, I take it, man's way of responding to the total demand. "God's word is ALL," as R.S.W. says, and primitive man in order that the life He asks for may go to Him, slays the body and releases the life. Perhaps I ought to say a bit on that? but even in primitive sacrifice there are meal-offerings—the Evening Sacrifice of the Temple was "bloodless" and there is surely a reminiscence of this in the Eucharistic oblation? Yes— I think the death *is* the action from man's side, and the response of God is always life. It all begins in the rough in the jungle, but points towards some mystery of the Divine action which lies beyond us still. Meanwhile, for Christians, surely it *is* a "holy and living sacrifice"? and unless the offered victim typifies the self-oblation of the offerer, it is displeasing to God. This, it seems to me, is what the Prophets meant to denounce. Yes! I agree about attendance at Mass—it is of course *the* snag of all institutional religion but perhaps specially of that kind—and yet, I would not say that the pure act of worship was not in one sense an end in itself. I can't bear the "worship God because it makes us better" type of religion.

50 Campden Hill Square, W.8.
19 October, 1934.

To F.H.

This brings you my love and prayers and blessings for Wednesday's clothing—it is a day I always go to Mass so I will

[1] A chapter of her book *Worship*.

make my Communion specially for you. How I hope this act of oblation will bring great peace and growth to you and give to God something He can use for the furtherance of His Will. I had such a nice letter from the Rev. Mother, who seems very sure that it is all right.

As to Confession, you will of course have to conform to the custom of your Order and the directions of the Rev. Mother and this act of obedience *in itself* will be good and bring grace with it. The confession itself may and probably will, be just an unrewarding and uncongenial duty. There do really seem to be some souls who never find it anything but irksome. In such a case, having explained yourself to your Superior, act as you are told, but take it *very* simply. Mention plain faults, omissions, imperfect dispositions etc. which come to the surface in a brief self-examination, make an act of contrition and leave it at that. I understand it very well as I'm much the same myself and Baron von Hügel when he directed me never allowed me to go at all!

Oct. 29, 1934.

To Mrs. HOLDSWORTH.

I am just back from Pleshey, where I received your messages and the delightful gift of your *Memoir* of Mrs. Waterhouse. Thank you so *very* much for it. I have read it for the first time this evening and even in the state of mental and spiritual coma which follows conducting a large retreat, I have appreciated it greatly and so loved gaining a picture of the author of the *Little Book of Life and Death*—whom, to my great loss, I never had the opportunity of meeting.

How happy and interested she would have been to see the Franciscan revival within the English Church now, and the young men and women deliberately turning their backs on luxury and even comfort and taking the "£3-a-week vow" as Tertiaries, or, as Friars, keeping within the 13s. 4d. a week of the dole.

All Saints, 1934.

To M.C.

How nice to write to you on one of the nicest days of the year. . . . Oh, *how* I love All Saints and Wisdom iii. 6.[1]

All Souls, 1934.

To G.F.

The flowers stand in a row under the rood in the study and make a festival of holy beauty all to themselves. I read the Baron's lovely bit, "Look up! look up! what a glorious, touching company"—d'you remember? I always feel All SS. is his day. And to-day read through the Matins of the Dead. One of the most beautiful bits in the Breviary, I think, like a symphonic poem. . . . We got to the Zoo and the first thing I saw were Pelicans, who said quite clearly, "O beata solitudine!"—which of course they were not enjoying at the Zoo.

50 Campden Hill Square, W.8.
6 November, 1934.

To L.K.

. . . I think, about suffering, we can offer it to God for "a particular intention" without any suggestion of bargaining— which would, of course, be horrible. We offer it as a kind of prayer—sometimes the only kind we *can* offer—"I offer you this suffering which I accept and bear—I offer it as my prayer for so-and-so. Please take it and use it." Specially we can offer it surely—because we are "members of Christ," as an atonement for sin—this, I suppose, is what St. Catherine meant when she used to say to the naughty, "*I* will bear the burden of your sin." Offering it for a definite object will, of course, like all inter-cession, be in subservience to the Will of God—which makes it all right.

As to that spiritual suffering you speak of, I think it is what

[1] "As gold in the furnace hath he tried them, and received them as a burnt offering."

some souls, not all, are asked to bear and to offer—their share in the Cross—it's not the same at all as the kind that comes from feeling our disharmony with God. How much of it comes to each of us and for how long, is His affair, not ours—but we must accept it with gratitude and use it as well as we can. I agree that it is very likely that you will be given a good deal of it; and anyhow the radiant, consoled prayer of God's vivid Presence is rather a beginner's prayer really and sooner or later—when God sees you are strong enough—He is certain to use your power of prayer for His redemptive purposes and that is always painful. No one—not the greatest saint—goes on in that lovely light all the time. You will have just common grey weather and storm and fog and perhaps even intense darkness before you have done —that's all part of the "Leave all and follow Me." But it's all right. I would not forecast anything or try to look ahead or wonder how much you can bear—just leave yourself in God's Hand. "I am with thee, saith the Lord." If you feel a definite pressure to leave contemplative prayer, and pray for others— then you must obey each time. But where it is left to you, give a little time anyhow to acts of simple love towards God. It soothes and braces us to remember His Beauty and be glad of it even when we don't see it at all. I think that's all for the moment —except of course avoiding strain, getting enough fun and so forth.

50 Campden Hill Square, W.8.

13 December, 1934.

To A.M.J.

Thank you very much for your letter, and for writing as frankly as you have done. It is not easy to advise someone otherwise unknown on a sample letter, so if what I say does not meet the case, I hope you will write again. I have been during my life (I am now approaching 60) through many phases of religious belief and I now realize—have done in fact for some time—that human beings can make little real progress on a basis of vague spirituality. God and the soul, and prayer as the soul's life, and the obligation of responding to God's demand, are real facts—in fact the most real of all facts—and they are the facts with which orthodox religion deals. As to dogmas which you cannot accept—e.g. the Virgin Birth—it is useless to force' yourself on these points. Leave them alone for the time being, neither affirming nor rejecting them, and give your mind and will to living in harmony with those truths which you *do* see. This is the way—in fact the only way—to get further light.

For your own reading I think if you do not know them you would find Baron von Hügel's *Letters*, Dr. Temple's *Christian Faith and Life*, the *Letters* of St. Francis de Sales, and Grou's *Hidden Life of the Soul* valuable. You probably know the *Confessions* of St. Augustine, but if not do study it. When you speak of reading more than you practise in your life, you put your finger on a real source of spiritual weakness. You would benefit by a simple rule of life: so much *definite* time each day given to prayer and spiritual reading; *definite* acts of, e.g. charity, self-denial, patience, aimed at "mortifying" whatever your special faults of character may be. The "active" and "passive" sides of your nature are meant to collaborate, not compete! As to Holy Communion, consider that this is the way in which Christians have always drawn near to God, offered themselves to Him and received from Him spiritual food. Leave the more doctrinal side alone for the present, and go humbly, taking no notice of how you "feel." This really matters very little!

50 C.H.S.
Epiphany, 1935.

To L.K.

. . . I've found, myself, that the mark of the direction which is meant for one by God is, that it is never used up; one re-reads it at each stage and finds it applying in a new way one had not thought of before.

I think now, that one of the things you've got, quite gradually, to aim at, is some kind of harmony or balance between your outer and inner life, otherwise the strain will become too much. Plainly you are required at present to live both lives; and so in both you can aim at God, though in different ways. I think you have to learn not to pour yourself out too much in outward activities, relationships, etc., but maintain a certain reserve. This is an awfully important thing for one's inner peace; but it takes a lot of doing, so you must expect it to be a slow job. It is really of course an aspect of detachment—you are to love much and give yourself much and *yet* maintain an independence of soul, fully given to *nothing* but God. When you have got this inner stability you won't be so much troubled by that painful shrinking from people and external action; nor will these things spoil your prayer (when they are part of your job) because you won't lose yourself in them. But some degree of pain and loneliness you are sure to have. Try to arrange things so that you can have a reasonable bit of quiet every day and do not be scrupulous and think it selfish to make a decided struggle for this. You are obeying God's call and giving Him the opportunity to teach you what He wants you to know, and so make you more useful to Him and other souls.

Your letter sounds as if you had got a wee bit strained and fussy. Remember that "the Holy Spirit works always in tranquillity" and even the most devout fuss is not any good to Him at all. There will inevitably be great tension between the natural and supernatural sides of your life, yet even this must be drowned in the peace of God. I'm afraid this sounds very muddling but you will pick out what you want. . . .

50 Campden Hill Square, W.8.
24 January, 1935.

To A.M.J.

I am so sorry to have been slow in answering your letter and acknowledging the very kind gift of your poems. There seems to have been a lot to do lately and correspondence is in arrears. I was so interested in (your book) and think it is beautiful. It seems to me that what you say there is true as far as it goes but not the whole story—because, as well as our "psychic drive," which is of course the same drive whether we direct it to self-satisfaction or to God, there is something else, namely a real transcendental spark in us which, once it is awakened, can *only* be satisfied by God. It must take everything else with it, but is definitely *not* just Libido. It belongs wholly to the Eternal.

This too is the reason why you failed to be satisfied by New Thought and all that sort of thing. It leaves out the "supernatural spark" and the soul's thirst for God alone, and is, really, a very refined form of self-cultivation and self-satisfaction. I don't a bit want to press "orthodoxy" on you. I have every reason to know how difficult it is and how often it ruins and makes repulsive the truths it exists to proclaim. But I do very much want you to see that "poetry and romance" are not enough for religion. It asks an immense self-giving and some real austerity to respond to the yet greater self-giving of God.

Have you read Kirk's *Vision of God*? There is a good deal in it you would probably like. Also von Hügel's tiny *Life of Prayer* and Maritain's equally small *Prayer and Intelligence* repay very close attention. You want to get into your bones the realization that the first movement of religion is from God to us and not from us to God. I expect you know Otto's splendid *Idea of the Holy*; if not, *do* read it. If you have a difficulty about getting books I could lend you some of these. Do please write if you wish to, and don't hesitate to ask questions if it helps.

As to prayer, follow (at present) your own attraction towards God Pure: do what is real and sincere to you, not what is not. But keep well in mind that this is only *one* path, and try to turn sometimes with thoughts and affections to Christ, remembering it is still the Absolute God Who draws near to you in Him.

50 Campden Hill Square, W.8.
Shrove Tuesday, 1935.

To F.H.

I am afraid, my poor child, you have had a very stormy time—but so thankful you did not carry out the wild impulse to run off, and did do the only right thing and took all your troubles to Rev. Mother. There is still quite a lot of "private judgment" about you, and you won't be happy, truly and peacefully happy, in Community Life till *all* notions of taking things into your own hands are put right away. This is not in the least bit meant as a scolding—as I am sure you know—but even *now* I don't think you realize what "obedience" in the religious life implies. It means, for instance, that you cannot just ignore the order to study 3 hours—but if your timetable makes this impossible you must explain this to Sister B. and leave her to decide on readjustments. I think you are very lucky in having so kind and really understanding a Mother and I do so hope now that this crisis is over that you will be happier. You want at the moment a thorough rest, to recover from the exhaustion of the mental uproar: and nothing leaves such utter limpness behind. Sister M.'s death of course had a lot to do with it—that, and the monotonous nature of your work, without sufficient mental relaxation. So lie low and keep quiet so far as possible for the time being. I would so love to see you happy and tranquil in your work for God.

50 C.H.S.
Feb. 8, 1935.

To L.K.

. . . Thank you very much for the books. . . . This one I send now [*Spiritual Canticle* of St. John of the Cross] I think one of the loveliest in some ways ever written, so I hope you'll like it too. You'll see it has two versions of the same book. No. 2 is really, I think, the clearest and the best to read. . . .

I am interested you have been hearing Zernov. I have just joined the Anglo-Russian confraternity—not much use really as I am hopeless at societies and guilds and always forget their rules and prayers. But they have a magazine with very good things in it, and also I am most interested in the Orthodox Church. Next time you are in London we might try to go to the Greek Cathedral or Russian Church. . . .

I am sorry things have been difficult. . . . But do not add to all this by "always feeling" it must be your fault. I am sure this is not true and though humility and acknowledgment of one's *real* failings is good, the gratuitous eating of worms *not* put before us by God does not nourish our souls a bit—merely in fact upsets the spiritual tummy.

I am sure that you do genuinely try to deal with the situation

He has given you, but I doubt if the most superhuman care and sacrifice could entirely prevent these attacks. Take things a bit more "as they come"—do all you can in a spirit of love and quite peacefully say to God, "I'm very sorry I do not make a better job of it." After all, if you did make a miraculously good job of it that might not fall exactly within His plan for you, and might even bring with it a subtle temptation against humility. As to that tension between the inward and the outward life—yes, I think to some extent it *is* inevitable for a long time yet anyhow. So I would not worry about that but accept it as part of your material. No doubt as you do grow more supple you will, as you say, go in and out between prayer and work quite simply and without strain, being moved by God. But that is a good way ahead and at present simplicity and self-abandonment will consist in accepting quite quietly this fact of tension between the two sides of your life and offering that, like everything else, to God. When you catch the idea about "not pouring yourself out" over each thing—this will help to reduce the tension. But do not strain after an understanding of it. God knows the proper time for giving you new lights.

50 Campden Hill Square, W.8.
Feb. 15, 1935.

To Y.N.

I think this tiny book[1] (valuable out of all proportion to its size) will solve some of your problems. It is by the late Abbot of Downside, who knew more *really* about prayer than anyone I ever met.

As to your feeling (which everyone has at first!) that it is somehow wrong to leave intercession, etc., for this silent absorption in God (1) it is His call to your soul, otherwise you couldn't do it—and this takes priority of everything else. (2) As you go on you will find you can take the people you desire to pray for with you into the great stream of this prayer—and this is the very best thing you can do for them! For in this prayer

[1] *Contemplative Prayer*: now printed in Dom Chapman's *Spiritual Letters*.

it is the deepest part of the soul that operates—it is, as *The Cloud* says, a "work," a spiritual "action" and self-offering, and you can do it for others as well as for yourself. Don't *overdo* it—there is a certain amount of strain involved, even when it seems all peace and joy!

Do write at any time if I can be of any use to you. Meanwhile, there is really *nothing* to worry about! You will find a good bit rather differently put about the *Cloud* type of prayer in Grou—especially the section on prayer in *L'École de Jésus*.

50 C.H.S.
April 8, 1935.

To L. K.

... Thank you for sending back St. John of the Cross. I thought you'd like him! I hope you will like this too—or at least a great deal of it [*Spiritual Letters* of Dom John Chapman]. Its writer knew more about prayer *really* than anyone else I've ever met; and I think most of these letters are quite splendid. He was such a darling too—so utterly natural and free from all pious jargon and nonsense. ...

I am so glad you begin to see the point about a certain reserve in your soul kept only for God. Don't worry about it or "try" too much. Now the seed has been planted it will grow, as quickly as He wills, without your fussing about it! ...

Yes, it is "of faith" that God dwells in our souls "by essence of grace." Of course all spatial language is really unmeaning as applied to Him because He is pure Spirit and is present everywhere in His fullness. The mystics always say He indwells the "ground of the soul" below the level of everyday consciousness, utterly distinct from and yet more present to us than we are to ourselves. Some find it easiest to withdraw and find Him in their souls and others to turn to Him as if He were the sun: both true and neither adequate.

Dockray,
Westmorland.
Holy Week, 1935.

To the Same.

... We are 1,000 feet up on the fells, a lovely wild place with a darling old grey church, very small, growing out of the ground and so much prayed in by its dear and very humble priest and one or two others that it gives you a marvellous welcome. .... The weather is perishing cold and dreams of eiderdowns and woolly jackets haunt my prayers, but we are quite well!

18 May, 1935.

To G.F.

I'm getting along with "Personal Worship" [a chapter of the book *Worship*] ... but am afraid it's rather recondite and impracticable and know I ought to dilate on the rather emotional Christo-centric devotion which seems to colour most people's private prayers, but don't find it easy to tackle. L. tells me that their best conductor advised the staff "just to whisper the word Jesus on first waking up, and there was no limit to what it might effect." ... It's in the best Christian tradition, yet I'm sure its origins are emotional and imaginative; not, in the pure sense, religiousness.

25 May, 1935.

To the Same.

I am both glad and sorry you feel like that. Sorry because it is very painful and takes a lot of handling, and glad because, as the Abbot says, it is a "very good state" to be in! Anyhow, you cannot help it. Of course it's not imagination, though one's state of nerves, mind and body all have their effect. I am prepared to find in a year or two you are more fundamentally at peace than now. I feel in my bones one should be. Like the blessed in the heaven of the moon—perfectly content to see God only by reflection, and not as those in the heaven of the sun, because it is His will for them and the fact that He *is*, is enough. But some people . . . don't feel like that and presumably they are those who have to go further and (en route) fare worse. . . . When the interior stripping and readjustment is complete you should come back to ordinary life to find it more full of interest than ever before. It is the transition that is tough. How nice if we knew about our insides, instead of feeling our way about by rule of thumb as we have to do.

Ascension Day, 1935.

To Y.N.

I was so very pleased to hear from you again—and it is nothing but a joy and privilege for me, if I can be of any use in supporting and reassuring you.

All I can say—and I say it with as much certainty as a poor human can have in these matters—is that your prayer is *all right*. It is God's gift, not your work, and all you have to do is to forget all the jargon about union and aspiration and so on and respond to Him with humble love. You have only three points to bother about:

1. All strain must be carefully avoided and if there were physical effects of any kind, you must ease off. But I don't expect this.

2. *Some* vocal prayer, psalm or office each day and *some* reading and thought.

3. Take it with a light hand—quite ready to let it go, and accept aridity or anything else, if it is God's will.

I'm thankful you read Dom Chapman. I very nearly wrote and told you to. He knew more about *real* prayer than anyone I ever met. And much of what he says applies directly to your case. Do you remember among other things that he says this type of prayer need not *necessarily* mean a very high spiritual state—he has known souls attain greater sanctity by the "ordinary ways." This I think is very reassuring for those who are worried by finding their own prayer called by very high-sounding names! He makes fun of all these distinctions; and just insists that this simple contemplation leading on to the sort of prayer you describe, is the right thing for those called to it.

As a matter of fact, you have no choice! as you say you can do nothing but accept. What is worrying you isn't your prayer but the rubbish people talk about it! So carry on and be thankful!

> 50 Campden Hill Square, W.8.
> 27 June, 1935.

To D.E.

I couldn't answer your letter before, being at the Anglo-Russian Conference where one was kept very much on the run. It was thrilling and the Orthodox services quite unimaginably lovely.

Yes—I hope and feel *sure* H.'s great day[1] will be beautiful for all of us. I feel it is a great privilege to be so near her when she makes her great act of self-oblation; and there should be no room for small prejudices or regrets over what her personal friends may feel for the time being they have lost. She has grown up so wonderfully, hasn't she, since she turned entirely to God? One can only just admire and be thankful.

I am glad you have had some happy hours, and God has shown you something of His beauty and harmony. These are sometimes I think His way of encouraging and reassuring us and helping us along. No, I do not think it was imagination—though your senses and imagination were used as a vehicle for His message. I think it is important to realize that—it protects us from mere hallucinations. You receive the impress of the Heavenly Beauty, which is a true part of God's Nature, by means of the faculties you have—and your music is a translation into human terms of something which is truly there. It's an experience that does happen to people—Richard Rolle called it "angels' song or heavenly melody dwelling in the mind," and said quite a lot about it. Thank God for it—and don't dwell on it too much.

[1] A profession at Wantage.

30 June, 1935.

To G.F.

This morning was so queer. A very grimy and sordid Presbyterian mission hall in a mews over a garage, where the Russians are allowed once a fortnight to have the Liturgy. A very stage property Ikonostasis and a few modern Ikons. A dirty floor to kneel on and a form along the wall. . . . And in this two superb old priests and a deacon, clouds of incense and, at the Anaphora, an overwhelming supernatural impression.

50 Campden Hill Square, W.8.
6 July, 1935.

To LAURA ROSE:

. . . We went to Wantage that afternoon and Sister H.'s profession was Tuesday morning. A long service—8 to 10.30—but *most* beautiful and impressive, especially the moment when the black veil is given and as she kneels before the altar the Novice Mistress takes off the white veil and the Rev. Mother puts the black one in its place. Those who are to be professed are brought in in procession, with lighted candles in their hands, by their fellow-novices and just before the ceremony begins (after the Creed at High Mass) are each given a sheaf of lilies to hold. They receive the veil, the cross, the girdle with three knots and the ring from the Bishop, and finally each is crowned with a wreath of little white flowers. X. told me that she went in in tears, but when she came out she was simply *radiant* with joy—it was lovely to see her. (They are, I think, very satisfied with her, and told me she has a very deep prayer-life.) Her cross was a special one and had belonged to a very old and saintly Sister who died last year, and had been specially saved for her. She made her vows in such a firm clear voice—one could hear every word! Afterwards we all went up on to the downs with her and had a delightful picnic, with larks singing, and a Birthday Cake with one blue candle!

14 September, 1935.

To G.F.

As to the *devoirs* of the *troisième* sort, to such as me they only turn up as it were now and then, but then probably carry their own sanction with them. Like the "interior words which do what they say." As for instance certain jobs, as to which you *know* you are to take them, and certain kinds of prayer which you are pressed to do. These cases settle themselves. Those more on the border you would keep in your mind and ask for more light on until they cleared up. If they didn't clear up, the presumption would be that you were to use your common sense about them. Of course the more entirely surrendered and loving you were, the more sensitive you would become to these pulls and pushes. But in ordinary cases the "inspiration" must be checked by the general rules of religion, "the mind of the Church," and, I think, by reason and a sound mind too. Otherwise there is no defence against all the follies of "guidance."

28 October, 1935.

To THE SAME.

You must read Gore's Life. When he was dying the Archbishop visited him. He was very weak and kept sinking into half-consciousness and murmuring to himself, "Transcendent glory! transcendent glory!" Don't you love that? It reminds me so of when my friend E.R.B. was dying and kept saying, "*Such* music! *Such* light!"

Christmas Day, 1935.

To L.M.

I've had a lovely Lalique glass Madonna given me by one of my youngest—a most naughty and extravagant gift but what is one to do? It is such a strange thing, very modern and yet somehow very spiritual—like the Platonic idea of the Nativity, different in every light. . . .

50 Campden Hill Square, W.8.
Eve of Jubilee (May 5), 1935.

To D.E.

. . . You should take Fr. X.'s directions about sleeping, and a more ordered life, very seriously indeed. Of course, he expects you to carry out what he said! ! And, though I fully understand it is quite against your whole temperament, if you *would* make a simple rule and stick to it regardless, you would find it bracing and quieting, and would get all that really needs doing done! If as I expect you don't have breakfast till 8.30 or 9, three-quarters of an hour for prayer and reading could surely come before that if you go to bed in reasonable time? You once mentioned letter-writing as one of the things which kept you up late—it is also one of the things that should be disciplined, both as to length and frequency! No letter-writing after 10.15, as an act of obedience to God, would probably bring a quite new sense of leisure, and no one would be a penny the worse. It looks impossible till you do it, and then you find it is possible.

8 January, 1936.

To G.F.

. . . My Indian turned out such a pet and so touching. He was quite a pale and very gentle one, a Moslem professor of philosophy, and after various technical questions about mysticism, he suddenly said, "You see, madam, for me there is really a personal question, I have not the happiness of this experience of God, and I *cannot* live without Him any more," and tears came into his eyes. It was illuminating to observe that the fact he wasn't a Christian simply didn't make any difference at all.

Just read such a nice little bit about Luther. When he'd finished his Commentary on the verse in Romans about "all creation travailing together, etc.," he turned to his little dog and said exultantly, "Thou too shalt have a little golden tail!"

50 Campden Hill Square, W.8.
Quinquagesima, 1936.

To A.B.

As to your Lent—no physical hardships beyond what normal life provides—but take each of these as serenely and gratefully as you can and make of them your humble offering to God. Don't reduce sleep. Don't get up in the cold. Practise more diligently the art of turning to God with some glance or phrase of love and trust at all spare moments of the day. Read a devotional book in bed in the morning, and strive in every way to make the ordinary discipline of life of spiritual worth. Be specially kind and patient with those who irritate you! And make of this effort an offering to God. Instead of wasting energy in being disgusted with yourself, *accept* your own failures, and just say to God, "Well, in spite of all I may say or fancy, this is what I am really like—so please help my weakness." This, not self-disgust, is the real and fruitful humility. . . .

Please be very kind to yourself (Christians must always be kind to animals, including their own animal part!) and get quite well.

Lent III, 1936.

To L.K.

What you say in your letter seems to me all right: it means God has shown you a little more of Himself. Thank Him for it very humbly and let it gently soak in. That pure unmoved Godhead, the "wholly Other" in which we have no part is something which many of the mystics have realized and tried to describe. What *we* know or experience of course is only the tiniest fragment and always will be—how could it be otherwise? But when you say, at that centre, "God does not want us or our worship" —then I think you go beyond what we can possibly know. I think one must not speculate about it either way but just love and offer oneself, and carefully guard against the danger, always present with this kind of religious experience, of becoming too exclusively abstract and impersonal—moving *from* God to Godhead. Our immediate concern must always, mustn't it, be with God as He moves towards us, touches us, reveals Himself to us, in Christ and the Sacraments and in our experiences in prayer.

50 Campden Hill Square, W.8.
14 May, 1936.

To D.E.

... Have you read Aldous Huxley's Peace pamphlet, *What are you going to do about it?* The end part I think fine, and just what all of us ought to do for a start. Do get it: it consoles one a bit for all the Ethiopian horrors and Musso's "intuitively willed war" and the Church's tactful silence. It is all a horrible mystery; but more mysterious that, immersed in such a seething pot, we can know and desire the Love of God. It all seems to me, on a vaster scale, very like the contrasts of the 14th century: all the outbursts of violence and despotism and sin as the setting for the lives of some of those who have known most about God.

Christmas Day, 1936.

To G.F.

I do hope your Christmas has had a little touch of Eternity in among the rush and pitter patter and all. It always seems such a mixing of this world and the next—but that after all *is* the idea! ... We had a hymn this a.m. I'd never sung before—"the seraphs veiled their faces, but Joseph *was not scared*"—nice, don't you think?

50 Campden Hill Square, W.8.
Epiphany, 1937.

To F.H.

No—I am not at all upset that you have refused to be put up for election as Companion Sister. The awful thing would be to contemplate profession when *not* sure of your vocation, either from fear of displeasing Rev. Mother or any other cause. I am so glad you told her at once, when you saw you could not go through with it. You are, I think, one of the people who do best on a yearly vow which you *need not* renew, because you must feel free! I am afraid it has all been very painful for you but I am sure Rev. Mother and Sister K. understand the situation— probably better than you do. Now just wait quietly for a bit, and see where God is wishing to lead you. If later He grants you a firm desire to give Him your life in this Community, then accept the gift with gratitude whatever the cost to yourself. If not, then accept whatever else He puts before you. But whatever you do, don't fuss.

15 January, 1937.

To G.F.

Most of these things don't belong to your type of prayer, e.g. remembering about individuals when you are trying to worship the Lord. When you've got to attend to individuals it will be forced on you. I know it's awfully awkward and one feels a sweep when people mention how hard they have been praying for one and so forth, and one does not do the equivalent. But there it is.

"Just as you say, Lord" is a perfect intention, can't be beaten; is the same as St. Francois' "Yes, Father, yes and always yes." And anyhow I think there is always the implicit intention of "take me and make me what you want." This with, in active life, doing things for people "in the Lord" gives a perfectly sufficient objective and material for your soul. Every word you say makes me feel dead sure of this. All your discomfort really comes from the loving but drastic action of God on your soul. It may get worse still, but never mind. It's more than worth it and you ought to give thanks. . . . I know it all feels vague and waste of time . . . but all these doings and not doings are veils to the deeper action of the soul, which is what matters really, and, still more, humbling conditions in which the Lord can act.

19 January, 1937.

To the Same.

. . . In the end the tension should be resolved for Christians by really and actually finding the Lord *so* present in the visible that it is transfigured and the gap between it and the Invisible is closed; in fact by the complete eucharisticizing of life.

22 January, 1937.

TÒ THE SAME.

Seems to me, as the Lord requires us to live (as much as we can) eternal life in succession, that, when we are fully abandoned, the painful tension between the two will cease because we shall be adjusted to His will. It is an element in our growth, incidental to the fact that we are getting the idea but have not yet arrived. Don't you think so?

Am reading Maisie Spens. She is difficult, but *full* of stuff. A quite new angle on Our Lord's personality and action. Basic idea, that His sayings arise from and point back to his inner experiences and life of prayer. We shall like discussing it.

23 January, 1937.

TO MAISIE SPENS.

. . . Of course now that it[1] is walking about in its street clothes, so to speak, I am mainly conscious of the strands of thought I did not develop in it, though they are there in germ for anyone who will take the trouble to make them sprout! . . . If there is one thing I seem to have learned in the course of my spiritual wanderings, it is the oblique nature of all religious formulations without exception and the deep underlying unity of all supernatural experience. This does not prevent some ways being better than others of course and some doors opening more easily and directly on the Eternal. All this (for me) applies to prayer before the Reserved Sacrament . . . I still attach very great value to it. But I no longer feel able to put it in a class apart as a means of communion with God. Perhaps my dear Russians, with their extraordinary sense of the Presence in the Liturgy, and entire refusal to venerate the "Reserved Gifts," have had something to do with this. You must go to St. Philip's some Sunday morning when you are in London; though I think perhaps it is even more overwhelming when the whole majestic action is carried through by a handful of exiles in some shabby little room with the poorest of "church furniture."

. . . the open-air element [in Our Lord's prayer-life], which always seems to me so central to the Gospels and so sadly ignored by the over-Churchy.

[1] *Worship.*

255

50 Campden Hill Square, W.8.
Quinquagesima, 1937.

To F.H.

Rev. Mother came to see me on Friday, and told me that it was now quite decided that you should not continue your life with them. I am sure that both you and she are right in coming to a final decision about it and not postponing things further— but all the same, I know you must be feeling very unhappy and am so sorry for you. Never mind. You have given the life a good trial under exceptionally favourable circumstances and have, I am sure, learned a great deal both about your own capacity for responding to discipline and the absolute demands of a consecrated life; and that is in itself a great gain.

Had God honoured you by calling you to surrender your liberty and take the vows of religion it would, of course, have been a glorious thing; but humbly and frankly to acknowledge that this is not for you, and to put your future into His hand, is also very pleasing to Him, so you must not be discouraged.

[Feb. 22, 1937.]

To L.M.

Your letter on arriving at Jerusalem came to-day. . . . I gather therefrom that the journey was far from Perfect Joy . . . and hope you took a long rest in that upper room with the lovely view and the balcony which does sound all right. . . .

I was thrilled by your description of the Jewish dedication service. It sounds exactly like the Kiddush, the probable ancestor of the Eucharist. . . . Lovely the cook doing it! Of course he had to wear his tweed cap as all Jews must cover the head when they pray. Do try to go to a good Synagogue service while you are in Palestine—such an opportunity to explore these exciting Judeo-Christian connections. . . .

Nédoncelle's book on the Baron (the one M. translated) is published to-day by Longmans. It reads very well, is nicely produced and has a lovely photo I had not seen before as frontis-piece. The publishers in their blurb quote Archbishop Goodier

as saying that the Baron "is better understood through his inter-
preters than through actual study of his writings"! ! ! In other
words, mince is easier to swallow than a cut off the joint.
Well! Well!

50 Campden Hill Square, W.8.
13 May, 1937.

To D.E.

... Of course you can have Baker! Disregard his views on
illness and some of his more lurid acts of resignation. I think his
notion of the powers of the director excessive myself—the whole
object should be so to organize the life of the directed that he
(she) can walk alone. But this commonly takes a bit of time!

I've been thinking about hot water bottles and the Basques.
It reminds me a bit of an occasion years ago when Copec was
being launched, and L——, its rather ardent secretary, observed
at a meeting that if each of us sacrificed something we really
cared about Copec would bring the Christian revolution in.
Bishop Gore, who was in the Chair, said grumpily, "If I gave up
my pipe, what good would that do to the world?" At the time
I was all for L—— and displeased with the Bishop. But as a
matter of fact he was living all the time a life of complete self-
renunciation, doing his own room, very ascetic in Lent, observing poverty and so on and taking it for granted without fuss:
while L.'s idea was a gesture, out of which she got quite a bit of
kick! And Gore remains an enduring influence because of that
hidden dedication, not done *for* this or that but just as his life
towards God. And I think it is the quiet steady stuff that tells
in the long run, not the startling sacrifices and acts of "reparation." No doubt there are souls called to express their love of
God through these but they ought to be very careful about it!

Whit-Sunday, 1937.

To MAISIE SPENS.

Nicholas Zernov's idea [in an article in *Theology*, March, 1937]
seems to me, as to you, beautiful but very limited in scope—
few have the chance of going, e.g. to an Orthodox Liturgy, and

I   257

if they do, need special knowledge if they are to make much of it. Alas, there and at the Roman Mass they can't be communicants, which at once creates a barrier to real unity, doesn't it? I am sure it is good sometimes to join in the worship of other Churches, but this alone won't lead us very far. The basis of reunion must be interior, secret, out of the reach of all ecclesiastical controversies. I think you have had a wonderful inspiration in basing it on Our Lord's own prayer, which as you say includes and over-passes the sacramental, and indeed all else. But I have no light as to how the revelation you have received (for I am sure it *is* that) should be used—whether something should be published about it, or whether it should be allowed to spread like leaven. It is of course the idea of the Corpus Christi made real, concrete, not a mere notion, as to most people it is: a Praying Church as the actual Body of the Lord. I think you will have to wait and brood over it all a little longer and see if light comes. Things are moving in the supernatural world— don't you feel this in spite of all that seems so hostile to religion? And at any time we may be given the clue to all the separate messages and lights and they will fall into place as parts of one whole.

16 June, 1937.

To the Same.

[For the development of Unity in and through the Praying Christ:—] I do agree that . . . a widespread group of praying souls, Orders and individuals, is essential. Still more that these should belong to *all* Christian Communions. I think verbal contacts much the best but you will not be able to make enough of these for your purpose, so you will be obliged to do some by letter. This leavening process seems to me of the greatest importance; and time and effort spent on it well worth while. Note that an unusual number of Christians of all types caring for reunion will be in England this summer, at Oxford for the "Church and State" and at Edinburgh for the "World Conference." The Religious Orders should be most important for you. . . . Of course use my name if you feel it is any use in making contacts.

50 C.H.S.
Lammas Day [1937].

To L.K.

I am sure the disciplined life based on the Sermon on the Mount is not easy! After all, it was never intended to be, was it? If you can get an hour a day (as much as possible consecutive and in the morning) you ought I think to be able to handle the situation even though just now the "sacrament of the present moment" may take rather a knobbly sort of form. Still God is in it—and it is there that you have to find a way of responding to Him and receiving Him and are actually being fed by Him. Christianity does mean getting down to actual ordinary life as the medium of the Incarnation, doesn't it, and our lessons in that get sterner, not more elegant as time goes on?

As to deliberate mortifications—I take it you do feel satisfied that you accept *fully* those God sends. That being so, you might perhaps do one or two little things, as acts of love, and also as discipline? I suggest by preference the mortification of the Tongue—as being very tiresome and quite harmless to the health. Careful guard on all amusing criticisms of others, on all complaints however casual and trivial; deliberately refraining sometimes (*not* always!) from saying the entertaining thing. This does not mean you are to be dull or correct! but to ration this side of your life. I doubt whether things like sitting on the least comfortable chair, etc., affect you enough to be worth bothering about! But I'm sure custody of the Tongue (on the lines suggested) could give you quite a bit of trouble and be a salutary bit of discipline, a sort of verbal hair-shirt. I think God does provide quite a reasonable amount of material for self-denial, etc., in your life. This extra bit is for love.

Rothbury.
September, 1937.

To G.F.

... The Deaconess is an old Pet, and pretty hot stuff too. Said she always reckoned to have three hours in church every morning, of which the first hour is spent getting rid of distractions and "getting down to the stillness." She is going to pray for both you and me every day. I thought we might as well have the benefit of it. She must be *very* old as she casually referred to some work she did in 1882. Has double cataract and broken wrist, but makes light of it. . . . I felt very abashed on being told that everything she knew about prayer she learnt from me, as obviously she knew infinitely more than I do. . . . I told her I was rather having to leave off active work, and she said, "O well, God has something else for you. After all, it doesn't matter in the least *what* one does, so long as it is what He wants."

Wooler.
8 September, 1937.

To the Same.

. . . Wasn't Philippians (ii. 1–11) nice this a.m.? Especially the marginal reading about "being made originally on the pattern of God," wouldn't clutch at it but let it go. In Philippians I think a deeply mature Paul is writing to very immature pupils— which is perhaps why such deeps of meaning come gradually out of it that one never suspected at first: things as it were he couldn't help putting in because he had arrived at them, and they were just *there* for him.

Wooler.
September, 1937.

To the Same.

. . . How glad I am you went to darling Southwell. And did you see the listening Angel and the contemplative Hermit (whom I like even better) on the screen, and did they tell you how all the plants on those naturalistic capitals on the way to the Chapter House still grow round there? So nice to think of them all trooping into the Sanctuary to praise the Lord, and then remaining permanently.

As to your ascetical programme, I can only say with the American lady, "My, Signora, if that isn't just how I feel myself!" Still, the usual advice is to take one virtue at a time, and not cut off a bigger chunk of perfection than one can chew.

as from
50 Campden Hill Square, W.8.
22 September, 1937.

To A.B.

... I feel the regular, steady, docile practice of corporate worship is of the utmost importance for the building-up of your spiritual life: more important, really, than the reading of advanced books like De Caussade, though I am delighted that he attracts and helps you and feeds your soul. But no amount of solitary reading makes up for humble immersion in the life and worship of the Church. In fact the books are only addressed to those who are taking part in that life. The corporate and personal together make up the Christian ideal. You will find the "new attitude" you speak of—the simplicity, trust and dependence—can be kept up, and that your Communions will play a very important part here, giving support of a kind you can hardly get in any other way, reminding you too of the great life of the Church, engulfing your little life, and checking any tendency to individualism.

Sept. 27, 1937.

To M.C.

Now for the moment I have only got odd jobs. Greatly daring I've undertaken to give the Mercier Memorial Lecture at Whitelands College on Oct. 8, *Education and the Spirit of Worship*, and only hope I'll have voice enough when the time comes. Do think of it! I wonder whether you feel as I do that the most difficult thing about rocky health is not the bits when one is *really* ill and has something as it were to get one's teeth into, but the ceaseless uncertainty about whether one will be able to carry out one's undertakings and the general shortening of the working day! this isn't worth calling a Cross and I fear has no intercessory value at all! but it *is* a bit of a discipline! and perhaps has value in preparing for further and more useful suffering and stripping. ...

October, 1937.

To G.F.

Did G. tell you a jewel we got from the new list of tulips: "*The Bishop*. A bloom of great substance. Blue base with white halo, borne on a stiff and upright stem!"

Moreton.

1 November, 1937.

To the Same.

... A darling old saint of a thing—Fr. X.—came and said Mass. Before he began, after putting his things on the altar, he turned back, and said: "It's All Saints' Day! We are encompassed by a great cloud of witnesses. They are not witnessing how *we* are getting on with it—they are witnessing to what God meant and means to them! So we are to think of them in their myriads, surrounding the Throne of God, all standing on tiptoe and crying at the tops of their voices, Alleluia!" After which he went on to say Mass. Don't you think it was rather nice? And aren't you glad, although he is such a dreadful loss to pacifism, that Dick Sheppard arrived so quietly and comfortably in such good time for the Feast? Nice too that before going he won that victory for peace at Glasgow. . . .

Did you do 1st Vespers of All Saints with the proper psalms and antiphons? Very nice I thought.

Alexandra Hotel,

Lyme Regis, Dorset.

4 December, 1937.

To E.M.

... I have read the letter, and the paper you enclosed carefully; and I think the upshot of it all is, that you are still far too much inclined to make *feeling* the test of religion. All that matters in religion is giving ourselves without reserve to God, and keeping our wills tending towards Him. This we can always do; but to *feel* devout, fervent, aware of His presence, etc., is beyond our control. Everyone goes through "dry" times such as you are experiencing. They are of great value as tests of our perseverance, and of the quality of our love; and certainly don't mean that anything is wrong. All lies in how we take them— with patience, or with restlessness. As to the experience you describe, thank God for it; but don't worry if you never again have it. Such things do happen to many people from time to time, and especially at the beginning of a new phase in the spiritual life, but in this life such "awareness" is never continuous and its absence certainly does not necessarily mean that we are stopping it by our own fault. Just be simple and natural with God, ask Him to do with you what He wills, avoid strain and fuss of all kinds, and be careful to keep in charity with all men, and you will have done what is in your power. You say in your letter "below everything, I believe I'm in a way very quiet and happy"—well, *that*, not the fluctuating surface moods, represents your true spiritual state, and is the work of God. Give Him thanks for it and trust it and don't bother about the variable weather.

as from
50 Campden Hill Square, W.8.
5 Dec., 1937.

To Mrs. ERNEST MILTON.

I have read *Miss Bendix* with the greatest interest and only wish you had carried her theological adventures a bit further. I do see, however, why Macmillan's reader criticized the end as lacking in strength; and think also that the reason for this is fairly obvious. Where one is transcribing, or building upon, an experience of one's own, and has this experience very vividly present in one's mind, it seems to me most difficult to discover how far one has succeeded in presenting it objectively, so that it can be realized in its full strength by one's readers. "Apperception" comes into play here so strongly that hardly anyone escapes it. In the present case, I'm afraid you have *not* given the reader the full blast, as it were, of Miss B.'s vision of God as you yourself see and feel it. You will have to strengthen it somehow; but *not*, I think, by expansion.

p. 134. I think you ought somehow to make clear that the underlined sentence is Miss B.'s own composition; it reads rather as if she and you thought she was quoting the Athanasian Creed! I like *very* much the section with alternative passages from Flammarion and the Psalms. Where the strengthening seems to me to be needed is in the earlier sections of Part II.

If Miss Bendix is intended to be an ordinary devout Anglican, rather "High" but not "Extreme," then the way she spends Holy Week needs a little revision.

p. 65. She wouldn't probably take a tea tray with egg upstairs for breakfast, as she would be *certain* to attend the early Communion service on Maundy Thursday; and a "fasting breakfast" taken *after* she had been to church would consist only of bread and butter and tea.

Good Friday—the fast ends at 3 p.m. and tea with a boiled egg on returning from the 3 hours' service is the normal thing. Why does she get ready so early for a service that doesn't begin till noon? Also most people, I think, have a cup of tea in the morning, and bread (dry) unless their practice is of exceptional severity.

p. 70. There are proper Psalms for each day in Holy Week: she would read, not 119, but 56 and 64 on Thursday morning, 23 and 109 in the evening, and 22 on Good Friday morning (Lady Day, if it occurs in Holy Week, is "transferred" till after Easter).

p. 157. The quotation looks like St. Augustine: but it was not Augustine who said (according to the best opinion) *Credo quia absurdum.* I *think* it was Tertullian, but am away from home at present and can't look it up.

On the last page of all, the mixed scraps from the Nicene and Athanasian Creeds which come to her mind rather look as if they were quotations from a single source.

But these of course are mere details, which are easily enough adjusted if you agree. The communication of Miss B.'s total experience to the reader, in its fullness, is a very different matter!

On the whole, my inclination would be towards slightly tightening-up and condensing the sunset part, and developing and elucidating the last page a bit. I've told you my impressions with brutal frankness as I am sure that is what you want and it is much too serious and beautiful a work to be insincere about.

Lyme Regis.

1 February, 1938.

To G.F.

I go into chapel for Evensong every day. It makes a nice fixed point, and now I'm getting into the rhythm of it and feeling the curious effect of a daily Office, which I had not experienced for a long time now, not having stayed at convents. You do not feel it if you only go now and then. But done every day it becomes a complete act in itself, within which you feel the action of the Church. Rather nice, though slightly spoilt by the curate's passion for adding some second-rate collects at the end; especially a very horrid one about putting the whole weight of our burdens on the bosom of God for the night. I wonder what Otto would have thought of that.

Ash Wednesday, March, 1938.

To THE SAME.

I feel Lent awfully difficult, being unable to lay my hands on anything specific to do or renounce that is not (a) obvious to the world or (b) hostile to health! I'm sure spiritual "mortifications" are the real ones, though without going so far as to say the others do not count. After all, Our Lord's Lent consisted of forty days of exclusive attention to God under austere conditions and resisting the "devil's" offers of things that compete with God— and that must be the ideal; quite impossible, of course, in its completeness for us. I'd never have *dared* to be as sweeping as Z. is about "not lessening your time of communion with God for any human being." After all, everything done in charity *is* communion with God; and therefore it is all right if charity *really* calls us to leave or reduce prayer for the sake of someone else. Don't you think so? . . . It's all fearfully difficult and I see more and more the reason for the Religious Life and Enclosure. I don't see how anyone *really* is going to teach and remain at the deeper levels whilst living in the world. Even this month here, not very well used, is enough to show the immense difference solitude makes. But that, of course, may only be at a certain stage. And the Baron would say if and when it was really required, we could trust God to provide it, and if He didn't, we must carry on tranquilly without.

April 6, 1938.

To V.T.

As to School Prayers; of course they are immensely important and quite plainly part of your job and you must put as much into them as you can and really pray in them. But the fact remains, doesn't it, that this is a bit of work? You are doing your best to help along and join in the corporate worship of the school— but it is not the normal channel taken by *your* personal communion with God and I still don't feel we can reckon it in, when considering how much time you are able to give to that. I should think you want more, not less, of this personal communion in order to "put your back" into school prayers and help to make them what they ought to be. You are more likely to make them your own, if they are well supported by secret prayer.

May 10 [1938].

To Laura Rose.

. . . I was so much interested in your letter about K. [a young girl]. I agree with you she has the genuine spiritual nature and will need to be very carefully guided. It isn't surprising, indeed at her age quite wholesome, that during this last year she should have concentrated most on active life and seemed to lose her prayer to some extent, and that the intense feeling about Our Lord also is less vivid. I think if I were you I would start at once to make her realize and make central the truth that these vivid impressions will vary much and may even depart altogether without there being anything (necessarily) wrong with her spiritual life. In fact if she wants it to be deep and mature, she must never make this the important thing. I think she has great self-knowledge for her age; and I would tell her at once, He comes to the soul when He wills and that soul needs it, but never continuously in this life. We are always in His presence but He not always in ours, isn't it so? Tell her it is all right to love people all she can, so long as she loves with and in God and does not clutch at them. But in times of prayer she must subordinate thoughts of others to thoughts of God Himself—otherwise they *do* become hindrances.

I would love to have her in a Retreat if it were ever possible. I don't think she would find it too difficult; anyhow there would be lots she could understand. Tell her to make a little meditation each day on something in the Gospels, picturing the scene and herself there, looking at and listening to Our Lord.

50 Campden Hill Square, W.8.
St. Barnabas (11 June), 1938.

To the Rev. George D. Reindorp.

I meant to write you a line yesterday with my good wishes for this morning, when I thought of you so much: and above all to thank you for your letter from Fulham. How splendid that everything cleared up for you like that and you were able to make your Confession too. I felt in my bones you ought to do it, but hesitated to press too much and disturb you to no purpose and am so glad now I just left it in God's hands. It has been a crucial week for you, hasn't it? When you had to make the choice which will now colour all your life—whether you will be (*a*) A real priest, offered to God, standing before His Altar as a sacrifice to Him, to be used for His people's needs—with all the effort and difficulty this *must* involve, or (*b*) A thoroughly nice young Clergyman. How splendid that He pressed you to choose (a). Having done so, you can feel quite sure that although there will be very hard and dreary bits to get through, in all real necessities He will provide the support and light you need. . . .

I thought it was so very specially kind of you to come round on Sunday afternoon and did wish I could have seen you. Will you please remember you are *always* welcome here, and have only to say when you want to talk, or just sit for a bit and get your breath! It is sometimes useful to have an auxiliary home.

50 Campden Hill Square, W.8.
26 October, 1938.

To C. S. Lewis.

May I thank you for the very great pleasure which your remarkable book, *Out of the Silent Planet*, has given me? It is so very seldom that one comes across a writer of sufficient imaginative power to give one a new slant on reality: and this is just what you seem to me to have achieved. And what is more, you have not done it in a solemn and oppressive way but with a delightful combination of beauty, humour and deep seriousness. I enjoyed every bit of it, in spite of starting with a decided prejudice against "voyages to Mars."

I wish you had felt able to report the conversation in which Ransom explained the Christian Mysteries to the eldil, but I suppose that would be too much to ask. We should be content with the fact that you have turned "empty space" into heaven!

50 Campden Hill Square, W.8.
3 November, 1938.

To the Same.

Thank you so much for your letter. But I don't think even you can rehabilitate "Condescension," especially where Admiration (in its full significance) was meant. It sounds as though you suspected me of being a terrestrial sorn, instead of just an elderly mouse.

I should not worry about the scientific view of the Cosmic Rays. Perhaps the rays Ransom felt came more directly from the heart of God and so had a vivifying effect on those fit to receive them. Anyhow, as you say, Heaven would no doubt be death to most of us—hence the necessity of Purgatory. Did you ever read St. Catherine of Genoa about that?

If ever you are in London and feel able to come and see me, it would be a great pleasure to make your acquaintance.

> 50 Campden Hill Square, W.8.
> Advent IV [1938].

To D.E.

. . . The Cats' Crèche . . . is too enchanting, and will be lit up at tea time on Christmas Eve, and be the success of the day! Thank you so much. My Irish Margaret gazed at it, and then said, "See the little cats making their offering to Our Lord, and sure it's Himself is fond of animals!" After a pause—"I should think the lady who made this is a good-living person."

Letter of thanks from the Campden Hill Square Cats, enclosed in above

HONOURED MISS,

We both thank you most purrily for our beautiful Crib expressing as it does in drama our Deepest Feelings, otherwise so often unperceived. We note that, like the story of Daniel in the Lions' Den, the lesson for us is one of Self-control. It is as you say the abnegation of will involved in walking up with a *live* mouse that really counts (in fact, the offering of a *dead* mouse often involving a certain temptation to Pride). Gazing upon this scene, and making it the material of our meditation, we hope in time to learn the real nature of the sacrifice of a troubled spirit, and perhaps the other bit will happen later. It may interest you to know, dear Miss, that as a matter of fact, owing to weight and well-fedness, Victims are not often come by. The local mice and birds continue their careers unhindered. Fish, we agree, is different. But then, they have that Upstairs.

Now, dear Miss, with rubs and purrs, and hoping your Christmas mat will be provided with all your pet foods,

We are,
Your affectionate cats,
TONY PUSS.
PHILIP ARGENT.

50 Campden Hill Square, W.8.
April 12, 1939.

To S.P.

I shall be only too delighted if I can be of any help about your prayers. But I am rather frightened of giving detailed advice to anyone I do not know personally: as every one differs in temperament, capacity, etc., their prayer must differ too. So please take anything I say with a grain of salt.

I think an hour in the morning is enough at present and should not be added to; so the question is, how to use it best. Without being too rigid, or watching the clock, try dividing it roughly into 3 periods of about 20 minutes each.

(a) Will be given to a short N.T. reading and a meditation based on it, leading to

(b) Prayer, including adoration, intercession and a review in God's presence of the duties, etc., of the coming day, especially the contacts which may be difficult, or uncongenial jobs.

(c) Spiritual reading.

The point about this plan is that the meditation leads on naturally to prayer; and as soon as you perceive it has done this, you can drop it (because it has then done its work) and continue with that intercourse with God which it will have set going. And, on the other hand, if it is a "bad day," the meditation gives you something definite to do and a subject to attend to and think about which will help to control wandering thoughts.

As to subject, there are lots of books which provide set subjects, points, etc. But I think myself the best and simplest way is just to take some point from one's daily N.T. reading, either the appointed Church lesson or whatever it may be, and, asking God for His light, to brood on it in His presence till it leads you into acts of penitence, love, worship, as the case may be.

No fixed rules can safely be laid down, because some people are more imaginative and others more logical in their ways of meditating and each should follow their *attrait* and not try to force themselves into a particular method. Prayer should never be regarded as a science or reduced to a system—that ruins it, because it is essentially a living and personal relationship, which tends to become more personal and also more simple, as one goes on.

Have you read *How to Pray* by J. N. Grou? I think that is one of the best short expositions of the essence of prayer which has ever been written; and of course there is much in his *Hidden Life of the Soul* too, which would be very useful to you.

On a much lower level, but still extremely good within its own limitations, is a small book called *How to Meditate*, published by S.P.C.K. in *Little Books on Religion* (2d.!); its directions are extremely clear, without being too rigid.

Beware of the elaborate arrangements of Preludes, Points, and so on which are set out in some devotional books; they only lead to unreality. And do not try to go on too long—ten minutes for the actual meditation will probably be enough at first.

If there is anything else you want to know, please do not hesitate to write again, or else come in one day for a talk when you return to London.

50 Campden Hill Square, W.8.
27 April, 1939.

To C.D.[1]

Thinking over our talk yesterday afternoon, I felt that perhaps it might be a help if I jotted down one or two points for you to consider at your leisure, without the worry of trying to remember just what was said! But if on the other hand you don't feel the need of this—then please ignore this letter.

(1) I am sure you ought to go very slowly and quietly—not only for the sake of your mind and body but still more for that of your soul. God in revealing Himself to you, put you at the beginning of a long road, and you must go at His pace, not your own (or mine!). "Tarry thou the Lord's leisure: be strong and He shall comfort thy heart: and put thou thy trust in the Lord." That is a grand verse for you.

(2) Make up your mind from the first to ignore the ups and downs of the "spiritual climate." There will be for you as for everyone sunny and cloudy days, long periods of dullness and fog, and sometimes complete darkness to bear. Accept this with courage as part of the Christian life. Your conversion means giving yourself to God, not having nice religious feelings. Many of the Saints never had "nice religious feelings"; but they did have a sturdy self-oblivious devotion to God alone. Remember old Samuel Rutherford: "There be some that say, Down crosses and up umbrellas . . . but I am persuaded that we must take heaven with the wind and rain in our face."

(3) Beware of fastidiousness! You are highly sensitive to beauty, and whatever branch of the Church you join there will be plenty of things that offend your taste, although they are religious meat and drink to less educated souls, who are also the children of God! Those dreadful Protestant hymns for instance! (The Roman ones if anything are worse—but I don't suppose you have ever heard such popular favourites as "Daily, daily sing to Mary" or "Sweet Sacrament I thee adore"!). *You* interpreted the heavenly music as rather like the best plain-chant.

[1] A convert to Christianity who, at the beginning of the correspondence, had not been baptized: and eventually joined the Roman Church.

But if God had given the same experience to the charwoman, and He is no respecter of persons, *she* would probably have been reminded of "Onward, Christian Soldiers" or "Abide with me." The Church must provide for all her children at every level of culture and this is a discipline which it is often hard for the educated to accept! It provides splendid training in charity and humility.

(4) I think you ought to have a very simple and unexacting rule for your devotional life; so as to get some order into it, but without worry and strain. Waking early as you do, I think you could at least spend 10–15 minutes with God either waiting silently on Him, praying or adoring, reviewing in His presence the duties, etc., of the coming day, or reading and brooding upon a psalm or a passage in Thomas à Kempis. Also in the last quarter- or half-hour of your afternoon rest, you could do this or read a devotional book. I think you would gain by getting familiar with the psalms, making a list of those that help your prayer and using one at least each day. Psalms 25, 27, 42, 63, 51, 103, 116, 130, 139, 145, 148 for instance; 134 is a nice bed-time psalm!

Read a little of the New Testament every day.

(5) On the England or Rome question, *The Anglican Armoury* by H. Beevor gives that side, and *The Spirit of Catholicism* by Karl Adam, the best view of the Roman position—but the author is considered very liberal! And more appreciated by Anglicans than R.C.s. In a book of mine called *Worship* I have a chapter on the Anglican position in which I have tried to state what seems to me the truth of the matter: and also some chapters on the Eucharist.

50 Campden Hill Square, W.8.
3 May, 1939.

To the Same.

I quite understand your feeling that a quite definite rule, even though a light one (as it must be) would be a help to you at present. Without it, especially in the earlier stages, one does waste a lot of time and energy wondering what one shall do and what book one should read!

I suggest something like this:

(1) *Morning.* A psalm, taken slowly and "broodingly" as material for prayer, preceded by the proper liturgical introduction:

> O Lord! open Thou my lips, etc.
>
> O God make speed to save us
> O Lord make haste to help us
>
> Glory be to the Father—etc.

Make a list of psalms you feel you can use in this way, and allot them to the days of the week, and stick to them! After this you will probably be led into prayer or worship of God, and go on to review the coming day in His sight, especially any difficulties, etc., and offer it to Him. Then a New Testament reading. For the present, I would take a Gospel, and read through it steadily.

This will probably be enough for the morning.

(2) During the latter part of your afternoon rest half an hour's reading: decide on a book, and go on till it is finished! Dr. Temple's *St. John* is suitable, or Grou. This is to be devotional reading of a kind that nourishes your spiritual life; not reading for information "about religion" but leading you more deeply into the world of prayer. You can read *about* theology, etc., at other times.

(3) At night, a glance back at the day, with an act of penitence for any fault you notice *without* exploring, a short prayer and a few paragraphs of Thomas à Kempis.

Even this may be too much at present; if it strains or tires you, reduce it at once. The only other thing I would suggest is, try to form the habit of remembering God, with a few words of love or worship, at odd moments during the day. You will find that this is very steadying and refreshing.

I should think it would be a good thing to have an interview with an R.C. priest if opportunity arises, before seeing Father X., but *he* (the R.C.) won't share your view that the question of which Church you join is unimportant! Because for him Rome is the only Church. I quite agree with you that "belonging to God and Christ" is what really matters—but it is, really, as members of God's family, the Church, that we must fully belong to Him. But von Hügel will have taught you that!

If you do decide on the Church of England make up your mind to accept it as a whole, for what it is, a "Bridge Church" which can include both those whose emphasis is Catholic and those whose emphasis is Evangelical, so long as they accept the only true basis of Catholicity—the Scriptures, the Creeds and the two Sacraments. Don't be sectional and anti-Protestant! Just quietly leave what doesn't suit you and feed your soul on the things that nourish it.

July 11, 1939.

To T.S.[1]

I read your letter with great interest and sympathy. It seems to me that the fact that your work has had this very sharp and distressing set-back is no argument at all against its being God's will. Most of the spiritual rebirths within the Church have begun in a very small way, and gone on for a long time in a small way, and have had very great difficulties and unpopularity to contend with; but looking back on them now, we do see in them the action of the Spirit, do we not? which must have been very hard for those who worked in them to realize at the time.

Consider the Tractarian Revival. The Church of England before it happened was at the lowest possible ebb sacramentally and liturgically, and it must have seemed incredible that a handful of ardent souls could make any real difference. And then, when it had begun to get going, there was the crushing blow of the secession of Newman and his friends to Rome. That seemed like complete failure, and indeed many people did despair, yet in spite of it the movement struggled on and recovered itself and now there is hardly an English parish untouched by its influence; and the present real revival of the religious life is entirely due to it.

So don't despair, or give up the struggle to hold real retreats and training in the spiritual life, even for a handful of people:

---

[1] A woman engaged in Retreat work.

our Lord began with a "little flock" and it is still the true method of renewal. From your point of view it may all be very patchy and unsatisfactory and you may never see "solid results" and yet it *is* the Spirit's work. As for the hostility and disapproval, that will go on too and must be borne.

As regards your further question whether the spiritual life *can* be lived apart from the Sacraments, God will care for His own, and will make up in other ways to the really desirous what they can't at present receive through the sacramental channels of the Church. Remember too that the frequency of communion in the Roman and Anglican Churches is quite a recent development. In the Middle Ages such a thing was unknown—as of course it is in the greater part of the Orthodox Church now. Three times a year was the usual thing for laity, though Mass was always the principal Sunday service. Therefore it can't be *essential* to the supernatural life. In teaching prayer and adoration you are bringing souls into touch with the supernatural, and teaching something all can and should do, in their own homes or perhaps meet for in small groups: whatever the custom of the official Church. As you say, individuals must make their own life of prayer and so leaven the rest. This too has always been a Christian method and happened throughout the history of the Church in a greater or less degree. We can't tell how much retreats mean to those who come—on the evidence, a great deal to some, less to others; but we must be content to work in faith.

So taking it all round, if you possibly can, remain . . . and stick it out! That is of course, unless you become aware of a steady and continuous pressure from God to move elsewhere. This work has come into existence for His purposes and the fact that you are now faced with a very discouraging situation, doesn't matter a bit. . . .

IV

1939–1941

Unlike nevertheless, much unlike, is the savour of the creator and of the creature, of everlastingness and of Time, of light uncreate and light illuminate.—*Imitation*, III, 39.

Highden,
Washington, Sussex.
18 Sept., 1939.

To L.M.

I knew you would be feeling the horror of the whole thing intensely; it is all so awful, one dare not dwell on it. One of the things I mind most is the thousands of humble little families . . . being ruined straight off by the exodus of people from the towns, shops, schools and so on. . . .

21 Sept., 1939.

To the Same.

You sound very busy and useful . . . far more than we are here! So far I have not found anything to do. The village being 1½ miles away and petrol so short, seems to make it difficult. Hubert works hard all day in the kitchen garden, which is under-staffed and of course very valuable now as a source of food.

I went to London last Friday for a night to get warm clothes, books and so on; had rather a disastrous trip as on the way up, just after leaving Richmond Park, an oncoming car on the opposite side of the road, suddenly swerved right across and crashed violently into us. My car was half wrecked, all one side stove in, petrol-tank and back axle smashed. By a miracle E. (our refugee), who was driving, was unhurt. I got a black eye, bruises, a bad shaking and a wrench to my back—not serious but very tiresome. . . . The bother is we shan't have the car for some weeks . . . which cripples us dreadfully here, 6½ miles from shops and train.

277

We have all decided to make this our headquarters for the winter. I don't feel quite sure it's wise. . . . Of course it is healthy and quiet and there is nothing to take us to London as the war has brought all Hubert's work to an end . . . meanwhile we shall have to economize as severely as we can. . . .

Highden.
Oct. 3, 1939.

To M.C.

I hope your Newcastle boys are being good and responding to (your country) atmosphere and you are not getting overdone. We go on here—I feel a bit troubled about it as we are just safe and comfy in heavenly country, but not being any use! there seems no job for us—the village hums with helpers and we are nearly two miles from it. . . .

I am just finishing off my little book on the Lord's Prayer. It is queer finishing a book now, that was written mostly in the summer. One's whole outlook seems so changed in proportion, and the terrible sense of universal suffering and ruin seems to get into everything.

I feel by turns (a) that one should fight against this oppression and (b) that it is to be accepted as one's share in the pain and horror of war—there's almost a feeling of guilt attached to enjoying things. I wonder so much what you feel about it?

We've got a kitten! black and white fluffy, of farm origin but full of friendliness.

Highden,
Washington, Sussex.
15 October, 1939.

To A.B.

I think from what you say, you are doing very well with your prayer. Everyone finds it difficult now, with all the distractions and anxieties that crowd on us. Nevertheless these are the circumstances in which we are now called to serve God; and the very best thing we can do to help the world's suffering is to lift it up to Him. Our own suffering and anxiety too can be dedicated and united to the Cross. "Christ did not come to save us from trouble but to show us how to bear trouble."

Do you know this bit from Gerlac Petersen's *Fiery Soliloquy with God*—

"Let every circumstance and event find thee standing firm like a square stone. . . . So much the more precious and glorious is virtue before Our Lord as agitated by contrary and diverse storms, occupations, tumults and conflicts, it shall be found more constant; nor has it ever truly taken root in us, in time of rest and tranquillity, if it shall fail in time of tribulation. . . . For to him who bravely conquereth and not to him who avoideth the fight or dissembleth will be given the hidden manna and a new name."

> Highden House,
> Washington, Sussex.
> 25 Oct., 1939.

To D.E.

I'm not a bit surprised you do get fits of furious revolt against this whole horrible and senseless business. Things like the *Royal Oak*, if one dares to stop and think what it means, are enough to upset anyone! But I am sure the only safe and sane way just now, is to keep the imagination sternly in check, turn to God in blind faith, hold on to Him in the dark as well as you can—or better, let Him hold you. You won't, however, be able to get away from feeling the suffering and the darkness. So best accept them, join them to the Cross and offer them to God. It is a very hard time for realists, who can't be content to "pay themselves with words." The world is subject to the law of consequence and must pay for its deliberate departures from God. Yet in and through all that, His Hand is over individuals, bringing them out at last by strange paths into His Light.

I have tumbled into quite a lot of work here: a weekly intercession service in the Parish Church beginning next Wednesday at 3. Also a weekly religious lesson in the School, 11–14-year-olds, 33 of them, taking the place of the Vicar, who is too ill at present. This *terrifies* me as I have never taught children. I begin Monday week and if you can give me any tips as to how you would tackle the job I would be most grateful. The Vicar wants me to teach them about Prayer—do you think they will ever listen or take any interest? The schoolmaster wants "The History of our Prayer Book"—more concrete but not easy to make very thrilling. If it isn't an abject failure I'm to have a class of evacuee girls, 12–14, later, but as they come from a Council school all doctrine is strictly forbidden.

Highden House,
Washington, Sussex.
11 November, 1939.

To Theodora Bosanquet[1]
My dear Editor,

Here is the review of Cat Books. I have tried my best but it is my first effort and I am very young; do please be lenient to its defects.

Hoping this finds you well and frisky as it leaves me at present,
I am,
Your obedient Kitten,
Michelangelo van Katzenellenbogen.
p.p. E.S.M.

Highden House,
Washington.
17 November, 1939.

My dear Editor,

Thank you so much for my Proof, and your kind letter. All these attentions are very gratifying, and deepen the purr. Please also thank Miss Moore for her amiable words.

As to my signature, I am not usually known as Underhill—I am the common property, if one may use such an expression of a Cat, of three families. I have heard them mention drawing lots for me when they leave the district. The one I call Mummy

[1] Literary Editor of *Time and Tide*. The following five letters refer to a review written by a Cat member of the Highden household, E.U. acting as amanuensis when necessary.

suggests perhaps "p.p. E.U." would clarify the situation sufficiently, or even E. Underhill if you think this really necessary.
We leave it all to you.

With grateful purrs,

Your affectionate Kitten,

MICHELANGELO VAN KATZENELLENBOGEN.

Highden,
Washington.
22 November, 1939.

DEAR T.B.,

The request for Michelangelo's photograph is just to hand.
He is much excited, but regrets that so far no portrait exists.
However earnest attempts will be made to secure a portrait
to-morrow and we hope a print may reach you on Monday. His
moods and motions being unpredictable it is impossible to say
whether anything fit for publication will result. Your telegram
put the whole tea table in a flutter and nothing else was spoken
of for some time.

In haste to catch our very infrequent post,

Yours ever,

E.S.M.

If no portrait available I will let you know.

Highden,
Washington.
23 November, 1939.

MY DEAR EDITOR,

Alas! a wet dark day has put an end to *any* hope of getting
my portrait into the paper. I am terribly disappointed. Had I
realized these possibilities earlier, I would have got into touch
with a Press photographer. Perhaps some other time!

Your regretful Kitten,

MICHELANGELO.

Lawn House,
12 Hampstead Square, N.W.3.
Christmas Day, 1940.

HONOURED EDITOR,

Your magnificent card—intended of course for me—has given great pleasure to all. And as you say, what a *lesson* it conveys, what a *warning*!

> Ah, better far to dwell alone
> One Ball, one Basket, and one Dish,
> Than midst a maze of twitching tails
> To share the rationed Fish.

My own work entirely. I am leading a very careful life now.
With love and purrs,
Your affectionate,
MICKIE.

Highden House,
Washington, Sussex.
21 November, 1939.

To E.N.

From what you say in your letter, I don't think you are really the sort of person who should go to Confession at all frequently. I should think two or three times a year quite enough. Confession should be kept for real sins and persistent faults, whether of omission or commission; and not be used for exploring the soul, trying to disentangle one's own inward states, etc.—a proceeding which only encourages self-occupation and does not really get one anywhere. The best way to take the "darkness and left aloneness" is not discussion, but a generous and humble act of acceptance of the state in which God has placed one's soul, however useless and frustrated one may feel, and an act of trust that in this darkness and incapacity He is training us to a more perfect self-abandonment. The fact that you feel "empty and useless" is not "material for confession"—it is really rather a good state to be in because so destructive of self-esteem. Probably physical health has something to do with it too in your case! And as you say it is the conditions "deep down" that really matter.

Highden House,
Washington, Sussex.
28 December, 1939.

To E. I. WATKIN.

It was a great pleasure to have news of you again. One of the distresses of our present condition is the way one's friends are scattered and the difficulty of keeping in touch. We, as you see, have left London for the present, and are sharing this house on the downs with some great friends.

Don't you find these times very difficult for pacifists? The war seems to enter into everything, and there are few things that one can conscientiously do. Most of my quasi-pacifist friends are becoming more warlike, apparently feeling that provocation is more important than principles and that the only way to combat sin in others is to commit sin ourselves. The attitude of the Anglican bishops has also been disappointing, though a great many of the clergy *are* strongly pacifist.

31 December, 1939.

To MAISIE SPENS.

I am sure a book which clings all the time to "the theocentric basis of interpretation" and approaches Christianity from the Godward side, is more than ever needed now, when we are so plainly approaching a crisis which only the deepest understanding and most heroic and other-worldly acceptance of the Cross can resolve. At present the whole attitude of the Church strikes me as getting steadily more sub-Christian, more and more forgetful of absolute standards and inclined to regard the B.E.F. as the instrument of the Divine Will. And as the earthly situation deteriorates—as it must—all this will get worse, unless some vigorous movement is made in the opposite direction. However it has generally been in times when the temporal outlook was darkest, that the great swings back of the human spirit towards the Eternal have taken place. The gist of all this is that I think you should make these new insights central for your work, and the more supernatural, absolute, and non-utilitarian you can make it, the better it will be! I particularly like what you said about physical suffering: that it *is* God's Will, and yet also is *never* His Will. That paradox has to be held on to all the time— so that we can accept even evil and imperfection as penetrated, in spite of themselves, by God's over-ruling Will and Grace and turned thus to His final purpose, though still remaining in themselves, and until redeemed, contrary to His intrinsic Will for life. . . .

Highden House,
Washington, Sussex.
12 January, 1940.

To E. I. WATKIN.

I delayed thanking you for the kind gift of *The Catholic Centre* till I had time to read it carefully, which I have now done with much enjoyment. What a fine, broad and deep book it is! And how I hope it will go home to those to whom it is really addressed. The chapters I specially liked were those on Ecclesiastical Materialism and on Immanence and Transcendence, and the final pages on Adoration. I think your exposition of that glorious Whitsun Introit is splendid—it is difficult to say anything fresh about Transcendence but you have made a wonderful thing of that chapter. I was particularly interested in "The Problem of Suffering" as I have just been reading the Abbé Nédoncelle's *Souffrance*, and was so glad you emphasized (as I felt he did not) the irreplaceable supernatural value of suffering. This of course does not solve the problem, since only a minute proportion so far as we know of the world's anguish serves spiritual ends; but it does emphasize a deep reality which humanism tends to forget. But on the general problem I *can't* feel Father Rickaby's arguments are satisfying! To predicate impossibilities of God seems in itself such impudence!

I am sorry we do not agree about Peace. Although I quite agree about the stern element in Our Lord's teaching, the denunciations of Pharisees, etc., etc., still the numerous texts enjoining love of enemies, non-resistance, etc., do seem to qualify this strain in a sense that precludes war. And in fact the early Christians held that they *were* debarred from war, didn't they? Of course Christendom has never had the nerve to apply this teaching without qualification, right up to the point of national martyrdom. When it does, perhaps the Kingdom of God will come.

Highden House,
Washington, Sussex.
Jan. 18, 1940.

To FATHER GEOFFREY CURTIS, C.R.

The coming of the Church Unity Octave reminds me that I have never answered the letter which you wrote to me in November, and which I enjoyed so much. And now your article in the current C.R. brings you back so vividly to my mind.

That real growth of unity among Christians of which you speak is one of the few consoling elements in the present situation, isn't it? and must surely mean the first beginning of a drawing-together and casting down of barriers. The warm interest in the Papal Encyclical among Anglicans and even Nonconformists, seems to me very remarkable—and there seems to be a real increase of elasticity among the Romans themselves. Such a book as E. I. Watkin's *Catholic Centre*, which I've just been reading, in spite of some special pleading, shows it in a marked degree. And so does a new book which has very much impressed me: Dom Aelred Graham's *Love of God*. I wonder whether you have seen it?

I liked your article *immensely*, particularly the passage on p. 9, about the offering of all sufferings for the re-integration of the Body of Christ. It is this sense of the sacrificial worth of suffering that one rather misses in de Tourville (and also in Abbé Nédoncelle's *La Souffrance*, which I expect you have seen). Perhaps this is what you mean when you say that he (de Tourville) does not leave the door open to a life of reparation, and also what Fr. Northcot felt the need of. But of course the whole of that little book[1] is taken from letters addressed to two penitents, both of them plainly of the self-tormenting scrupulous type, and there is nothing to show that he would not have made far harder demands on souls of a different kind. He seems to make a great appeal at the present time, judging by the way the English translation has been received. But I agree with you, that in spite of his great merits—realism, confidence, simplicity, etc.—there are large tracts of spiritual experience on which he throws no light, and depths which one instinctively feels to exist, especially in respect of suffering, which he entirely ignores. All the same, he is a splendid tonic for certain states of soul.

I do wonder what you thought of *La Souffrance*. There too, I couldn't help feeling that the supernatural had been sacrificed to the sensible—I mean the common-sensible; and also that there was disproportion in the long section given to "suffering through friendship." And again that putting of the sufferings of the Saints in a special class and allowing redemptive value to them alone, is surely wrong? The sufferings, whether "deserved" or "undeserved" of all Christians surely have or can have redemptive value in their own small way? the doctrine of the Mystical Body must mean this.

It seems to me part of the transforming power of grace, that even suffering caused by our own silliness or sin can be turned to the purposes of God. But he (Nédoncelle) doesn't seem to think that.

Yes, I am still entirely pacifist and more and more convinced that the idea that this or any other war is "righteous" or will achieve any creative result of a durable kind, is an illusion. But I notice that a good many of my pacifist friends are showing a tendency to compromise! and certainly it is difficult (for instance) to say what one thinks the Finns ought to have done. . . .

I hope you keep well and find a little time for Father William.

---

[1] *Pensées Diverses*, by the Abbé de Tourville.

Highden House,

Jan. 18, 1940.

To S.T. (a member of the Prayer Group).

I am so glad you are going to try to reduce the tension in your own life. The important thing, psychologically and every other way, is to get that one clear day in the week, without theology! this will do far more to get rid of strain and feelings of saturation than reducing hours of work on the other days.

About "mortal sins"—they are the same as the "deadly sins"; and if persisted in, inevitably separate us from God. According to Catholic teaching, these are the only sins we *must* confess; and if we die without repenting and being forgiven for them, we are lost. But committing a mortal sin is not as easy as it sounds—because it must be done deliberately and our *will* must consent to it. This does not happen very often to people who are trying to live a Christian life; e.g. we get angry, are possessive, greedy, lazy, etc., more through weakness and yielding to sudden temptation, than by deliberately doing these things when we *could* have refused to do them! So we have to distinguish between the *sinfulness* which makes us constantly commit faults, and be conceited, impatient, envious, etc., and the Sin of persisting in these things when we need not; not trying to resist. The Seven Deadly Sins, if you look at them, are all forms of selfishness; so what it boils down to is, that if we deliberately persist in selfishness, we shall inflict mortal injury on our soul and finally lose God. Which, after all, is what one might expect, is it not?

On the other hand, if we love God, and constantly turn to Him, this is practically a safeguard against mortal sin, for in His presence we cannot be deliberately self-assertive, angry, envious, avaricious, etc., even though we may sometimes be tempted to the faults which are as it were the "baptized forms" of mortal sins—self-esteem, impatience, clinging to our possessions, grabbing the things we enjoy, etc.—because these tendencies are rooted in our nature and can only really be vanquished by God's grace. But falls of that kind are "venial" not "mortal" —we do not want to do them and we are sorry when we have!

The second volume of Archbishop Temple's book on St. John is now out and seems *very* good. So I suppose [you] will take that up, after reading the one on Ephesians which you have in hand now.

> Lawn House,
> 12 Hampstead Square, N.W.3.
> May 20, 1940.

To L.K.

I was so glad to hear from you. This 2½d. business has reduced my letter-bag to nothing and will I can see tend to isolate people in the most horrible way just when we most need to keep together.

I didn't write to anyone for Whit. this time as I've been seedy again and was in bed and discouraged from writing. However, I'm up again now though still in my room. This fragile plant business is beginning to pall upon me but no doubt it is a good plan!

I expect your prayer-cum-knitting is also a good plan so long as you get enough sleep (I do not think 6 hours *is* enough, with all you have to do.)

The great difficulty (to me) just now in prayer, is that directly you quiet your mind all the frightful things that are happening batter against it and make it impossible to steady yourself on God, which is the most important thing one can do for the world and for all those overwhelmed by the violence—and there I think something done with your fingers probably helps. I feel a great concern, don't you, for the dying and for those who are suffering the extremity of fear, as if one should try to hold on to them, and keep them linked to the Perfection of God? . . .

There is nothing Pacifists can do but take their share of the agony and pray for the future we shan't live to see. I must say it's not an easy creed to hold on to, in view of Norway, Belgium and Holland. In fact it *can* only be held for supernatural reasons and by a supernatural faith that love *is* the ultimate reality and must prevail.

How satisfactory it must be for X. and in fact all religious, to have their jobs so clearly defined now. No "practical" distractions but nothing to do but put their whole weight on to the spiritual scale, feeling quite sure *that* kind of action is not wasted.

Have you heard that Y. is giving up . . . and going into a contemplative Order? . . . It is rather like the 12th century when the horrors of the outward life caused hermits and anchorites to spring up everywhere. Perhaps we are about to see a great return to the contemplative life. It's about the only thing strong enough to conquer Hitlerism. Meanwhile I suppose that next Sunday we shall see a dreadful explosion of patriotic Christianity. I do hate these "days of prayer," don't you? Such a flagrant making use of God.

22 June, 1940.

To Maisie Spens.

The only thing that pulled me up, as it often has in other writers, is the description of the Crucifixion as "the very worst that can possibly happen." If by this you mean Absolute Holiness enduring the full punishment of evil, perhaps it is a permissible phrase. But as it stands, it always seems to me an exaggerated statement: the cross was endured by hundreds of malefactors throughout the Roman Empire. It was a commonplace, not a *ne plus ultra* of suffering. And Our Lord endured it for three hours only, whilst 24 was a usual time for the victim to survive. It seems to me that perhaps it is truer and more impressive to think of Him as enduring the *ordinary* lot of the individual condemned under the law. Of course in a way capital punishment is the "worst possible" but it hasn't a unique character. . . .

I think perhaps the war has tended to increase religious unity among ourselves, don't you? But it has also increased a good many other less desirable things. Feeling against aliens, even refugees, is becoming obvious everywhere and hatred of the enemy is increasing all the time. The News Bulletins with their glorification of bombing are enough to destroy the moral integrity of any society.

Lawn House.
June 8, 1940.

To L.K.

I am still in my room but am up at last; but allowed to do nix and hardly move as everything makes me breathless. It transpires that the long illness destroyed the elasticity of my lungs and that takes ages to come back (so far as it does come back). Meanwhile one just has to stay put and submit to having everything done for one. I can't say I like it much but it seems to be the Lord's idea for the present moment. . . .

Mickie has two entrancing kittens, Spitfire and Hurricane, and the family basket lives in my room quite a lot and is very engaging and helps to keep our minds off the war.

Dunkirk was so absorbing that for days one could think of nothing else. An acquaintance of Hubert's took his motor-boat there and says it was the finest week-end he ever had in his life. He came back with the boat riddled with shot.

What is so fine, and suggests that somehow our people have a certain amount of Christianity in their marrow even if not outwardly believing, is the way everyone agrees about the wonderful behaviour and unselfishness of the men—all quite patient, no pushing or attempt to get off before others, though it was "each man for himself."

Hampstead.
Trinity IV, 1940.

To M.C.

I have a feeling just now that one should try to make contact with one's friends not knowing how long normal communications will be possible to us, or what the next few weeks may bring. This shattering triumph of the evil will leaves one dazed and unable truly to realize anything. I suppose the Romans felt a bit like it, when Attila swept down on them and suddenly broke their security to bits. . . . Do you notice now how everything in the liturgy seems to have a new and piercing application? especially of course the Psalms and many of the collects too.

I am glad to think of you tucked away in the comparative security of the N.W. and surrounded by all the summer loveli-

ness. Everyone tells me the country has never been more beautiful and peaceful over against the destruction and hideousness
which is all we seem able to produce. Yet even war, it seems, isn't
spiritually sterile. . . . Were you not thrilled by all the accounts
of the patient endurance and unselfishness at Dunkirk?—no one
pushing and trying to get away first—and the splendid work of
the young Chaplains, going about those awful beaches helping
the men and giving the Sacraments. There was something supernatural in all that, an eternal quality triumphing over the horror
—and if our whole civilization has to be smashed under the Nazi
heel, that is what will survive. . . .

I can't settle to writing, can you? One is too conscious of
living on the brink of the precipice for it to have any reality. . . .

Lawn House.
June 20, 1940.
To L.K.

Thank you so much for your letter: I do think one values
these contacts with those one loves just now, when "earth's
foundations tremble" as never before. I feel more and more it is
all a great purging action of God, beyond our control, and using
the Nazis as His instruments. The way in which all initiative,
energy, surprise, is on their side, never on ours, is most extraordinary. . . .

Don't you think this is a lovely bit from De Caussade? It
seems to fit the present moment rather well:

"Let us remember these great truths: (1) There is nothing,
however small or apparently indifferent, which has not been
ordained or permitted by God—even to the fall of a leaf.
(2) That God is sufficiently wise, good, powerful and merciful
to turn those events which are apparently the most calamitous
to good and the advantage of those who know how to adore and
accept with humility all that His Divine and adorable will
permits."

Lawn House,
12 Hampstead Square, N.W.3.
June 27, 1940.

To W.V.

Yes, aren't the Psalms extraordinarily apposite just now? They seem to have come alive in an entirely new way. . . .

As for "merit" it is a horrid phrase but I feel it does stand for a spiritual reality; ultimately, the extent in which the Spirit of Christ indwells and dominates any particular soul or (the same thing) its entire submission to God's Will.

8 July, 1940.

To Maisie Spens.

I'm sure it is the sense of that coincidence of Majesty and Mercy [of God] and of our real position over against it which is wanted now—and this is part of the lesson which God's present action through history is to teach. Only apparently when everything is reeling do we begin to perceive the over-ruling presence of the Eternal Being. Don't you feel now that out of what at first was utter confusion bit by bit the Divine purifying purpose is beginning to emerge? Fear and bewilderment are giving place to a sort of hushed expectancy, as if people were beginning to realize the superhuman character of that which is taking place.

Lawn House,
Hampstead.
Aug. 12, 1940.

To S.T.

It was lovely to see you here and I do hope you will come again when you can.

As to W.'s views on Intercession, I entirely agree with you. . . . After all, Intercession is *not* asking God to do difficult things for Mr. Jones or Mr. Smith (though as you say sometimes when we are deeply concerned we can't help doing this). It is offering your will and love that God may use them as channels whereby His Spirit of mercy, healing, power, or light, may reach them and achieve *His* purposes in them. We can't do it unless we care, both for God's will and also for "the whole family of man"— but that certainly does not involve knowing all the details about everyone who asks our prayers. God knows the details—we need not. Probably the best kind of intercession is a quite general offering of oneself in union with our Lord—and that is what the total prayer of the Church for the world is. He prays in and through us, lifting up into the supernatural world all souls and causes and setting them before God's face—and it is our privilege to share that "lifting-up" process. Of course there is and must be a wide variety in the way people pray. For some, "crude petition" about Tommy's exam. or Aunt Jane's bronchitis is the only sort that is real. We each do what we can, mostly very badly. The point is that we do it with faith and love and offer it to God, who will take from it that act of will and love which alone really matters, and use it where and how He chooses. Perhaps the prayer we make here may find its fulfilment the other side of the world. Perhaps the help we were given in a difficult moment came from a praying soul we never knew! It is all a deep mystery and we should be careful not to lay down hard and fast rules. The variousness with which Grace works is one of the most wonderful things about it. It is a living and personal energy, not a machine, and makes a response of love to all our movements of love—even the most babyish. But our power of interceding for those quite unknown to us is very closely connected with our membership of the Church—it is her total prayer in which we take part. As individualists we could not do it with any sense of reality. I think we have to try to keep two sorts of Intercession going—this share in the Church's prayer and also our personal self-offering for persons or causes about which we care deeply—the corporate and individual sides of full religion.

Lawn House,
Hampstead.
Oct. 6, 1940.

To Mrs. HOLDSWORTH.

Thank you so much for your beautiful little book.[1] I waited to read it at leisure before writing, knowing that in your case this was a safe thing to do, as indeed it proved.

I am so grateful for much you say in it; for though I am not yet half through the sixties, illness *plus* age has come to mean a very thorough limitation of freedom and general slowing down and dependence on others; none of which is altogether easy to a person who prefers to do everything for herself at express speed!

But it's a marvellous discipline and introduces one to a complete fresh series of tests and opportunities and involves the discovery and acceptance of so much devoted kindness.

I specially loved your Sea of Honey and Sea of Peace, and that serenity and joy which so many people are letting slip now, just when the poor world needs it most. In one's desire to take one's share in the universal suffering, it is so easy to forget the positive value of joy. . . .

We are living here with friends and have shut up our own little house for the present, as it seems better just now to be part of a larger family. But it is a "warm spot" and we are bombarded from 8 p.m. to daylight regularly. I am afraid Falmouth too has had a bad time. What tragic folly and sin!

12 Hampstead Square, N.W.3.
23 October, 1940.

To NESTA DE ROBECK.

I have long been meaning to write and ask how you are getting on. We miss you and your visits so much though glad to think you are away from the noise and destruction that surrounds us and seeing something of this lovely autumn. "And wherever He passed He touched all things to beauty." It's so difficult to remember that among the swishes and thuds and shakings!

[1] *Seas of the Moon.* Friends Book Centre, 1940.

This household has remained very lucky and so far nothing has touched us, and we are now quite settled in to a basement and ground-floor existence. The whole district is practically without water since the Highgate Power Station was blown up last week. We fill buckets from the main in the morning and live on it as best we can during the day. However there is a certain odd satisfaction in being reduced to primitive conditions and having to practise abstinence about something one has always taken for granted. Sitting very loose to possessions and much simplification of life is certainly one of the lessons the Lord is going to teach us through the war, and we are beginning to get on with it now. Travelling facilities change almost from hour to hour as stations are bombed and roads closed, and shops are getting less and less able to deliver anything; so that a peculiar mixture of prudence and resignation is required in the conduct of life!

Underneath all this muddle and horror, however, I do have don't you? a queer underground feeling that something new *is* being prepared? a more realistic view of religion, a fresh sense of the overwhelming majesty of God, a shifting of emphasis to a more organic Christianity—not just socially but *supernaturally* organic. All sorts of separate little struggles seem to be going on in this direction, especially amongst the younger clergy, and the same trend appears in most of the new theological books, both Catholic and Anglican. With us it is all mixed up with the liturgic revival, which has now rather got its bit between its teeth and threatens to snuff out individual prayer altogether. What a pity it is that religious thinkers always seem to find it necessary to bang about between extremes instead of keeping steady and trying to remember the inclusiveness of God.

Lawn House,
Hampstead.
Wednesday [undated, 1940].

To D.E.

. . . He [Father Z.] seems to have been rather useful this time, and really got hold of your situation. I love the bit about it being grand to feel bedevilled and identified with all the sin and evil because that is like Christ—unconditional sacrifice of everything, even the most precious thing, our instinct for holiness and peace. I think you are very privileged, and standing up to the cost marvellously well. But it *is* costly, and naturally his first concern must be to protect your nervous and physical health. The compensating craving for some shelter and love seems just natural and rather humbling but not in the least sinful. No point in increasing strain by trying to behave more heroically than we really are, and rejecting the helps that nature provides. If Lawn House can give a bit of shelter and cherishing, we shall feel very pleased, warmed through and honoured.

I communicated some of your letter to M. who sends her very best love and says in her opinion there is no hard and fast difference between consecrated and unconsecrated—whatever is offered even in a roundabout way is taken and consecrated by the Lord. I think the Baron would have agreed with that.

All Saints, 1940.

To Maisie Spens.

... It [London] really does feel like living in the Inferno, perpetually confronted by the folly and wickedness of men. . . . Christians never (or hardly ever) seem able to take the gift of Power seriously, but when they do wonderful things happen— e.g. the Curé d'Ars. And that sense of impotence you describe is I feel sure almost universal in the Church at present, and is absolutely crippling in effect. I think your linking up of the gift of Power with Unity is fine, and gives a basis for intercession which many, baffled by the usual theories, will be able to accept. (It is astonishing how prevalent the crudest notions of intercession—"asking God for things," etc.—still are even among the clergy—and perhaps specially among the clergy!) . . .

... Ruysbroeck's great passages on the "fruitive unity of the Godhead," I have always thought to be among the most profound and inspiring writings of the medieval mystics.

... It is because our Christianity is so impoverished, so second-hand and non-organic, that we now feel we are incapable of the transformation of life which is needed to get humanity out of its present mess. . . . It all comes back of course (*a*) to the lack of a concrete, realistic faith; (*b*) to a failure to realize what Unity really involves. Yes, I do understand your distinction between trying to visualize and grasp all the sufferings and horrors, and accepting the pain of them. At the beginning of the war I tried to do the first, with deplorable results. The second is done *to* one rather than *by* one, which makes it all right, and is simply one's share in the life of the Church at this time.

Nov. 27, 1940.

To L.M.

There is so much to say about the sacrificial side of Christianity suitable for Lent and Passiontide, and it all fits in so well with much that is happening now, that you ought to find plenty of material.

I suppose there never *was* a time when people were more completely called to abandonment or encouraged to look beyond the world for the clue to life.

I enclose with this Maisie Spens' last utterance,[1] which I think *most* remarkable—one might make a good set of addresses on that theme, don't you think?

Gwynedd turned up on Saturday after a long absence—she had had the typhoid inoculation and been made rather ill by it. She told us that early one morning after a recent raid the head of their local Toc H heard a knock on the remains of the front-door, went down and found a stocky figure in mac. and tin-hat, who said, "I just looked in to see whether you were all right here." The head replied that they were; and the visitor said, "I'm glad to hear that. Carry on; and God bless you."

It was Winston Churchill. It appears he often goes out alone in the early morning and looks round districts where the blitz has been bad.

[1] *All Power is Given.* S.P.C.K., 3d.

Dec. 7, 1940.

To THE SAME.

I am trying to put together some Retreat notes and will send them soon, but I doubt their being much use to you. It is so difficult to use other people's material. I thought: 1st day, The preparatory conditions of the spiritual life—interior Poverty, Chastity and Obedience.

2nd day, The essence of it, the life of Faith, Hope and Charity.

Lots of scope and deals with fundamentals which I feel a retreat should always do, don't you?

Lawn House,
12 Hampstead Square, N.W.3.
St. Stephen, 1940.

To NESTA DE ROBECK.

Your lovely gift arrived on Christmas Eve and I began to read it at once. Thank you so very much for it. I think it is a most valuable book and casts a lot of fresh light on St. Francis's method of direction. I, certainly, had not realized how thorough was his dislike of rule-keeping and every sort of rigidity. It would do some modern directors and superiors good to ponder it! I think the whole section on "Characteristics of Salesian religious life" excellent both from the religious and psychological point of view. It is really much the same in principle as De Caussade's *Abandon* brought down to "brass tacks." The last half I have not read yet. I think what always puts me off St. Francis slightly is the fact that he is so exclusively the Apostle of the upper classes, and takes so seriously the position and duties of the Best Set. One is reminded so often of Wilber-force—"Yes indeed, my dear Duchess, as your Grace so truly observes, God is love." But all this no doubt he would claim as an example of his own doctrine of vocations—and certainly French society in his time badly needed an evangelist. And of course the great lines of his doctrine are of universal application and a great pity it is that they are not more generally applied. Müller brings them out in a remarkable way, doesn't he? Far better and more convincingly than Bremond, for instance: and shows so clearly their theological implications. It is odd to realize that on his showing St. Francis must almost have disliked St. John of the Cross! at any rate for general consumption. It *is* a good book and I'm so very grateful to you for it.

Christmas Day, 1940.

To U.V.

It was a great joy to hear of you and know how all your family are doing. How proud you must be of them—but I fear anxious too . . .

I loved your quotation about "the wild-weather of His outlying provinces"—most beautiful; I wonder where it comes from?

Lawn House,
12 Hampstead Square, N.W.3.
1 January, 1941.

To E. I. WATKIN.

Thank you so much for your Christmas letter—I had heard of you through Maisie Spens to whom you have given so much pleasure. . . . The paper on Christian power, which I understand you have seen, . . . seems to me extremely fine. I am glad it is going into the *Guardian* though I could wish it a wider circulation than that luckless paper ever seems able to achieve. I hope it will do better under your friend's editorship. There is room for a really intelligent paper representing the Anglican central position.

I am sorry I did not see your article on the Collet MS. Little Gidding has always interested me, but I found the Ferrar Papers rather disconcerting when they were published! The clash of temperaments in that strange household must have been terrific and very unlike what one understands as the religious life!

I wonder how *Pax* is getting on. So many of my fellow-pacifists seem to have fallen from the absolute position and think that Hitler's wickedness justifies participation in the war; but when we have won it they will be pacifists again. I cannot feel, however, that committing sin to cure sin is either Christianity or common sense, and the steady increase in bombast and self-righteous heroics is very displeasing, isn't it? Perhaps we have reached a level of collective sinfulness in which we *cannot* do right. I quite understand your deep satisfaction that your son is a monk. I remember his interest in theology as a boy, and wondered then which way his life would turn. How very interesting that he should have found those Winchester relics!

I am supposed to be writing a book on Christianity and the Spiritual Life for the Christian Challenge Series; but feel quite unable to get on with it—partly because a long stretch of ill-health has reduced my vitality, partly the difficulties of living in someone else's house, as we are doing now, with only a few of my books, and partly the general disturbance of the times!

I have just read C. S. Lewis's *Problem of Pain* in that Series, and think it *excellent*.

I am so glad you are working. Everyone likes *The Catholic Centre*. Father Biggart, C.R., preached on it a few weeks back at St. Augustine's, Queen's Gate, and told everyone to read it. The book on Lauds and Compline will be good to have and I hope you will soon find a publisher.

Lawn House,
12 Hampstead Square, N.W.3.
13 January, 1941.

To C. S. LEWIS.

When *Out of the Silent Planet* appeared, I was so excited by it that I had to write to you, and received a very kind reply. I hope this event, though long forgotten, may serve as a re-introduction now, because *The Problem of Pain* over which I have been brooding for the last week or so, has impressed me deeply, and opened up so many paths for exploration, that I feel I must talk to you about it.

The subject is one that I have thought about a good deal, which is why I am particularly grateful for your book and for the way in which you have related the fact of suffering to the eternal background of our life. Myself, I cannot get much beyond von Hügel's conclusion, that Christianity does not explain suffering but does show us what to do with it. To me the most satisfactory theory—and I am glad to see it is one that you are willing to accept—is that of a cosmic or angelic Fall, infecting the world with sin and its consequences. We can't, I think, attribute all the evil and pain of creation to man's rebellious will. Its far-reaching results, the suffering of innocent nature, the imperfection and corruption that penetrate all life, seem to forbid that. The horrors of inherited insanity, mental agonies, the whole economy of disease, especially animal disease, seem to point beyond man to some fundamental disharmony between creation and God. I sympathize a good deal with the listener who replied to every argument on the love of God by the simple question, "What about cancer in fish?"

It is your chapters on Human Wickedness, and Original Sin and the Fall that I so specially admire and feel to be immensely important and illuminating. I hope they will be widely read and digested by the clergy, especially those who keep on insisting what fine fellows we really are; and so reduce the amount of sentimental rubbish poured out from their pulpits, and deepen their conceptions of human personality. Original sin, which in my bright and clever youth I regarded as pure nonsense, now seems to me one of the most profound and far-reaching of truths. And your treatment of it is particularly valuable and satisfying because you have kept so clear of the mere theological say-so, and related it to our total experience of life. Our generation has a specially good chance of grasping this fact and all it implies if the psychologists will let it! I was very much impressed, too, by your picture of Paradisal man. It is this capacity for giving imaginative body to the fundamental doctrines of Christianity that seems to me one of the most remarkable things about your work.

Where, however, I do find it impossible to follow you, is in your chapter on animals. "The tame animal is in the deepest sense the only natural animal . . . the beasts are to be understood only in their relation to man and through man to God." This seems to me frankly an intolerable doctrine and a frightful exaggeration of what is involved in the primacy of man. Is the cow which we have turned into a milk machine or the hen we have turned into an egg machine really nearer the mind of God than its wild ancestor? This seems like saying that the black slave is the only natural negro. You surely *can't* mean that, or think that the robin redbreast in a cage doesn't put heaven in a rage but is regarded as an excellent arrangement. Your own example of the good-man, good-wife, and good-dog in the good homestead is a bit smug and utilitarian, don't you think, over against the wild beauty of God's creative action in the jungle and deep sea? And if we ever get a sideway glimpse of the animal-in-itself, the animal existing for God's glory and pleasure and lit by His light (and what a lovely experience that is!), we don't owe it to the Pekinese, the Persian cat or the canary, but to some wild free creature living in completeness of adjustment to Nature a life that is utterly independent of man. And this, thank Heaven, is the situation of all but the handful of creatures we have enslaved. Of course I agree that animals too are involved in the Fall and await redemption and transfiguration. (Do you remember Luther looking up from Romans viii. 21 and saying to his dog, "Thou too shalt have a little golden tail"?) And man is no doubt offered the chance of being the mediator of that redemption. But not by taming, surely? Rather by loving and reverencing the creatures enough to leave them free. When my cat goes off on her own occasions I'm sure she goes with God— but I do not feel so sure of her theological position when she is sitting on the best chair before the drawing-room fire. Perhaps what it all comes to is this, that I feel your concept of God would be improved by just a touch of wildness. But please do not take this impertinent remark too seriously.

I have run on far too long and must not weary you with my comments on your Heaven and Hell chapters, both of which I admire immensely—especially that on Heaven, which is a fitting conclusion to an impressive and beautiful book and lifts your thesis once for all to the level at which alone it has full significance. Thank you so much for it.

Lawn House,
12 Hampstead Square, N.W.3.
27 January, 1941.

To L.K.

... Thank you so much for letting me see all these.[1] I have enjoyed them, even though the result of the whole thing seems to me rather inconclusive. I was specially interested in Dr. Temple's answers to queries though I must say, in the teeth of Our Lord's remarks about riches, that "vocation to share the life of the wealthy in a spirit of detachment" made me smile. Once you were *really* detached from wealth, you would simply be unable to bear it a moment longer surely.

I thought the synopsis of Sir R. Acland's speech awfully good and am not surprised he made an impression. . . . But I quite agree with you that what people want from the Church and always have wanted are precise and simple directions on what they can and should do *now*—not only as regards special points like birth control or military service (and she can't even make up her mind about these) but about use of time and money, Christian conduct of business, education, etc. I don't agree with you, however, that Our Lord made the full demand for absolute surrender on all. He obviously made a great distinction between the "multitude" and the "little flock," and I think recognition of that, and a call to become part of the little flock (but, as you say, *in* the world) is probably what we need. Things like the Franciscan Tertiaries and the Jeunesse Ouvrière Catholique and the Filles de Marie are looking in the right direction. But it must not be only a devotional demand but something practical and far-reaching. I think it will come—we are only at the tentative stage now—and so far as possible one should throw one's weight in that direction.

[1] Papers about the Malvern Conference.

12 Hampstead Square.
Wed. in Holy Week, 1941.

To the Same.

This brings you my best love and all blessings for Easter.
I do hope you are now a bit less tired and over-strained and will
be able to enter into something of the supernatural peace and
wonder, even in your crowded and Martha-ish life. I was dreadfully sorry not to be able to answer your last letter; just then the
germ which had been rambling round the house attacked me and
turned to asthma and bronchitis and the Dr. sternly forbade
all letters and has now only partly raised the ban.

Well, I do largely agree with your R.M. It is always a difficult
problem to decide, when only external "good works" seem to
put a stopper on one's interior life, whether this *is* God's call to
the soul or one has made a mistake and chosen an unsuitable
job. If you are strong enough to stick it out, the mere fact of its
being very uncongenial does not matter. But the desire for self-
sacrifice may easily lead one into temptation that is too much for
one's delicate interior processes. After all, the very best thing
one can do for one's neighbour as well as for God, is to keep
spiritually alert, and anything which checks prayer is to be held
in suspicion. I may say practically everyone I hear from finds
that war-work does this: and you, with your inclination to go
"all out" on your jobs and not keep an inner reserve, are
particularly vulnerable!

But I cannot agree with Fr. A. about Mass without Communion. Bishop Frere and Baron von Hügel were solidly
against this and I hope you will take their deep and wise view
on this. . . . Quite right not to strain and struggle when prayer
is difficult; but just make a simple motion of abandonment to
God. But as to Communion, both would say it is something
done by God to us, not by us towards God; and even though
we felt actually repelled we must still receive it. I feel no doubt
at all that this is right; and is a deeper, simpler, more direct view
of our relationship to God than all the stuff about Church
discipline, etc.

Meanwhile a holiday is clearly indicated as soon as you can
contrive it: and in the future better management of your

resources and a certain moderation in your self-giving. This does not mean "ca' canny."

Of course all these suggestions must be laid before God who will then (if you can give Him time and opportunity!) show by His pressure on your soul how you should act. But to have got yourself into a jam in which you can no longer feel that pressure, is to destroy the chief source of your usefulness to Him!

12 Hampstead Square, N.W.3.
27 April, 1941.

To E. I. WATKIN.

Yes, I have never felt any inclination to change my views about the war. As horror is piled on horror it becomes more and more clear that one cannot fight evil by the use of evil. Of course I think *none* of us have any idea of what the real and spiritual events are, which have this awful repercussion on the surface of life. We are witnessing Armageddon without knowing what Armageddon really means and so have not the material for forming a considered judgment on what our own action can and should be. But to adhere to the Eternal God, and help others to steady their lives in the same way, must always be right. I understand so well and sympathize with your own feeling that you had not sufficiently given yourself to your original *attrait*. But I suppose the principle of *abandon* means that we always envisage our situation as it is *now* and give ourselves to God in that, without considering the past?

Indeed I will pray for you "according to my poor cunning" and hope you will for me. Our future seems very dark and uncertain as so much we thought permanent has fallen away.

30 April, 1941.

To MAISIE SPENS.

. . . the whole idea of the Communion of Praise must be free and loose-knit and nothing in the way of an "Order" attempted. Apart from all else this would at once bring in denominational difficulties, and give the idea of some specially intense group in contrast to the rest of the Church. I feel so sure myself that this movement and others like it—i.e. Brother Edward's "daily waiting on the Holy Spirit"—are small surface manifestations of some great movement in the supernatural, some vast and transforming action of the Spirit, which will end the present chaos, and also the divisions of the Church. . . . People hardly seem to realize *how* remarkable it is that Cardinal Hinsley and the Archbishop and the Free Church people should be writing letters and acting together in the interests of the Christian life. Yet this is happening more and more, and is I'm sure one of the manifestations of the great things preparing in the Invisible World.

. . . Of course printing is terribly difficult now but we must get a lot of it done if possible, if the *central idea* of union in adoration, with all that flows from it, is to be made known—and I'm sure it is intended to be made known.

May 3, 1941.

To K.N.

People sometimes get St. John of the Cross by the tail! Self-occupation, including religious self-occupation, is always wrong, though often disguised as an angel of light.

This is the first thing I should say—Just plain self-forgetful-ness is the greatest of graces. The true relation between the soul and God is the perfectly simple one of a childlike dependence. Well then, *be* simple and dependent, acknowledge once for all the plain fact that you have nothing of your own, offer your life to God and trust Him with the ins and outs of your soul as well as everything else! Cultivate a loving relation to Him in your daily life; don't be ferocious with yourself because that is treating badly a precious (if imperfect) thing which God has made.

As to detachment—what has to be cured is desiring and hang-ing on to things for their own sake and because you want them, instead of offering them with a light hand and using them as part of God's apparatus; people seem to tie themselves into knots over this and keep on asking themselves anxious questions on the subject—but again, the cure is more simplicity! They *must* shake themselves out of their scruples. The whole teaching of St. John of the Cross is directed to perfecting the soul in charity, so that all it does, has, says, is, is transfused by its love for God.

This is not a straining doctrine, though a stern one, as of course it does mean keeping all other interests in their place and aiming at God all the time.

5 May, 1941.

To C.D.

... No—I had not heard of the meetings you mention; but I never do go to meetings nowadays nor, I fear, have I much belief in their usefulness. All this discussion about a "Christian Society," a "New Christian England," etc., seems so entirely on the surface, doesn't it? And shows no realization of the drastic changes and awful sufferings which must be endured before anything of the kind becomes possible. I agree with you in thinking Hitler a "Scourge of God"—but it is idle to begin to think yet of what we shall or can do when he has finished his course! Probably very little of what we know as the ordinary framework of life will survive.

The new life when it comes, I think, will not be the result of discussions, plans, meetings, etc., but will well up from the deepest sources of prayer. I see some signs of the beginning of this movement, and one is the new and marked tendency of the various Christian bodies to draw together and work together. You may have seen some of the writings of the Abbé Couturier on this. I think it one of the most religious phenomena of our times. A great friend of mine, Maisie Spens, a very unusual person and something of a prophetess, is greatly concerned in it, and during Lent she got a number of R.C. and Anglican Communities to offer their whole prayer for this intention of spiritual unity. Of course a great many individuals of all denominations also joined in. The next period of special prayer begins on June 27 and ends on the Transfiguration: I should be so glad if you cared to take part. I enclose a copy of one of her "meditations" in case you are interested.

12 Hampstead Square, N.W.3.
12 May, 1941.

To MILDRED BOSANQUET.

Yes—I am still a pacifist though I agree with you about the increasing difficulty of it. But I feel more and more sure that Christianity and war are incompatible, and that *nothing* worth having can be achieved by "casting out Satan by Satan." All the same, I don't think pacifists at the moment should be controversial, or go in for propaganda. The nation as a whole obviously feels it right to fight this war out, and must I think do it. I think Hitler is a real "scourge of God," the permitted judgment on our civilization; and there are only two ways of meeting him—war, or the Cross. And only a very small number are ready for the Cross, in the full sense of loving and unresisting abandonment to the worst that may come. So those who see that this alone is *full* Christianity should be careful not to increase the disharmony of life by trying to force this difficult truth on minds that are closed against it, and will only be exasperated by it. At present I think one can do little but try to live in charity, and do what one can for the suffering and bewildered. We are caught up in events far too great for us to grasp, and which have their origin in the "demonic powers" of the spiritual world. Let us hope that the end of all the horror and destruction may be a purification of life!

Lawn House,
Hampstead.
Easter IV (1941).

To E.N.

Don't worry about your prayer! Everyone I know feels in a "rotten state" and general condition of muddle and distraction. The situation is a bit too thick for us—but we must just do our best! I am sure a quite general waiting on God, and giving oneself and all one cares about totally and trustfully into His hands, should be the substance of it. A very deeply spiritual woman I know says that the Lord's Prayer, Gloria Patri, and Behold the handmaid of the Lord, are the only prayers she can use now! Though it may seem play-acting because our feelings are over-strained and numb—so long as we pray not as individuals but part of the Church, it shares the reality of the Church's total prayer—and as the essence of that total prayer is "Thy Will be done" this overrides our inevitable human desire for victory.

I will try to remember your poor friend though I'm terribly bad at intercession for individuals.

Lawn House,
12 Hampstead Square, N.W.3.
Whitsunday, 1941.

To Z.A.

Will you accept the enclosed if it appeals to you?[1] and tell anyone else who might care for it. It is part of the Reunion Movement begun by the Abbé Couturier; who considers reunion *can* only begin by union in prayer and thence spread to the surface. Many R.C. and Anglican communities have taken it up eagerly and Maisie Spens who is much concerned with it has written some really remarkable pamphlets I'd like you to see.[2]

5 June, 1941.

To Maisie Spens.

I have been immersed in Kierkegaard—some new ones in English lately published, and all of his latest period, when he was much more spiritualized than in the first part of his career. At his best he really is superb—and just what all are needing now, though too drastic in his demands ever to be popular.

Trinity, 1941.

To M.C.

You have been so much in my mind lately and I've been meaning to write—but it's extraordinary that tho' I live such a quiet life now, mostly in one room, the arrears of letters never get done. You as billeting officer must be very busy—what an

[1] An invitation to join in forty days of prayer.
[2] *All Power is Given* and *As One in Praising*. S.P.C.K., 3d. each.

exacting but as you say very *very* worth while job. This mixing-up of people, specially children, will surely be one of the few good things to come out of this time of horror. I feel more and more to be living through the Apocalypse. I remain pacifist but I quite see that at present the Christian world is not "there" and attempts to preach it at the moment can only rouse resistance and reduce charity. Like you I think the final synthesis must reconcile the lion and the lamb—but meanwhile the crescendo of horror and evil and wholesale destruction of beauty is hard to accept. . . .

TO A FRIEND

1923–41

Heavenly King, Paraclete, Spirit of Truth, present in all places and filling all things, Treasury of good and Choir-master of life: come and dwell within us, cleanse us from all stains and save our souls.—*Liturgy of St. John Chrysostom.*

Jan. 19, 1923.

. . . As to the "degrees of prayer," it is not really uncanny, for most of us travel by that road more or less, though of course we each feel our own experience to be unique! As you recognize yourself there do read *Les Graces d'Oraison* by Poulain and *Holy Wisdom* by Augustine Baker. It's not in the least "out of order" that you should find yourself at the levels of the "simplicity" and the "quiet"—but you may, probably will, lose these, perhaps more than once, before they become truly established and habitual. That vivid awareness could not go on all the time—it has to grow steadier. But the great thing is not to try to do too much of yourself, but leave it to happen. Of course too it is of primary importance for anyone committed to this way of life, to set aside, so far as possible, the same time each day for prayer and recollection, and it is also far better to do it always in the same place. This time should be so used, whether you are in the light or not—at least ½ hour daily. It is essential to you as training if for nothing else. I mean this of course in addition to any ordinary morning and night prayers. Do not be too much cast down when the joy goes, will you? It is the steady course, not the ecstasy, that counts in the end. . . .

Jan. 25, 1923.

I am not a bit unpleasant about sins and penances . . . but apt to be disagreeable on the church question. I stood out against it myself for so long and have been so thoroughly convinced of

311

my own error, that I do not want other people to waste time in the same way.

Nothing can save you from narrow intensity and "vertical-ness" if you reject all the corporate and institutional side—always rather repugnant to people of our temperament. I do not mean that perpetual church-going and sermons (!) are necessary, but *some* participation in the common religious life and some sacramental practice. In the long run you will find it has a steadying and mellowing effect, and will help too to carry you over the blank times. You will find regular training a great help too. A simple rule, to be followed whether one is in the light or not, gives backbone to one's spiritual life, as nothing else can. You should fix it now, during this time of peace and joy; and let it be decidedly less than you feel you can do now. . . . If you fall later into a state in which you cannot, without strain, practise meditation or mental prayer, you can spend the time in spiritual reading, only try always to keep it intact and not use it for other things.

It is no trouble to write to you—but a great pleasure and privilege; and easy, because you trust me enough to write intimately, for which I am very grateful. Only please never assume that what I suggest is necessarily right for you, if you have a distinct feeling against it.

Feb. 7, 1923.

But you MUST settle down and quiet yourself. Your present state if encouraged will be in the end as bad for you spiritually as physically. I know it is not easy to do. Nevertheless it will in the nature of things come about gradually and I want you to help it all you know. If you allow rapture or vehemence to have its way too much, you risk a violent reaction to dryness, whereas if you act prudently you will keep the deep steady permanent peace, in the long run more precious and more fruitful than the dazzling light. But you won't do it by direct struggle—did you ever quiet a baby, or your dog, or any other excited bit of life, by direct struggle? You will do it, please, by steadily, gradually and quietly turning your thoughts and prayers not so much to the overwhelming joy and wonder, as to the deep steadfastness of God, get gently accustomed to it, at home with it, *rest* in it. Let your night prayers be rather short, very quiet, more or less on a set form, not too "mental" and in the line of feeling of Psalm xxiii. Let yourself sink down into God's Love in complete dependence, and even though the light does seem to rush in on you, keep as it were the eyes of your soul shut, intent on falling asleep in Him. . . . During the day, doing your work, etc., it is I know very hard not to be distracted and absorbed. But remember you have no more right to be extravagant over this than over any other pleasure or craving. It is true you can and probably will find a balance in which you will live in a quiet spirit of prayer, able at all leisure moments—and in the middle of your work—to turn simply and gently to God. But this will come only when all vehemence is eliminated.

Consider the sequence of daily acts, and your external interests as part of your service, part of God's order for you, and as having a proper claim on your undivided attention.

Take *special* pains now to keep up fully or develop some definite non-religious interest, e.g., your music. Work at it, consider it an obligation to do so. It is most necessary to your spiritual health; and you will very soon find that it has a steadying effect. "Good works" won't do—it must be something you really like for its own sake. (When this prescription was given to me by the wisest of saints, I objected strongly, but lived to bless him for his insistence! Now I hand it on to you.)

Otherwise, just for the present, do go as quietly as you can, about your work, etc., I mean. Avoid strain. If you could take a few days off and keep quite quiet it would be good, but if this is impossible at any rate go along gently, look after your body, don't saturate yourself the whole time with mystical books. I know you do feel tremendously stimulated all round; but remember the "young presumptuous disciples" in the *Cloud*! Hot milk and a thoroughly foolish novel are better things for you to go to bed on just now than St. Teresa.

Remember as a general rule, running right through the spiritual life, that the more any particular aspect or exercise

313

attracts you, the more ordered, regular, moderate should be your use of it.

Don't have any lurking fear that you will lose the light by this kind of discipline—just the opposite, you will steady and tend to retain it.

February 21, 1923.

It is physically as much as spiritually I want you quieted and normalized. The body must not be driven beyond its strength. . . . Your nerves and mind have been subjected to an abnormal strain and must be wisely looked after for a bit. Otherwise just gently encourage the quieting-down process in all possible ways and give outlet to your new zest in your active and mental as well as your purely religious life. I would never dream of calling you a Young Presumptuous Disciple! What am I to use such language? "An infant crying in the night" as the poet said. I merely wanted to draw your attention to what happened to those who "travailled their fleshly hearts outrageously in their breasts." The Choral Society sounds quite a good outlet!

If you should find you tend to dry up during your fixed time of prayer—I don't mean merely become passive—*don't* try to tune yourself up again, but at once take to congenial vocal or book-prayers with intervals of silence if you like; nothing forced.

I look forward so much to seeing you. Give me as much notice as you can, when you want to come.

March 1, 1923.

I am delighted to hear of the novels, but please leave St. Teresa, Ruysbroeck and Co. alone for a bit and don't deliberately practise mental prayer either. I know this is a "hard saying" and I don't mean I want you to put any strain on yourself to keep off it, but don't encourage yourself in it. . . . So long as you feel "peaceful and rested" well and good—just stay there and be content. You see, the whole point is, there is as you know quite well, a psychic as well as a spiritual side to all these experiences—and it is in your case the psychic side which has been too fully roused and upset your equilibrium. The spiritual side is always deep, quiet, peaceful, humbling. All this you have and this is the valuable part and absolutely safe. Keep close to that and gently move away from the vivid, passionately rapturous type of reaction. It is not God but your too eagerly enjoying psyche which keeps you awake and tears you to bits with an over-exciting joy. This was inevitable for a bit—but please get away from it now!

You will think I give nothing but unpleasant lectures. However I promise not to refer to the subject when you come, unless you do first!

But do be limp and get well.

May 2, 1923.

I was wondering when you would write again, but never dreamed of that lovely keepsake falling, as it were, out of the letter. . . . It is beautiful and I do like it so much.

Some of your letter I like too, but not the part confessing that you are still really ill and plainly in a condition when a little spiritual vegetation would suit you better than the demanded revision of your rule of prayer. I still think one or at most 1¼ hours in the day for deliberate continuous prayer is sufficient; it is as much, and probably more than you will manage without strain when this exceptional illumination fades—and that is the real test. It may be in two or three separate portions, as you like. I do not count short 5-minute recollections or aspirations during the day. These you are quite free to do so long as they do not interfere with necessary activities. In fact the occasional momentary prayers are excellent and should become habitual. As to reading, something rather less advanced and more concerned with laying solid foundations than the *Sparkling Stone* would be better I should think, and please do not *only* read mysticism. Balance it with some good logical stuff; and use the New Testament as material for meditation in preference to anything else; it is steadying, and after all, if the other things do not lead you back to that, they are not much good.

I think a Retreat of not more than seven days would be very

good for you. . . . Most of the conducted Retreats are only about three days but you can usually stay on a bit longer as a private retreatant and get the benefit of the silence and general atmosphere. . . . Do take care of yourself—I mean your body, not your soul! make up your mind to some sort of complete rest. The tramp steamer sounds nice.

June 27, 1923.

The Retreat House I always go to is Pleshey. I do advise you to go to a conducted Retreat; you are more sure of unbroken silence and you get the atmosphere better. But by all means stay on a day or two by yourself afterwards. . . . No restrictions except a general warning against over-intensity. . . .

Go to Communion as often as you can and weave the idea (and practice) of spiritual communion into your prayers. You've got to get rid of that obsession of sin, you know; it's a crudeness, an inferior sort of humility at best—and really rooted in a disguised self-occupation! I've had it badly so I know all about it. Look at Christ and not at yourself. Regard the inclination to useless remorse as a temptation. There is not much to choose between the best and the worst in us, seen in the spiritual light, is there? Just let the love of God wash over the whole thing. It's the only Christian attitude.

Now as to your rule of making Christ the ultimate arbiter as to the spirit of every action, of course that is right. As to the concrete fact of each action, don't fall into excesses. If He did not go to Italy, He visited His friends, obviously enjoyed beauty, satisfied the poetic and imaginative outlook so clearly reflected in the Gospel. You are to be both world-accepting and world-renouncing. This He clearly taught and teaches.

Also kindly re-read and ponder the parable of the Two Camels in *Ferishtah's Fancies*—a very wise work! This need not count as spiritual reading, though it is. And get as long and complete a holiday as you can and regard it as your first religious duty to keep quiet and in a state of gentle acceptance and not bang about.

The Chapel — Pleshey Retreat House

October 7, 1923.

Do bring yourself to realize that a life of complete surrender, inward poverty and correspondence with Our Lord, has been and can be lived without the use of physical penances. . . .

If you are feeling so much as you say the attraction of Holy Communion and beginning to have the idea that a more Catholic type of practice may be God's will for you, I should very deeply regret any action on your part which shut you off from this possibility. I have felt all along that a regular sacramental practice was what you needed and now you begin to see what it means it is doubtful whether you will get on in the long run without it. I shall never say one word to press you to join the Anglican or any other church. You must only do so if you clearly feel it is God's call for you. Do not confuse the issue with scruples about Holy Communion being a "spiritual self-indulgence." You know at the bottom of your heart it is nothing of the kind and is not to be resorted to for its sweetness but as a positive source of strength. If you do become a regular and frequent communicant you will have to do it with absolute determination to continue it steadily in darkness or in light and will find in this a degree of discipline you probably do not realize yet. . . .

After being myself both a non-sacramentalist and a sacramentalist, there is no doubt at all left in my own mind as to what is the simplest and most direct channel through which grace comes to the soul.

November 6, 1923.

I am so dreadfully sorry for you and do not suppose anything I say will cheer you up much. But I do want you to realize that this was *absolutely bound* to happen sooner or later—not merely to you, but to any soul whatever. No one—not the saints—has ever had continuous illumination: and the very vividness of your experience has to be paid for by a corresponding reaction. I am so glad you realize it was not "quite right" or peaceful enough. I knew it—but the least hint that it had a psychic element seemed to upset you. I believe you do not know at all yet, though you will, what the deep and true peace really is.

Now do, my very dear child, take this grand, indeed crucial opportunity rightly. You've desired suffering—this is your opportunity of suffering and of testing the purity and disinterestedness of your love. Your whole spiritual future depends on how you take this trial. If you are quiet and steady I do not suppose the darkness will long be unrelieved. Read again St. John of the Cross, *Dark Night*, Book I; I think you will see where you are. A more blessed place to be really, than in the midst of "sensible consolations"—which, however entrancing, are mere snares unless they lead to self-loss.

Now as to practice. Keep up, however it repels you, regular Communions (once a week if you can, not more); other churchgoing I leave to you. Quite short morning and night prayers. No strain. No attempt at mental prayer. But please keep intact the time you had for mental prayer; do needlework, gardening, any quiet and congenial work in it, but don't melt it into your day—and if the unsought impulse to prayer then comes to you, yield gently to it. Make no struggle to recover fervour. . . . Above all, remember all the time, God is moulding you as much in darkness as in light and turn to Him with gratitude and acceptance.

November 16, 1923.

The more you can avoid strain, remain quiet, trustful and accepting, the sooner light will return. Offer what you suffer in this darkness to Christ, it's worth offering, and if you do this, the worst of the sting will go.

I do not think either St. John of the Cross *or* your director (a pretty pair! why not Jehovah and a black beetle?) fails to realize that you feel very small indeed. It would be most deplorable if you did *not*! Any soul feeling the dark side of the Divine action is necessarily overwhelmed with its own "nothingness." All the same, what he says does apply to you and what you are suffering is what countless others have borne before. Of course the sense of being forsaken is the worst bit, as it was the worst bit of the Cross. I shall be glad if you emerge from this to a more moderate and quiet type of experience, for indeed these sudden and violent alternations are enough to tear you to bits and you must take real care of yourself. . . . Do not struggle for concentration in reading. That mental deadness is part (a psychic part!) of the whole condition of exhaustion in which you now are. But all parts of it can be turned by you to great spiritual profit, if they bring you to a perfectly quiet and patient waiting on God's will for you. . . . Think of yourself as a child in a dark room from which the light has been taken, in order that you may quiet down and sleep a little. Love took away the light and at the right time will bring it back.

November 24, 1923.

Do arrange your life to get in as many Communions as you can, for thus you will get really, though not directly in consciousness, the strength you have been getting in contemplative prayer. You have been relying too much on experience and not enough on the facts of faith, which is the path you have now got to follow for a bit. When you feel that impulse to prayer, try to stay as it were in the dark for a bit with God and accept the conditions under which you have now got to live. Quiet acceptance and common-sense are the way to get fervour back again. Repulsive programme, isn't it?

December 14, 1923

It's not the least use reintroducing the physical penance question. As you were so insistent I even went so far as to ask Baron von Hügel (who is my "final court of appeal" on all questions of the inner life) in an impersonal way, what would be the correct advice to give on this point; and he replied, to leave all severe penances alone, their renunciation being a far more wholesome discipline than their use. Considering that he has directed hundreds of souls of all sorts of different types and is himself a saint, I do not think you can go against this, can you? You are quite mistaken if you think anything of this sort would bring back fervour and light: on the contrary, keep quiet, do not concentrate on religion, let the reaction spend itself and in the end, all will be well. You are in God's hands and He can't hurt you. Do rest your soul on that. As to "God's absence"; it is of course illusion; it is He who casts the shadow that distresses you so.

Do not hesitate to write if it helps.

January 26, 1924.

How I wish I could get out of your head the idea that the love of Christ is "withdrawn" from you and that you have "no spiritual life." You are far more truly living the spiritual life holding on through this darkness than when you were enjoying yourself in consolations. And one proof of this is that people come to you for help and you are able to deal with them. Why be vexed about that? It is extremely good for you to do it, as well as a blessed privilege. Certainly do not tell them "you have no spiritual life" or indeed unless inevitable, anything at all about yourself! There's no occasion to feel hypocritical, and even when, as so often happens, those who come to us for advice are so immeasurably better than we are ourselves, keep it all on impersonal levels. God sends such work and will help you to do it.

February 25, 1924.

Ovaltine! gentle aspirations! no strain and no fixed rule! preference given to secular interests! Be one-tenth as kind to yourself as you were to me and you will do very nicely. . . . It was such a perfectly happy week and I loved every moment of it, both the sacred and the profane!

The poem[1] *will* come true for you—not "perhaps"! I am not dissatisfied, though it is horrid to have to stand by and see you suffer. But it is the sort of pain which is one of the greatest of the soul's privileges and makes "affirmative religion" look

[1] These verses were found written on the fly-leaf of a copy of *Immanence* after E.U. had left.

pretty thin. How can we expect God's action to be other than
torture to us; weak and unpurified and yet sensitive things as
we are?

> Come with birds' voices when the light grows dim
>   Yet lovelier in departure and more dear:
> While the warm flush hangs yet at heaven's rim,
>   And the one star shines clear.
>
> Though the swift night haste to approaching day
>   Stay Thou and stir not, brooding on the deep:
> Thy secret love, Thy silent word let say
>   Within the senses' sleep.
>
> Softer than dew. But when the morning wind
>   Blows down the world, O Spirit! show Thy power:
> Quicken the dreams within the languid mind
>   And bring Thy seed to flower!

E.U.

May 20, 1924.

Of course a life of adoration and surrender is not selfish!
What next in the way of scruples? Do you think the seraphim
Isaiah saw were monuments of spiritual self-indulgence? If that
is your call it is a very blessed one and to be received with deep
gratitude in spite of the suffering it must entail. But I am grieved
for all the physical pain, though somehow when you are not
too overcome by it to do anything but just bear it, it too can
open up heavenly vistas with the Cross at their far end. I
wonder whether beads will help you at all just now—usually I
rather dislike them—but when ill and weak one can drowsily
run them through one's fingers as a link to one's aspirations;
keeping thus gently recollected without strain I find. DON'T
do it if it tires you ever, or if you find it is no help. But in case
you do find it nice I send you a heavily-blessed Dominican
rosary I got for a friend of mine now dead, who came as near
sanctity in her ten years as a Christian, as anyone I've known.
I'd love you to have them anyhow.

One can make endless devotional patterns on them. I rather
like this one:

Anima Christi or *Jesu dulcis memoria* on the Cross, and on the small beads *O Sacred Heart of Jesus! in Thee is all my trust* and the *Paternoster* on the big beads; or if that is too long, *If Thou wilt that I be in Light, be Thou blessed for it; and if Thou wilt that I be in darkness, still be Thou blessed for it! Light and darkness, life and death, bless ye the Lord!* . . .

Glad you like Otto; he has got hold of something *real*, hasn't he? I was sorry he trailed off into Luther when he might have illustrated from real saints; and of course he does not get the intimate, penetrating other side, the sacramental and homely —just as "irrational" as the "numinous" and perhaps in a way more productive of abject feelings!

June 20, 1924.

You need not have worried about penances and mortifications need you? When the hour strikes they are there all right; and so on with everything else, only never the expected thing. It is lovely to think you are happier inwardly, though still so "tried and tempested" outwardly. Sink down gently into that self-abandoned peace all you can, it is there that your real treasures are hid.

As to Communion, well it would have been a solace to you: but it is the comfort, not the grace, you are missing. "Every time we think with love of the well-beloved, He is once more our meat and our drink." I love that bit, don't you?

Yes, as you say, the vastness does open up more and more and we shrink more and more; and get more our real shape and size in the process. It is when one gets a glimpse of the Completeness and Perfection of God's operation right through, that it is so lovely, isn't it? Then we cease to matter and at once we are in Him and quite happy, even though not consciously "consoled."

August 7, 1924.

I'm very glad to hear you have managed to get recollected again. The sort of prayer you describe is all right, I am sure. In fact you ought to make up your mind to it as your average prayer and a great deal to be grateful for at that. Anything beyond is an added grace and never to be expected continuously and in your present state of health would be far too much for you. So stay quiet and be content with that sense of dim nearness, won't you? You do not require sugar-feeding now and so aren't having it. No! I don't mind much about your rule. Only avoid all strain and just remain quietly with God as long as you feel called so to do. Let your side be entirely response and acceptance—no forcing of the situation—and that will be all right.

As to what you can *do*: I feel pretty confident, and all the more since you've had to weather this darkness, that your real call is contemplative: and this fits in well enough with your physical situation, doesn't it?

Now, contemplation which is exclusively of the *à deux* type certainly does run a grave risk of falling into spiritual selfishness. But a true contemplative vocation (whether lived in or out of the world) is surely not this at all. It involves (in the end— gradually—never with violence) the development of a spiritual force by which you exercise not only adoration, but also mediatorship—a sort of redemptive and clarifying power working on other souls—a tiny co-operation in the work of Christ.

This is the thought I'd like you to keep before you. And it will cover not only everything you have to suffer, physically and every way, but actual work in and for other souls. It is only to my mind when thus understood, that the vocation to prayer achieves real greatness. Of course the side of personal communion and adoration remains primary—through that comes the food, power, impetus and peace—but all that comes thus is to be used again, eventually, for the purposes of God.

I do not mean you are to change your prayer at all *now*, or struggle to do intercessions, etc. But regard your present phase as educative, and respond to it faithfully and quietly. The rest will come at the right time. You may have more time for this quiet receptive prayer; but on days when you feel dry, exhausted etc., you are quietly to drop it.

"Where Thou art, there is Heaven" is a nice little aspiration I think, don't you?

I am glad you like Lucie-Christine. But if you read her carefully (and after all it is only *extracts* from her *Journal*) she has plenty of times of obscurity and desolation. Yes, her fervours do make one blush like the "Golden Fountain" lady. But after all she never meant 'em to be printed poor dear, and French is an unfortunate language. Even St. Catherine of Siena in modern French would look pretty bad!

August 28, 1924.

After your remarks about Fénelon and health (with which I rather agree!) I suppose further reference to this subject would be tactless. Otherwise descriptions of invalids driving in the cows *are* calculated to provoke a "Surtout, chère Madame, évitez les fatigues!" The Baron dosed me with Fénelon at one time, till I told him that a Perfect Gentleman giving judicious spiritual advice to Perfect Ladies was no good to me—since when his name has not been mentioned between us! . . .

You must expect and accept fluctuations. You won't mind them nearly so much after a bit. . . . Try not to be torn to bits by the longing, it's so bad for you and so useless—and you are just as much there really in the dark as in the light, aren't you? Heaven would still be Heaven if we had to go in with blinkers on.

Perugia.

Feast of the Exaltation of the Cross.

You know quite well it is Fénelon's moderation and avoidance of introspection that is so good for you; and not his gentility! I too am much more at home among cows and pigs than elsewhere and so glad you had a little of their company. . . .

I am sure you ought not to kneel! Like you I always want to and find it much harder if one doesn't. But it is possible to cure oneself of that! The most contemplative person I know always sits and shuts her eyes: like Rolle! It is just habit and you had better begin to acquire it. So handy in many ways, especially for short snatches of recollection when one may be interrupted. Shutting one's eyes and thinking of oneself as kneeling before the Cross is sometimes rather a help. . . .

Do not overdo things or forget how necessary it is to keep external interests going if you want to avoid the spiritual *ennui* which comes from overstrain. When I said more time for prayer, I didn't mean *all* the time!

September 24, 1924.

. . . the prayerful attitude is more valuable for you than long concentration on the prayerful *act*, which is only one way, and not *the* way of living the contemplative life.

October 24, 1924.

I've given two addresses this week, or rather the same one twice . . . on the need for Retreats and all that they stand for. . . . I spoke of Joy, and the Chairman said "Miss Underhill has told us we must be Cheerful Christians." I nearly yelled "I didn't!!" Imagine it! Like putting the loveliest of the angels into Jaeger combinations!

. . . Do not fuss about using this part of your life well! Of course you will "keep on" as you call it, or rather, He will keep on with you. There are times when "suffering the divine action" is the main part of one's job. . . .

I never got much value out of Pascal except the *Mystère* and the *Amulet* myself. . . .

Holy Innocents Day, 1924.

Do you like this aspiration which came to me on a tiny card, "Lord! for Thy great pain, have mercy on my little pain!" I think it's rather a lovely one: it is from Margery Kempe.

The other new one I have liked is, "I lose myself, wondering at Him"—from the old Cowley Saint, Richard Benson.

THE LETTERS OF EVELYN UNDERHILL

Yes! though I'll never believe God likes or means illness *per se*—I am sure in its weakness and suffering it is among the most valuable ways in which He can work on us and we complete our surrender to Him. Although conscious recollection is often beyond us, we *do* then remain in true interior solitude with Him and are obliged to suffer His working on our souls.

Of course because you've been trying to take it right, it has not impaired (but improved) you as an instrument of His purposes. . . .

January 25, 1925.

I'll bring or lend you when we meet St. François de Sales' *Letters* which are full of splendid, sane stuff. As for Thérèse de l'Enfant Jesus, she is NOT a model for you! A "case" inclined to tepid and agreeable paths who read it, asked me whether she was to regard it as "murder or suicide?" and I certainly think, without daring to criticize the special calls of the saints, that there is an element of this sort in it.

As to self-abnegation: be ready to accept every mortification and sacrifice God asks of you in unruffled peace—but No Cross-Hunting! Your consecration means tranquil abiding in love with Christ, through ups and downs and lights and darknesses—just as they come, without self-will, doesn't it? But requests for yet another dose of powder without jam, are only inverted self-will! *Far* the best way to deal with self-love, is to let it die of starvation because you are wholly concentrated on His love, within which you can safely love all things, from your dog to the Seraphim, can't you?

April 16, 1925.

NO! prayer for other people is emphatically not an extra; but part of one's daily rule. It must come within the two hours for prayer and meditation. Sorry! But after all, if one is spending the time with God, does it matter very much exactly how one is spending it?

July 16, 1925.

The Conference about "deepening the spiritual life of the Church" was a most interesting and illuminating affair. A mixture of eminent and progressive ecclesiastics of all parties (4 Bishops and quite a bunch of Canons) with boys and girls from the Universities (who told the Bishops without any tact or reserve just what they thought about the Church), representatives of Missionary Societies, Studdert-Kennedy, the Superior of Cowley and so forth. Most of the mature persons freely confessed to feeling "spiritually impotent and tired"; but when we were all asked to give $\frac{1}{4}$ of an hour a day to prayer for the objects of the Conference, a surprising number were alarmed by this dreadful demand! And after a little discussion there was a plaintive yelp from one clerical collar to presiding Bishop: "My Lord! is this $\frac{1}{4}$ of an hour to be *in addition* to our ordinary devotions?"

We now form a more or less permanent body and meet again in October. Everyone on it I think is really keen, though the way they put things might suggest to an outsider that there are at least 12 different religions in the English Church. We meet in the Jerusalem Chamber and have silent prayer before the High Altar of Westminster Abbey at 10 p.m. which is rather wonderful. . . . Oh yes! I am sure it's true we each have to discover (with help) all the real things for ourselves and don't really understand what we read—though we often think we do!—till we have managed to practise at least some of it. . . .

August 28, 1925.

. . . I do realize that a long quiet time alone with God would probably help you a lot. But it must be quite without strain and have opportunities for relaxation and safeguards both against intensity and monotony. After all, if you had been able to leave the world . . . you would not have been allowed to spend all your time praying. But you would have a life considerably relieved from distraction and external claims, and so more consistently recollected. And this I think you may certainly have for some weeks on end, if a suitable place can be discovered. . . .

Venice,
September 14, 1925.

I agree with you about Poulain; *no* account of "states of prayer" reduced to a system can be really accurate, because we are not machines and each go within certain general limitations our own way; and may have transitory gleams of "higher states" whilst still only really belonging to the lower degrees, and so forth. After all, his *présence de Dieu senti* as a criterion of "mystical prayer" is much too general. For as we all know, this may vary from a faint sort of certitude to an overwhelming experience, and there's no point at which one could say "here the supernatural begins."

November 10, 1925.

Do not please assume and dwell on the idea that this illness and suffering is necessarily God's special visitation to you and therefore ought to go on. It is raw material simply; an opportunity of acceptance and consecration, and therefore capable of becoming an immense grace for your soul, an opportunity of adoration from the Cross. But humanly speaking, your life is to pass on and through it, taking all reasonable means of cure and making yourself fit for service to whatever else God's providence contains for you, isn't it?

Epiphany, 1926.

I am deeply interested in your Chemical [student]. . . . As to his recent remarks, I think I would say Catholicism did not *produce* Torquemada but gave his natural ferocity a theological outlet. It is the old choice between a religion wide enough and human enough to embrace all sorts, and one narrow enough and lofty enough to be content with Gentlemen Only. And it is the big room-for-all-sorts kind that produces saints, isn't it? Would he really condemn an apple-tree that occasionally tolerated a bit of blight, and in spite of it produced a good average crop and here and there a Prize Specimen? While he is at it, he had better condemn the whole Universe—but it is really no use being more fussy than God! . . .

My latest case is aged 64 and says, poor lamb (sheep perhaps), that ever since 17 it has been longing for an answer to prayer but never had one, in spite of listening! Almost as if she expected a sort of spiritual telephone, and—"What is wrong?" But what can one say?

Sunday before Ascension, 1926.

I am so grieved that you have been wretched physically and spiritually too. Of course the two things are closely connected but that I know does not make the spiritual desolation any easier to bear. The right and only way for you to take it is to relax all effort, make no attempt to keep your rule, but wait as quietly and peaceably as you can and dwell on this and kindred subjects as little as you can. I wish your nature craved less for emotional satisfactions; for it is that very largely which causes this intense suffering in you. After all the sense of Christ's presence, though a joy and support, is not the essence of religion. Nor would the Cross be the Cross without that feeling of darkness and abandonment by God. You can, you know, turn all this into a redemptive sacrifice; and if you are able to do that, it is worth all the consolations in the world. But you must do it quietly, and check the propensity to dwell on your own spiritual pain. It is much the same with bodily suffering. There too, one can either explore and emphasize it, allow oneself to be obsessed till it is nearly intolerable; or, stand away from it and let it happen and so kill the worst of the sting. You have got, probably, to let this thing happen for a bit; and the more quietly you can do this, the sooner light will return. If you have Tauler's *Inner Way* read the sermon on the Martyrs and see what can be made of such a situation! You told me you felt called to suffer for Christ. Well! here is the suffering— far more prevailing too than crude physical austerities and I don't think, if you take it that way, you can resent it, can you? Never mind if you did "feel rebellious." Do not agonize over this. Accept it too as part of the suffering and then just leave it.

Go to Communion when you can; but make no efforts to achieve any sort of realization. These in your present phase always defeat themselves and increase the sense of conflict and strain.

No more now. Let me know how you get on. And do not lose hope or allow yourself to consider the idea of losing hope. That is the one thing which is never allowed surely, and which takes away the whole value of the sacrifice to which you are called.

September 5, 1926.

This is just to send you my love and say I hope you will have a really and deeply happy time at [the Convent]. I entreat you to enter on it in as simple, expansive, non-intense mood as you possibly can, turning steadily away from all self-abasing and self-analysing sentiments and remaining gently passive and ready for everything, or for nothing.

Horning.

September 14, 1926.

Now as to your Confession. If you are genuinely sure that you wish it because you feel it to be God's will for you, by all means do it. But do not do it to please the Rev. Mother or abstain from doing it to please me! These motives should not ever be thought of in connection with a Sacrament, should they? I think possibly, if you feel a real inclination to do it, it may be a good thing and help you to escape from this morbid sense of sin and confusion of motive, etc., which obsesses you.

Be quite clear with yourself that only definite committed sins are to be confessed. The fact that you feel "wlatsome"[1] and are always brooding over it is merely an unfortunate piece of foolishness, to which the Church does not extend absolution. I remember the Baron saying to me under similar circumstances, "The Sacrament of Penance was not created in order that you might discuss your unfortunate character. You can't be absolved for not having a sense of humour!"

[1] A word used by Hilton.

330

I should be very sorry for you to make a practice of frequent confession or anything else requiring detailed self-examination because I am sure it would increase your self-occupation. But *one* confession, without soul-scraping of any kind and with a clear determination to let bygones be bygones when it is over, may really pacify and clarify your soul. . . .

50 C.H.S.

October 29, 1926.

I think you have lately made a distinct advance in this [Prayer] even though it is "without salary" (but at any moment you know the arrears may be paid in full) and that you are most distinctly to follow quietly but faithfully where you are being led. You are also quite right to leave formal prayer as you say, when impelled to, and go and do "something useful" in that same spirit. That you are able and inclined to do this, is in itself a sign of growth, Persevere gently along this line.

As to "that which you are going to transmit will be relative to that which you are able to receive"—Yes! But not "consciously receive"! You are, in such a disposition as you describe, as wide open as you know how to be towards God, and so receiving all the while. That remark was not directed to your type but to the sort of people who practise constant fussy intercessions without that essential background of contemplation which is, though it may not give you any particular satisfaction, well established now in your life. And if this self-oblation to God *does* take the form of suffering (though here you have to guard most carefully of course against any morbid assumption that particular sufferings "come from God" and must be endured and not alleviated) still this is supremely material which can be utilized for His redemptive work in souls. When it comes, use it thus—but *never* deliberately seek it. I do not think it necessarily a coincidence that your "difficult child" came round thus. It is seldom possible to do much with really crucial cases without at least being fully willing to suffer, mentally or otherwise. . . . The mere tension and effort needed tend to produce it. Anyhow in all this I take it you will be perfectly safe to follow your *attrait*, so long as you are reasonable, and do not overstrain yourself and keep non-religious interests alive as much as you possibly can.

As for asking for special things for special souls, don't you think it is rather a case of first offering oneself and them to God, and then as it were letting oneself be used to work His will on them? Of course in some cases the issue is quite clear—e.g., rescue from temptation: in which case you simply try in union with His will to work this. First give yourself to God; then direct your whole attention, as it were, from within the Cross, on the person for whom you have got to pray. This probably comes to the same thing as what you describe. Anyhow, don't force yourself to a particular method, but follow your call. Goodbye for now. I am very glad you wrote about all this, though you don't need direction on it really, except a judicious use of the curb! . . .

Heiler is in England and coming to tea next Sunday. Yes! isn't Père Charles a pure joy? I love the meditation on the *Benedicite* so, and feel when David [her cat] suddenly sticks his nose into my face that, like the frogs and the *escargots*, he can *enchanter ma prière*. Your dog too should be good at this!

My last addition to Andrewes is from St. Anselm:

"Lord! teach me to seek Thee and show Thyself to me as I seek: for I cannot seek Thee unless Thou teach me, nor find Thee unless Thou show Thyself."[1]

July 18, 1927.

In view of all you say I think:

(*a*) Daily Communion would be spiritually permissible provided it was not too much for you physically; but it must be one of your chief duties to reduce physical strain as much as you possibly can.

(*b*) Extra times of prayer are not necessary. You must use

---

[1] E.U. used an edition of Andrewes with blank pages on which she used to write prayers which specially delighted her. But each new prayer had to be on probation for some time before she admitted it to her collection.

your judgment as to how much and what kind, best enables you to keep in the generalized state of prayer you describe.

(c) Community life probably not suitable and almost certainly too much for your health. The best thing seems to me at present what you suggest: your normal life, with longish but not strenuous retreats from time to time.

You will probably always find your special type of prayer pretty exhausting and therefore the careful preserving of your strength is of the very first importance. For this reason, considering your health, I do not feel definite fasting would be a safe asceticism, except in the form of leaving out something you like and replacing it by something you do not care for. Fragile persons are never allowed to fast.

For the rest, you have I fear quite enough physical suffering to give material for the exercise of patience, surrender, etc. Be moderate! Great privileges must be handled wisely. . . .

In the train, Liverpool to London.
Eve of All Saints.

Both shows are safely over and I really felt very happy, thanks to good backing up. We had 28 at Watermillock. . . . I had lots of interviews and many of them were perfect dears. . . . I had to submit to a long discussion on Spiritual Healing [after the Retreat was over]. These people seem so cocksure abou what God means and wills and all the rest of it and so over-impressed by the importance of physical robustness, don't they? X. considered the Saints would have been so *much* more useful if they had been full of beans and had lived longer and gone about and met more people. I said, from that point of view a mere three years ministry in Galilee instead of a prolonged tour through the Roman Empire did seem a pity. But he did not seem inclined to deal with this argument and only made a vague noise. . . . History teaches these people nothing—they seem unable to distinguish between quality and quantity. . . .

. . . At Liverpool I had the Bishop's vestry all to myself! Think of that! . . . One simply darling person, an aged Quakeress, 86, Dr. Thomas Hodgkins' widow, and Violet Hodgkins' mother: light simply streamed out of her. She came in to see me and held my hand and said, "I hope, my dear, while you are watering our souls, you get a few drops for yourself?" I said, "Well, I have to give most of my attention to holding on to the can!" At which she laughed and kissed me.

Advent Sunday, 1928.

Had an interesting lunch sitting next the Archbishop [of Canterbury] on Wed. He pleased me greatly by saying the only really important thing for Clergy was to make a Retreat every year: and then told me a tale of an utterly lonely, poverty-. stricken one in an utterly irresponsive village, with an ill wife and no servants, who rang his own Church bell daily, said his offices and made his meditation and never lost heart; and then added quietly, "*That* is the true evidence of the Supernatural." Nice, don't you think?

April 16, 1929.

As to what you say about the times in Chapel, I think what you do is ample, and also that the sort of prayer you describe, however unsatisfying it may be to you, is perfectly all right and you have no cause for depression about it. . . .

I think regularity in the *Opus Dei* is important. In your own times in Chapel, when it is a strain, I should not attempt actual prayer but read a bit and just be there—it will suffice. Also reduce the early morning half-hour if it tires you for the day and certainly DON'T get up earlier. . . .

My Bishop too thinks I do not get enough time for myself when conducting, but it really is impossible! As to Intercession, I do not believe anyone really knows much about it, except in experience, and it's best to follow your *attrait*. But in leading Intercessions, one is bound to provide a certain amount of framework. It is all a very difficult problem. People as a whole are so much cruder than one realizes. . . .

July, 1929.

I am so glad you liked your Retreat and am sure the quiet bit you had alone in bed upstairs was just what you needed most and the discoveries you made are the true ones.

We all tend to mix up peace with *feeling* happy, and joy with enjoyment! And the effort and tension and strain you *would* put all your stress on, stopped the simple, tranquil sort of acceptance which does make burdens light! And as to advising people, if it is put into one's hand, one just has to do it in simple trust that if one keeps as quiet as possible, God will do it through one and that one's own insufficiency does not matter much. . . .

I think it was lovely your Reverend Mother asking for your prayers. After all, if we never prayed for those who are streets above us, our list would become uncommonly short. . . .

January 26, 1931.

It seems to me perfectly all right—for after all you are doing what you can and can't do otherwise—and to do this is to please God. And what *is* "sitting in the Chapel looking at the Crucifix" but a form of passive prayer? I am sure my Abbot[1] would say the same. Isn't he a darling?—the simplicity of the saints.

December 7, 1931.

As to your prayer, I am sure you must avoid everything that strains you or keys you up; that it ought to be mostly a quite gentle self-yielding towards God; a loving and docile *abandon* and feeding your trust in support even though you do not *feel* support.

"Adherence" rather than effort. Remember Maria's, "Jesus can use everything: and though I am afraid I am not alert enough, He can make something even out of my weariness." After all, to give ourselves quite simply is all we are asked to do and there is nothing reprehensible in resting in the Lord! so long as it really *is* in Him!

[1] Dom John Chapman, Abbot of Downside.

July, 1933.

(After one of E.U.'s Retreats.)

I do not think the addresses should be shattering, because the achievement can never be general but must be the result of our various poor little efforts, decorated as it were by a handful of saints, like the almonds on a cake! And it's lovely to think that after all our lives can contribute to the total of the *Corpus Christi* however small. F. von Hügel's " Joy for the others— the lovely constellations of the spiritual heavens." I wish you would try that and not feel tormented by what seems to you the smallness of your own achievement. I am sure we are meant to be at peace about ourselves, whatever we are like!!

August 1933.

A hard month's work is not the time to examine one's doubts! I think a better plan is Julian of Norwich's, "It was said unto me: 'Take it generally'" i.e. although one may be in the dark about details and unable to draw a neat line between what is realistic and what is symbolic, one's whole life, work and sense of obligation witnesses to the general truth of the super- natural and our relation to God; and detailed investigation of the way the relationship is maintained, etc., is on the whole less fruitful and less pacifying than this general trustful adher- ence. The *test* is not of course our understanding of this or that, but the effects produced by the bits of work we are given to do —or rather, which are done through us. And the more you let yourself be a channel, a kind of spiritual Robot, the less you will "do it on your nerves" and the quieter you will be. This, not merely doing less, is the point, isn't it? When things are very thick, it is more important to maintain this spirit (by occasional aspirations, etc.) than to wear yourself out with trying to keep your times and do everything.

March 1934.

Yes! it was lovely at Wantage and I am so glad we were there together for it all went so perfectly. . . .

As to dark prayer being deeply satisfying, I am sure for many who are put to it in a queer way it *is*. Dom Chapman says so too—that although one seems to know and do nothing, yet one comes away sure of having been praying somehow, and pacified.

Where the prayer is real suffering as you describe, that is a special case and (very likely) a special vocation, a prayer in the Cross. Of course that is not, at least on the surface, pacifying, but agonizing; and yet if it is your contribution, your share in Christ's action, then it is (or can be) satisfying in the deepest sense. I feel if you saw it more from that point of view, as a painful and sacred kind of intercession, it might take away some of the strain of it. You would go to it as one might go to the painful privilege of doing a hard, even torturing job for someone that one loved. On the theory of the Church's total prayer, your suffering avails for other souls.

April 25, 1935.
(After 10 days in the Lakes.)

It *was* a nice time, wasn't it? the heavenly little Church gave it a sort of special benediction! . . .

The Abbot's *Letters* are a god-send.[1] I knew they would enlighten you as to the meaning of your own state and that alone is an enormous relief of strain and bewilderment. His calm matter-of-factness is so reassuring and also his sense of the fundamental queerness of things existing at all—which I have always had very strongly

I still think you distress yourself unduly and also quite un-profitably by dwelling on the sight of your own unworthiness. . . . It is at best a distorted sight and no index at all of your real state. Drop it quietly as much as you can and simply turn away from all self-scrutiny of every kind. In one of his letters to me which Dom Hudleston did not print the Abbot said, "I have lots of monks here who are always ill because they are always thinking about their own insides!" Quite a lot of truth in that! When you feel the blues coming on, at once go and do something which takes your whole attention (not something religious) or write and tell me about it! This sometimes acts like a charm!

[1] *Spiritual Letters* of Dom John Chapman.

Septuagesima, 1936.

Don't think about being good! If you accept the very tiresome stuff the Lord is handing out to you, that's all He wants at the moment. "Let not your heart be troubled" if you can help it, is the best N.T. bit for the moment I think; but the more bovine or merely acquiescent you are the better. I know this will strike you as thin advice, but it is all I can give. Drop religion for the time being and just be quiet and wait a bit and God will reveal Himself again, more richly and closely than ever before. . . .

February 26, 1936.

Have been reading for the first time, Pusey, and am amazed to find what a fine, deep creature he was. Full of the mystics, very averse to all mere ritualism and Romanism, and his letters of Direction are splendid, quite in the St. François de Sales tradition. He strikes me as much bigger spiritually than Newman, though not so brilliant.

Maundy Thursday, 1936.

[Written when she had to cancel a Retreat and disappoint many people and when her correspondent also had to give up a bit of work.]

If your physical presence were absolutely necessary from God's point of view, then He would arrange for it! This idea always comforts me a lot when I can't do things though perhaps you will think it rather austere! . . . I hope you are more comfy and freer from pain. Sometimes I think the resurrection of the body, unless much improved in construction, a mistake!

Advent Sunday, 1936.

My love and blessing for your Retreat. I hope and believe it will be a time of peace for you and, if you will avoid all strain and let your soul slowly become tranquillized, you will begin, like the cats, to see a bit in the dark.

I do see that you must be constantly tempted to escape the pain of darkness by losing yourself in activity but I am not at all sure that it is a good thing to do. Physical exhaustion then reacts on your spirit and so we get a vicious circle! Do let this time be an entire withdrawal from work, the world, people and the rest; an abiding in the emptiness where God alone is. I will be thinking of you much and shall expect you on the 6th anyhow, whether in the Pink or in the Drab and whatever the angle at which you are carrying the tail.

Eve of the Annunciation, 1938.

So terribly sorry if you have to leave off ... These losses of liberty *I* think are among the hardest demands of the Lord. At least I feel them so, but perhaps they are meant to drive us bit by bit into the solitude with Him, which He requires of us.

Just sitting or kneeling in Church and apparently doing nothing at all is a very good prayer. It is God's prayer in us, we are just the vessels and so feel nothing. If that is your main trouble, you ought to be quite pleased; it's a form of *oraison passive* and should be settled into and no straining after anything else!

Maundy Thursday, 1938.

I was so glad to get your letter and hear all went so very well with the Retreat, I thought it would! But it does all sound as if it had been very specially lovely. I only hope you have not had a very bad reaction from the inevitable fatigue. The Sunday always is the easy day if things are going right; Saturday, as it were one hauls them into position and Sunday they go along under their own steam. . . . It will be very nice to see you. I can't tell you how pleased I am about the Retreat!

Trinity V, 1938.

You are now to rest quietly till God hands you out your next job. Who knows what? His unexpectedness is one of the most attractive things about Him!

Trinity VI, 1938.

I am afraid you are going through a very bad bit of readjustment just now—that feeling one is no use any more, is horrible but *is* a temptation of the devil. Remember Huvelin's "Notre Seigneur a gagné le monde non pas par ses beaux discours par le sermon sur la montagne, mais par son sang, par sa douleur sur la croix"—which must have seemed utter failure, a *finis* to "being of use." In various degrees I am sure we all have to make that transition. You and I have both been allowed a good run of active work, but the real test is giving it up, and passively accepting God's action and work, and the suffering that usually goes with it. It will mean not only interior growth for you, but also in the end, a closer union with God and greatly increased power of helping souls. . . .

No one, not the greatest saint, is irreplaceable. It is a greater act of trust and love to give your work into fresh hands than to struggle on with increasing damage to health. I know it must be increasing anguish to you—but after all, Our Lord Himself had to leave His work to 12 quite inferior disciples. We have to learn to accept for ourselves all that this means, before we are really abandoned to God.

Ascension Day, 1941.

This intense craving for activity, freedom, doing work, is natural to you and me and hard to give up. But it is quite clear that it is something one must be prepared to give up if one is really to be "abandoned." And praying for people, however dryly and inadequately, may and often must be an exchange for instructing them! "Our Lord taught great perfection on the Cross"—doing nothing at all, but just accepting the situation and offering it to God.

Glory be to the Father and to the Son and to the Holy Spirit: and upon us, weak and sinful, be mercy and grace at all times.—*Liturgy of the Syrian Jacobites.*

INDEX

LIST OF CORRESPONDENTS

SUBJECTS